PEACE UNDER FIRE

Dedicated to everyone—Palestinian, Israeli or International—who has lost their life, their health, their livelihood, their home, their liberty, in the struggle for justice, freedom and an end to the Occupation.

PEACE UNDER FIRE

ISRAEL/PALESTINE

AND THE

INTERNATIONAL SOLIDARITY MOVEMENT

EDITED BY
Josie Sandercock, Radhika Sainath
Marissa McLaughlin, Hussein Khalili
Nicholas Blincoe, Huwaida Arraf
Ghassan Andoni

VERSO
London • New York

First published by Verso 2004

1 3 5 7 9 10 8 6 4 2

Verso
UK: 6 Meard Street, London W1F 0EG
USA: 180 Varick Street, New York, NY 10014–4606
www.versobooks.com

Verso is the imprint of New Left Books

ISBN 1-84467-007-4 (hardback)
ISBN 1-84467-501-7 (paperback)

British Library Cataloguing in Publication Data
Peace under fire: Israel/Palestine and the International Solidarity Movement
edited by Josie Sandercock … [et al]
  1. International Solidarity Movement 2. Pacifists – Palestine
  3. Arab–Israeli conflict – 1993 4. Al-Aqsa Intifada, 2000–
  I. Sandercock, Josie
  956.9'4054

Library of Congress Cataloging-in-Publication Data
Peace under fire: Israel/Palestine and the International Solidarity Movement /
edited by Josie Sandercock … [et al.].
    p. cm.
  ISBN 1-84467-501-7 (pbk.: alk. paper) – ISBN 1-84467-007-4 (hardcover:
  alk. paper)
  1. Arab–Israeli conflict 1993–Peace. 2. International Solidarity
  Movement–Political activity. I. Sandercock, Josie.

  DS119.76.P42 2004
  956.05'3–dc22

                                                            2004006225

Typeset in Bembo
Printed in the USA by R. R. Donnelley & Sons

CONTENTS

PART TWO: REOCCUPATION   43

EDITORS' NOTE

This book tells two stories. One is of the first two years of the International Solidarity Movement (ISM); the other is of the Israeli military occupation as witnessed by the thousands who have come to live, work and resist in solidarity with the Palestinian people.

The book is woven together from contemporary eye-witness accounts, press releases, interviews and newspaper articles. There is no new writing; the reports appear here as they were written at the time. The structure of the book is broadly chronological, but each chapter has a specific theme. We hope the book will be as easy to dip into as it will be to read from cover to cover.

The hardest part of the editorial process was deciding what to leave out, with so much that has happened and hundreds of excellent reports from activists, journalists and others. We have had to shorten many of the pieces included, in part to maintain the focus of the chapters in which they appear, but mainly to make space for other voices to be heard. Where pieces have been shortened, this is indicated in the text. The interested reader might wish to look up the full articles, most of which can be found easily on the internet, many on the ISM website—www. palsolidarity.org. The website also provides links to many other internet resources about the conflict.

Other than shortening reports where necessary, we have tried to maintain a light editorial touch with only minimal changes to the original texts, such as correcting typing errors and making the spelling of place names consistent to aid clarity. ISM press releases have been kept strictly intact with no amendments, although personal telephone numbers have been removed. The photographs chosen to illustrate each chapter come from a variety of sources, some from professional photographers and journalists, many from photographs and footage taken by activists using ordinary cameras and camcorders.

This book focuses on the first two years of ISM; as we were submitting the manuscript reports were still coming in from Freedom Summer 2003 and a few from the Olive Harvest campaign which followed. We have included just one report which is more recent than the rest. Changes to a manuscript are difficult to make at such a late stage, but this one was important. It can be found in Chapter 13.

We would like to thank all those activists, journalists and friends who have written about ISM and given us such a rich variety of material to work with, and all those who helped us compile the manuscript.

— Gabriel Angelone, Raph Cohen, Neta Golan, Lisa Nessan, Flo Razowsky, Leila Sansour, Michael Shaik, and Elana Wesley for their help in tracking down articles and photographs, and for their invaluable advice on the manuscript as it evolved.

— The many authors and photographers whose work we have used—too many to list here—for giving us permission to use their work.

— *Al-Ahram*, Al-Jazeera, Associated Press, bitterlemons.org, the Corrie Family, the *Guardian*, the *Herald-Sun*, the *Independent*, International Press Center, *In These Times*, the *Miami Herald*, the Middle East Research and Information Project, the *New York Times*, palestinetoday.org, *Q News*, rafah.virtualactivism.net, Reuters, *The Other Israel*, The Tom Hurndall Foundation, *UCSD Guardian* and the *Washington Post* Writers Group for giving us permission to reproduce articles and photographs.

— Mariam Said for giving us permission to use an article by her late husband, Dr Edward W. Said, as the foreword.

— Gavin Everall, Jane Hindle, Andrea Stimpson, Tariq Ali and all at Verso for having the idea for the book and then helping us to make it happen.

March 2004

FOREWORD

THE MEANING OF RACHEL CORRIE
Of dignity and solidarity
by Edward W. Said

In early May, I was in Seattle lecturing for a few days. While there, I had dinner one night with Rachel Corrie's parents and sister, who were still reeling from the shock of their daughter's murder on March 16 in Gaza by an Israeli bulldozer. Mr. Corrie told me that he had himself driven bulldozers, although the one that killed his daughter deliberately because she was trying valiantly to protect a Palestinian home in Rafah from demolition was a 60-ton behemoth especially designed by Caterpillar for house demolitions, a far bigger machine than anything he had ever seen or driven. Two things struck me about my brief visit with the Corries. One was the story they told about their return to the US with their daughter's body. They had immediately sought out their US Senators, Patty Murray and Mary Cantwell, both Democrats, told them their story and received the expected expressions of shock, outrage, anger and promises of investigations. After both women returned to Washington, the Corries never heard from them again, and the promised investigation simply didn't materialize. As expected, the Israeli lobby had explained the realities to them, and both women simply begged off. An American citizen willfully murdered by the soldiers of a client state of the US without so much as an official peep or even the de rigueur investigation that had been promised her family.

But the second and far more important aspect of the Rachel Corrie story for me was the young woman's action itself, heroic and dignified at the same time. Born and brought up in Olympia, a small city 60 miles south of Seattle, she had joined the International Solidarity Movement and gone to Gaza to stand with suffering human beings with whom she had never had any contact before. Her letters back to her family are truly remarkable documents of her ordinary humanity that make for very difficult and moving reading, especially when she describes the kindness and concern showed her by all the Palestinians she encounters who clearly welcome her as one of their own, because she lives with them exactly as they do, sharing their lives and worries, as well as the horrors of the Israeli occupation and its terrible effects on even the smallest child. She understands the fate of refugees, and what she calls the Israeli government's insidious attempt at a kind of genocide by making it almost impossible for this particular group of people to survive. So moving is her solidarity that it inspires an Israeli reservist named Danny who has refused service to write her and tell her, "You are doing a good thing. I thank you for it."

What shines through all the letters she wrote home and which were subsequently published in the London *Guardian*, is the amazing resistance put up by the Palestinian people themselves, average human beings stuck in the most terrible position of suffering and despair but continuing to survive just the same. We have heard so much recently about the roadmap and the prospects for peace that we have overlooked the most basic fact of all, which is that Palestinians have refused to capitulate or surrender even under the collective punishment meted out to them by the combined might of the US and Israel. It is that extraordinary fact which is the reason for the existence of a roadmap and all the numerous so-called peace plans before them, not at all because the US and Israel and the international community have been convinced for humanitarian reasons that the killing and the violence must stop. If we miss that truth about the power of Palestinian resistance (by which I do not at all mean suicide bombing, which does much more harm than good), despite all its failings and all its mistakes, we miss everything. Palestinians have always been a problem for the Zionist project, and so-called solutions have perennially been proposed that minimize, rather than solve, the problem. The official Israeli policy, no matter whether Ariel Sharon uses the word "occupation" or not or whether or not he dismantles a rusty, unused tower or two, has always been not to accept the reality of the Palestinian people as equals nor ever to admit that their rights were scandalously violated all along by Israel. Whereas a few courageous Israelis over the years have tried to deal with this other concealed history, most Israelis and what seems like the majority of American Jews have made every effort to deny, avoid, or negate the Palestinian reality. This is why there is no peace.

Moreover, the roadmap says nothing about justice or about the historical punishment meted out to the Palestinian people for too many decades to count. What Rachel Corrie's work in Gaza recognized, however, was precisely the gravity and the density of the living history of the Palestinian people as a national community, and not merely as a collection of deprived refugees. That is what she was in solidarity with. And we need to remember that that kind of solidarity is no longer confined to a small number of intrepid souls here and there, but is recognized the world over. In the past six months I have lectured in four continents to many thousands of people. What brings them together is Palestine and the struggle of the Palestinian people which is now a byword for emancipation and enlightenment, regardless of all the vilification heaped on them by their enemies.

Whenever the facts are made known, there is immediate recognition and an expression of the most profound solidarity with the justice of the Palestinian cause and the valiant struggle by the Palestinian people on its behalf. It is an extraordinary thing that Palestine was a central issue this year both during the Porto Alegre anti-globalization meetings as well as during the Davos and Amman meetings, both poles of the worldwide political spectrum. Just because our fellow citizens in this country are fed an atrociously biased diet of ignorance and misrepresentation by the media, when the Occupation is never referred to in lurid descriptions of suicide attacks, the apartheid wall 25 feet high, 5 feet thick, and 350 kilometers long that Israel is building is never even shown on CNN and the networks (or so much as referred to in passing throughout the lifeless prose of the roadmap), and the crimes of war, the gratuitous destruction and humiliation, maiming, house demolitions, agricultural destruction, and death imposed on Palestinian civilians are never shown for the daily, completely routine ordeal that they are, one shouldn't be surprised that Americans in the main have a very low opinion of Arabs and Palestinians. After all, please remember that all the main organs of the establishment media, from left liberal all the way over to fringe right, are unanimously anti-Arab, anti-Muslim and anti-Palestinian. Look at the pusillanimity of the media during the buildup to an illegal and unjust war against Iraq, and look at how little coverage there was of the immense damage against Iraqi society done by the sanctions, and how relatively few accounts there were of the immense world-wide outpouring of opinion against the war. Hardly a single journalist except Helen Thomas has taken the administration to task for the outrageous lies and confected "facts" that were spun out about Iraq as an imminent military threat to the US before the war, just as now the same government propagandists, whose cynically invented and manipulated "facts" about WMD are now more or less forgotten or shrugged off as irrelevant, are let off the hook by media heavies in discussing the awful, the literally inexcusable situation for the people of Iraq that the US has now single-handedly and irresponsibly created there. However else one blames Saddam Hussein as a vicious tyrant, which he was, he had provided the people of Iraq with the best infrastructure of services like water, electricity, health, and education of any Arab country. None of this is any longer in place.

It is no wonder, then, with the extraordinary fear of seeming anti-Semitic by criticizing Israel for its daily crimes of war against innocent unarmed Palestinian civilians or criticizing the US government and being called "anti-American" for its illegal war and its dreadfully run military Occupation, that the vicious media and government campaign against Arab society, culture, history and mentality that has been led by Neanderthal publicists and Orientalists like Bernard Lewis and Daniel Pipes, has cowed far too many of us into believing that Arabs really are an underdeveloped, incompetent and doomed people, and that with all the failures in democracy and development, Arabs are alone in this world for being retarded, behind the times, unmodernized, and deeply reactionary. Here is where dignity and critical historical thinking must be mobilized to see what is what and to disentangle truth from propaganda.

No one would deny that most Arab countries today are ruled by unpopular regimes and that vast numbers of poor, disadvantaged young Arabs are exposed to the ruthless forms of fundamentalist religion. Yet it is simply a lie to say, as the *New York Times* regularly does, that Arab societies are totally controlled, and that there is no freedom of opinion, no civil institutions, no functioning social movements for and by the people. Press laws notwithstanding, you can go to downtown Amman today and buy a communist party newspaper as well as an Islamist one; Egypt and Lebanon are full of papers and journals that suggest much more debate and discussion than these societies are given credit for; the satellite channels are bursting with diverse opinions in a dizzying variety; civil institutions are, on many levels having to do with social services, human rights, syndicates, and research institutes, very lively all over the Arab world. A great deal more must be done before we have the appropriate level of democracy, but we are on the way.

In Palestine alone there are over 1000 NGOs and it is this vitality and this kind of activity that has kept society going, despite every American and Israeli effort made to vilify, stop or mutilate it on a daily basis. Under the worst possible circumstances, Palestinian society has neither been defeated nor has it crumbled completely. Kids still go to school, doctors and nurses still take care of their patients, men and women go to work, organizations have their meetings, and people continue to live, which seems to be an offense to Sharon and the other extremists who simply want Palestinians either imprisoned or driven away altogether. The military solution hasn't worked at all, and never will work. Why is that so hard for Israelis to see? We must help them to understand this, not by suicide bombs, but by rational argument, mass civil disobedience, organized protest, here and everywhere.

The point I am trying to make is that we have to see the Arab world generally and Palestine in particular in more comparative and critical ways than superficial and dismissive books like Lewis's *What Went Wrong* and Paul Wolfowitz's ignorant statements about bringing democracy to the Arab and Islamic world even begin to suggest. Whatever else is true about the Arabs, there is an active dynamic at work because as real people they live in a real society with all sorts of currents and crosscurrents in it that can't be easily caricatured as just one seething mass of violent fanaticism. The Palestinian struggle for justice is especially something with which one expresses solidarity, rather than endless criticism and exasperated, frustrating discouragement, and crippling divisiveness. Remember the solidarity here and everywhere in Latin America, Africa, Europe, Asia and Australia, and remember also that there is a cause to which many people have committed themselves, difficulties and terrible obstacles notwithstanding. Why? Because it is a just cause, a noble ideal, a moral quest for equality and human rights.

I want now to speak about dignity, which of course has a special place in every culture known to historians, anthropologists, sociologists and humanists. I shall begin by saying immediately that it is a radically wrong Orientalist, and indeed racist proposition to accept that, unlike Europeans and Americans, Arabs have no sense of individuality, no regard for individual life, no values that express love, intimacy and understanding that are supposed to be the property exclusively of cultures like those of Europe and America that had a Renaissance, a Reformation and an Enlightenment. Among many others, it is the vulgar and jejune Thomas Friedman who has been peddling this rubbish, which has alas been picked up by equally ignorant and self-deceiving Arab intellectuals—I don't need to mention any names here—who have seen in the atrocities of 9/11 a sign that the Arab and Islamic worlds are somehow more diseased and more dysfunctional than any other, and that terrorism is a sign of a wider distortion than has occurred in any other culture.

We can leave to one side that, between them, Europe and the US account for by far the largest number of violent deaths during the 20th century, the Islamic world hardly a fraction of it. And behind all of that specious unscientific nonsense about wrong and right civilizations, there is the grotesque shadow of the great false prophet Samuel Huntington who has led a lot of people to believe that the world can be divided into distinct civilizations battling against each other forever. On the contrary, Huntington is dead wrong on every point he makes. No culture or civilization exists by itself; none is made up of things like individuality and enlightenment that are completely exclusive to it; and none exists without the basic human attributes of community, love, value for life and all the others. To suggest otherwise as he does is the purest invidious racism of the same stripe as people who argue that Africans have naturally inferior brains, or that Asians are really born for servitude, or that Europeans are a naturally superior race. This is a sort of parody of Hitlerian science directed uniquely today against Arabs and Muslims, and we must be very firm as to not even go through the motions of arguing against it. It is the purest drivel. On the other hand, there is the much more credible and serious stipulation that, like every other instance of humanity, Arab and Muslim life has an inherent value and dignity which are expressed by Arabs and Muslims in their unique cultural style, and those expressions needn't resemble or be a copy of one approved model suitable for everyone to follow.

The whole point about human diversity is that it is in the end a form of deep co-existence between very different styles of individuality and experience that can't all be reduced to one superior form: this is the spurious argument foisted on us by pundits who bewail the lack of development and knowledge in the Arab world. All one has to do is to look at the huge variety of literature, cinema, theater, painting, music and popular culture produced by and for Arabs from Morocco to the Gulf. Surely that needs to be assessed as an indication of whether or not Arabs are developed, and not just how on any given day statistical tables of industrial production either indicate an appropriate level of development or they show failure.

The more important point I want to make, though, is that there is a very wide discrepancy today between our cultures and societies and the small group of people who now rule these societies. Rarely in history has such power been so concentrated in so tiny a group as the various kings, generals, sultans, and presidents who preside today over the Arabs. The worst thing about them as a group, almost without exception, is that they do not represent the best of their people. This is not just a matter of no democracy. It is that they seem to radically underestimate themselves and their people in ways that close them off, that make them intolerant and fearful of change, frightened of opening up their societies to their people, terrified most of all that they might anger big brother, that is, the United States. Instead of seeing their citizens as the potential wealth of the nation, they regard them all as guilty conspirators vying for the ruler's power.

This is the real failure, how during the terrible war against the Iraqi people, no Arab leader had the self-dignity and confidence to say something about the pillaging and military Occupation of one of the most important Arab countries. Fine, it was an excellent thing that Saddam Hussein's appalling regime is no more, but who appointed the US to be the Arab mentor? Who asked the US to take over the Arab world allegedly on behalf of its citizens and bring it something called "democracy," especially at a time when the school system, the health system, and the whole economy in America are degenerating to the worst levels since the 1929 Depression. Why was the collective Arab voice *not* raised against the US's flagrantly illegal intervention, which did so much harm and inflicted so much humiliation upon the entire Arab nation? This is truly a colossal failure in nerve, in dignity, in self-solidarity.

With all the Bush administration's talk about guidance from the Almighty, doesn't one Arab leader have the courage just to say that, as a great people, we are guided by our own lights and traditions and religion? But nothing, not a word, as the poor citizens of Iraq live through the most terrible ordeals and the rest of the region quakes in its collective boots, each one petrified that his country may be next. How unfortunate the embrace of George Bush, the man whose war destroyed an Arab country gratuitously, by the combined leadership of the major Arab countries last week. Was there no one there who had the guts to remind George W. what he has done to humiliate and bring more suffering to the Arab people than anyone before him, and must he always be greeted with hugs, smiles, kisses and low bows? Where is the diplomatic and political and economic support necessary to sustain an anti-Occupation movement on the West Bank and Gaza? Instead all one hears is that foreign ministers preach to the Palestinians to mind their ways, avoid violence, and keep at the peace negotiations, even though it has been so obvious that Sharon's interest in peace is just about zero. There has been no concerted Arab response to the separation wall, or to the assassinations, or to collective punishment, only a bunch of tired clichés repeating the well-worn formulas authorized by the State Department.

Perhaps the one thing that strikes me as the low point in Arab inability to grasp the dignity of the Palestinian cause is expressed by the current state of the Palestinian Authority. Abu Mazen, a subordinate figure with little political support among his own people, was picked for the job by Arafat, Israel, and the US precisely because he has no constituency, is not an orator or a great organizer, or anything really except a dutiful aide to Yasir Arafat, and because I am afraid they see in him a man who will do Israel's bidding, how could even Abu Mazen stand there in Aqaba to pronounce words written for him, like a ventriloquist's puppet, by some State Department functionary, in which he commendably speaks about Jewish suffering but then amazingly says next to nothing about his own people's suffering at the hands of Israel? How could he accept so undignified and manipulated a role for himself, and how could he forget his self-dignity as the representative of a people that has been fighting heroically for its rights for over a century just because the US and Israel have told him he must? And when Israel simply says that there will be a "provisional" Palestinian state, without any contrition for the horrendous amount of damage it has done, the uncountable war crimes, the sheer sadistic systematic humiliation of every single Palestinian, man, woman, child, I must confess to a complete lack of understanding. As to why a leader or representative of that long-suffering people doesn't so much as take note of it. Has he entirely lost his sense of dignity?

Has he forgotten that since he is not just an individual but also the bearer of his people's fate at an especially crucial moment? Is there anyone who was not bitterly disappointed at this total failure to rise to the occasion and stand with dignity—the dignity of his people's experience and cause—and testify to it with pride, and without compromise, without ambiguity, without the half embarrassed, half apologetic tone that Palestinian leaders take when they are begging for a little kindness from some totally unworthy white father?

But that has been the behavior of Palestinian rulers since Oslo and indeed since Haj Amin, a combination of misplaced juvenile defiance and plaintive supplication. Why on earth do they always think it absolutely necessary to read scripts written for them by their enemies? The basic dignity of our life as Arabs in Palestine, throughout the Arab world, and here in America, is that we are our own people, with a heritage, a history, a tradition and above all a language that is more than adequate to the task of representing our real aspirations, since those aspirations derive from the experience of dispossession and suffering that has been imposed on each Palestinian since 1948. Not one of our political spokespeople—the same is true of the Arabs since Abdel Nasser's time—ever speaks with self-respect and dignity of what we are, what we want, what we have done, and where we want to go.

Slowly, however, the situation is changing, and the old regime made up of the Abu Mazens and Abu Ammars of this world is passing and will gradually be replaced by a new set of emerging leaders all over the Arab world. The most promising is made up of the members of the National Palestinian Initiative; they are grassroots activists whose main activity is not pushing papers on a desk, nor juggling bank accounts, nor looking for journalists to pay attention to them, but who come from the ranks of the professionals, the working classes, and young intellectuals and activists, the teachers, doctors, lawyers, working people who have kept society going while also fending off daily Israeli attacks. Second, these are people committed to the kind of democracy and popular participation undreamt of by the Authority, whose idea of democracy is stability and security for itself. Lastly, they offer social services to the unemployed, health to the uninsured and the poor, proper secular education to a new generation of Palestinians who must be taught the realities of the modern world, not just the extraordinary worth of the old one. For such programs, the NPI stipulates that getting rid of the Occupation is the only way forward, and that in order to do that, a representative national unified leadership be elected freely to replace the cronies, the outdated, and the ineffectiveness that have plagued Palestinian leaders for the past century.

Only if we respect ourselves as Arabs and Americans, and understand the true dignity and justice of our struggle, only then can we appreciate why, almost despite ourselves, so many people all over the world, including Rachel Corrie and the two young people wounded with her from ISM, Tom Hurndall and Brian Avery, have felt it possible to express their solidarity with us.

I conclude with one last irony. Isn't it astonishing that all the signs of popular solidarity that Palestine and the Arabs receive occur with no comparable sign of solidarity and dignity for ourselves, that others admire and respect us more than we do ourselves? Isn't it time we caught up with our own status and made certain that our representatives here and elsewhere realize, as a first step, that they are fighting for a just and noble cause, and that they have nothing to apologize for or anything to be embarrassed about? On the contrary, they should be proud of what their people have done and proud also to represent them.

June 2003

PART ONE: BEGINNINGS

I

FOUNDING THE INTERNATIONAL SOLIDARITY MOVEMENT

HELPING TO BRING BACK HOPE
Talks given in Toronto by George Rishmawi and Neta Golan
by George Rishmawi and Neta Golan, 20 November 2002, ZNet

George Rishmawi

Thank you for being here. My name is George Rishmawi and I was born in 1973, in Beit Sahour. Parts of Beit Sahour are in what's known as "Zone A", other parts are in "Zone C", zones of occupied Palestine as designated by the Oslo agreement. It's a town of 13,000 people; 80% are Christians, and 20% are Muslims, but everyone is related and everyone knows each other. People know each other so well that it can take 15 minutes to walk 100 metres in Beit Sahour, because you are always running into your cousins, friends, and you have to stop and talk. Beit Sahour is also one of the sites of a nonviolent resistance movement against the Israeli Occupation, a community that refused to pay taxes to Israel in 1989, which I'll talk more about.

I have to say that it is a very different feeling being here in Canada. When I travel here, or in the US, or in Europe, it's a different feeling because I'm able to drive for hours and not be stopped at a checkpoint. It's a different feeling because here you don't

Photograph by Jamal Arouri, AFP/Al-Ayyam.

feel like someone is constantly trying to push you out.

I didn't really understand that I was living under Occupation until I was 8 years old. When I was 8 years old my cousin was kidnapped and killed by the Israeli army. He was 24 years old, and because he was a close relative, the "mourning house" was our house. Many people visited us in those 40 days of mourning, because at the time such a killing was still an unusual and rare event. It was then that I understood that we were living under an Occupation: an Occupation that steals your land, your freedom, your cousin away—and one day it could steal you away as well.

The first intifada started in 1987, and I was old enough then to participate in it. For a young person in Palestine at the time there were all kinds of options as to how to participate. Which party to join? Which tactics to apply? There were many different parties with many different ideas as to how to win liberation. I was attracted to a group that believes in education, in nonviolence. We worked based on the belief that by educating ourselves, we would give ourselves the power to face the situation, and the more knowledge we had, the more power we would have as well.

But of course I started by throwing rocks, chasing soldiers and running away from them, like everyone else. Like everyone else, I was arrested, in 1989. I'm a bit shy to talk about my experience in prison because I was only imprisoned for two months. My experience was not tough at all compared with my cousin's, or another cousin who was in prison for seven years.

Based on my experiences though, if I were the Israeli authorities I would not send any Palestinians to prison. Because it's in prison that you learn how resistance is absolutely necessary. You learn because in prison you feel the Occupation even more intensely. I was in prison and missed university. I missed Christmas, New Year's Eve, and my birthday. On New Year's Eve we were gassed by the army, in prison, because January 1 is the anniversary of the Fatah movement's founding in 1967, associated strongly with the movement for Palestinian Liberation. The prison authorities were worried about how the prisoners would react to the anniversary, so they put us under curfew and gassed us. We were under curfew in prison. It's strange, but true.

But before long I was out of prison, and back in the intifada. Around Christmas of 1991 there was a candlelight procession in Beit Sahour. I heard that there would be Palestinians, Internationals, and Israelis taking part in this and I knew I had to join it.

I wanted to join it so that I could talk to the Israelis, specifically, and tell them about the different kind of Christmas that I had had in prison. So I went, and I met those Israelis, and I did tell them about my experience, and they listened. I found out who organized the procession—it was the Centre for Rapprochement Between Peoples, that I had heard of because of the tax revolt in 1989. I joined it immediately.

I appreciated the idea of rapprochement because it gave me a chance to tell Israelis, without using violence, what I thought of the Occupation and what I had gone through. I believe that in some sense the violence that we are living comes about because people don't have a way of communicating this pain, these experiences, without violence. Palestinians are shooting in order to say "we don't accept the Occupation, we have a bad experience". The rapprochement centre provided another way for people to say this. So we organized dialogues between Palestinians and Israelis, but since 2000, with the second intifada, we have also been doing a lot of direct action, nonviolent direct action.

One of the important initiatives that rapprochement was involved in was the tax revolt in 1989 that I mentioned. In that year Beit Sahour refused to pay taxes to Israel, and they did so under a slogan. The slogan was: "No taxation without representation." This slogan might be familiar to you, but what happened next had a strong impact on me. Beit Sahour was seized by Israel. The army arrested 89 people and besieged the town. There was a resolution in the United Nations condemning Israel's actions in Beit Sahour, and it was vetoed by the United States of America. That was a clear message from the United States that what is good for us isn't good when other people do it, and it had an impact on me personally.

Israel confiscated goods, machines from small businesses, ovens right out of people's houses, in order to "collect the taxes" that Beit Sahour was refusing to pay. They took $5 million worth of goods and left the town with a damaged infrastructure. There was a loud cry among Palestinians then, because our nonviolent resistance was met very violently. There were Israelis coming in to break the siege and be with the Palestinians. That was part of an effort against Prime Minister Rabin's policy of "breaking the bones of the Palestinians". Our initiative was called "Break bread not bones". One day the military ordered the evacuation of all the Israelis in the town on the grounds that it was "dangerous" for them. Luckily some of the Israelis visiting us were rabbis, and they argued. It was Shabbat, they said—was the Israeli government going to be the only government in the world that impinged on the religious freedom of Jews by forcing them to travel on Shabbat?

In 2000, the rapprochement centre had another candlelight procession, the biggest since 1991, with 8000 people. After our demonstration there were several houses that were demolished by shelling. Why? The army claimed that there were snipers who were hiding out in the houses. But there were 160 houses destroyed, 240 families displaced, because when you destroy a home you displace more than one family. When your house becomes the source of your fear, when the children are afraid to stay in the house, you will want to leave, and so many people left even though their houses weren't destroyed.

On December 28 of 2000 we marched for removal of the military base near Beit Sahour. There was no justification for this base even in terms of protecting Israeli settlers. There were no Israeli civilians in the area. It was also an ancient site of graves dating back to the Byzantine era, of historical importance. Three hundred and fifty of us marched to the base, and there were no guards at the gate because marching to a military base was not something that was done, it wasn't something they were expecting. So we walked right in, and gave them our message: we meant them no harm, we intended no violence, but that they had to evacuate the base. They were shocked. This wasn't something that happened! They said they would consult with their superiors. On our way out, one protestor—an International, who they say was French but I still remember as a Canadian—climbed up a watchtower and planted a Palestinian flag. Palestinians wanted to do that but couldn't because they would have been shot, but this International managed to do it. This was a victory. There were 350 people marching, people of all ages, including kids, Internationals, Palestinians, some Israelis; no one even threw a stone.

The Israeli media put this on the 7 pm news—most people watch the 7 o'clock news. The commentary that went with it was: how did the army allow them to do this? This question was asked over and over. When the IDF [Israeli Defence Forces] spokesperson was interviewed, he said the base had been moved—200 yards away. Now 200 yards is not a major victory but it shows that they were concerned. We thought we could build on this. There were examples of successful nonviolent action, like the

Christian Peacemaker Teams in Hebron, so why couldn't we do the same? We planned for a campaign in April 2001.

In that campaign we had three major actions targeting the daily problems of Palestinians under occupation. The roadblocks, for example. These were a major problem, dividing the West Bank into 64 separate cantons. They make 15-minute journeys into journeys of three or four hours. Babies have been born at these road-blocks. People have died in ambulances at them. The roadblocks are for the settlers. The settlers can drive straight through them while Palestinians have to wait. So we did direct actions to take these roadblocks down. We had other campaigns of direct action.

Since April 2002—well, March 29, 2002 to be exact—the ISM has managed to establish a permanent international presence in some Palestinian areas. Staying in homes, in Balata in the houses of martyrs that are targeted for demolition. Riding ambulances and acting as a human shield, for students and teachers in schools. Sometimes Internationals have been shot at. In Beit Jala, there was some shooting even though the army knew there were Internationals in the crowd. We have been training people in nonviolence and in action in the Palestinian situation, and we've seen great improve-ments in the performance of our activists as a result. So today training is a fundamental part of what the ISM does.

The ISM is today a Palestinian-led, nonviolent movement. It isn't that Palestinians are the commanders. We have a consensus-based structure, with a core group that meets once a month but with the details left to the affinity groups. We have regional coordination, and a decentralized structure that depends on the local communities. Our goal is to help Palestinians do nonviolent resistance because when they do it without international accompaniment they are met with terrible violence. The inter-national presence enabled many families, this October, to go to their fields and harvest their olives, and open roadblocks. When the army sees that they're watched, they are less free-handed in how they treat people.

You are all invited to Palestine. When they see Internationals who have come, Palestinians feel hope, that others have come to share their hardship. Hope is very important for a people who feel their pain ignored, their voice unheard, their land taken away every day.

Neta Golan

My name is Neta Golan. I was born in Tel Aviv. My childhood was scary, and simple. There were good guys and bad guys. We were the good guys. The bad guys … could be anyone, but they were mostly Arabs. Now I'm a third generation Israeli: my grandmother was born in what was still called Palestine. My mother was born in 1948. And yet, I grew up in the shadow of the Holocaust. It was always my reference point, for everything.

As a child, I met Palestinians. They were there, working in construction or sanitation. But there was never a chance to meet as equals. Instead there were fears, being fed by the media, by what we learned in school. I learned always that we were defending ourselves from people who wanted to kill us.

It wasn't until I was 15 years old that I learned of the Occupation. It was during the first intifada, because before the first intifada Palestinians, the Occupation, simply didn't exist to us. The first intifada made it impossible for Israelis to ignore Palestinians. But I was raised on Jewish history, a history of oppression, dispossession, suffering ethnic cleansing, of being forced out of community after community. Could we really be doing these things to another people?

I couldn't believe it because I was a part of the consensus opinion in Israel, that we are morally superior. They are violent. We have purity of arms. If we do kill a civilian or an innocent, it's by mistake. Even if these mistakes happen every single day. I didn't believe it until I saw it with my own eyes. I refused to believe that a soldier would open fire on an innocent child, but I saw it. Unfortunately in Nablus where I live, I see it too often. When I would hear about a child being killed by a soldier, I would think—no, he must have thrown a stone, he must have been doing something that endangered the soldier and forced the soldier to shoot back. I wanted to believe that the children were throwing stones. But when you are in the West Bank, and you see a child throw a stone at a tank, you understand that if that child is killed, that is murder. And very recently, five Internationals were with Baha, one of the children who we knew well, and soldiers in an armoured personnel carrier picked him out from among the Internationals, shot him twice in the chest, and killed him.

As a child I wouldn't have been able to believe this. I would say "the proof of their violence is suicide bombing! We would never do something like that." One of my classmates asked me: "What's the difference between a suicide bombing and a Phantom jet bombing a refugee camp?" I said: "We don't bomb refugee camps." I couldn't believe the only difference between us and them was that we had better weapons. But I went home and asked my father. "Is it true that we bomb refugee camps with Phantom jets?"

"Yes. The terrorists think they can hide in the refugee camps, so we prove that they cannot," he told me.

But that wasn't even enough to change me, because the conditioning runs very deep. So deep that when I first went to the West Bank, during Oslo, I would have anxiety attacks. Once a week I would go, and every trip I would be filled with anxiety, filled with fear, thinking "they all want to kill me!" And it took at least fifteen minutes of seeing people going about their business, talking to each other, working, doing almost anything other than thinking about how much they wanted to kill me, before I calmed down. Seeing their openness, their willingness to accept me, their generosity, that has been the greatest gift of overcoming my fear—the chance to discover the wisdom, the beauty of the Palestinian people. Israelis who can't overcome their fear are much poorer for not having the chance to do that.

After a year and a half of this anxiety, it mostly went away. But as soon as things changed, when the political situation would become worse, I would fall back on that conditioning and become afraid again. In 2000, when the second intifada broke out, I was afraid. I was in Nablus and asked my fiancé "Am I being paranoid because I'm afraid?" He said "Yes!"

I am still shocked, sometimes, to discover what my government does, and to discover who the Palestinians really are and what they are really like.

During the Oslo peace process, I thought, along with most Israelis, "this is wonderful!" Because in Israel, there was peace. But when I heard from the Palestinians, I learned that there was not peace. There were, instead, settlements, losses in freedom of movement. Overnight in 1991 Palestinians lost the right to go to East Jerusalem without a permit. East Jerusalem is the capital, the heart of Palestine in every way: politically, culturally, spiritually, economically. Overnight they lost the chance to go there and in 1993 with the peace process, they waited to get their chance back. The resistance to occupation basically stopped. But peace never came. What came instead were the bypass roads, settler roads that surrounded all the communities, with the checkpoints and roadblocks.

Thanks to the bypass roads and checkpoints, it isn't just difficult to travel between cities in the West Bank: it's illegal. This wasn't the case even during the first intifada. Today the West Bank has been under siege, under curfew, for months and months. It's possible for the army to besiege the West Bank in this way because of the infrastructure of the bypass roads that was built during the "peace process".

People saw that the peace process was a smokescreen and that on the ground, the Occupation was expanding. Palestinians would tell me, first, "Nothing has changed, but we're waiting for things to get better." Next, they would say "Things aren't changing, and we can't stand this." For years I tried to tell Israelis that there was no peace process. Most Israelis didn't want to hear it. They would say these things take time. And when you have a job, a home, freedom, you have time. But when you have none of these things, for seven years, as Palestinians didn't have, you don't feel like you have time.

I remember in 1997, Prime Minister Netanyahu made the decision to build a settlement around occupied East Jerusalem, Har Homa. East Jerusalem is the capital of Palestine, but it had been surrounded by Israeli settlements. Har Homa was the final link in a chain that would totally surround East Jerusalem with settlements. For the Palestinians, this was read as proof that the peace process was over. There were non-violent protests. Palestinians and Israelis joined in. Feisal Husseini and others were there. The mountain that was to become Har Homa was squatted by activists.

Netanyahu gave the order to storm the mountain, kick the demonstrators off it, and bulldoze all the trees on the mountain to make room for the settlement. The night that happened I was devastated. Again I talked to my father, who supported the decision. "We can't allow them to tell us where we can and can't build," he said.

I'm not a prophet, but I knew hopelessness, desperation, when I saw it. And I saw it then.

"But what if there's another suicide bomber?" There hadn't been one in some time, by that time. He told me that it was a "calculated risk".

Hours later there was a suicide bombing. "Do you still think it was the right decision?" I asked him. "Yes, it was a calculated risk." I couldn't believe it, but I thought "he's upset, as I am, shocked by the bombing, he doesn't mean that."

Hours after that, our phone rang. My father answered the phone and when he hung up he was pale. My cousin had been killed in the bombing. My father took back what he said about the calculated risk. "I shouldn't have said that," he told me. "But the only person responsible is the bastard who did it."

The only person responsible. The "calculated risk" had disappeared. The context had disappeared. Just the bomber was responsible.

And the bomber was responsible. But so was Netanyahu's settlement policy. And the Israeli government, who are willing to pay the price—even in Israeli blood, my cousin's blood—for maintaining and expanding the Occupation.

And the international community, as well, for not reacting. In Israel, I was shocked at the international community's non-reaction. We kept thinking—there's no way the international community is going to put up with this. But they did. And they do, still.

The Palestinian nonviolent movement today faces an unprecedented situation, a level of violence that is unimaginable. The Israelis don't see it. I want to show you a day of siege in Jenin, basically a "non-news" item, where tanks roll around, shooting in the streets to announce curfew as people run in fear. This happens every single day and it's not news because most journalists don't leave Jerusalem except occasionally to go to Ramallah or Bethlehem.

In an environment like this, people won't join a nonviolent movement. That's why we need Internationals. We need people to join, to bring the attention of the international community to the situation. The intifada started with children throwing stones. They were answered with snipers. Some Palestinians reacted to this violence by shooting attacks on soldiers and settlers. They were systematically assassinated, starting in Beit Sahour, and nearly every assassination killed innocent bystanders as well.

I'm often in Balata refugee camp, and I want to believe that Israel believes that its actions are going to stop resistance but they have to know that they are making the situation so intolerable that non-resistance is a non-option. There were no suicide bombers from Balata until May of this year. In May there were assassinations of two young men who were Palestinian fighters, members of the armed resistance. For the people in these camps, these fighters were heroes who were defending their people. It was four days after these assassinations that a wave of seven suicide bombers came from Balata.

The oldest of these bombers was 18.

The operations were poorly organized. Many of them blew up on the way, failed in their missions. They were obviously acts of pure desperation. The Israeli Army knows they can't stop attacks like these. Arafat certainly can't stop them.

But there is one thing that can stop them. Hope.

In the first intifada, tens of thousands of Palestinians marched for an end to occupation. There were some bombings—but Palestinians stopped them. When Prime Minister Barak wanted to have elections in an atmosphere of quiet, he got his quiet by lifting the siege and opening up a few roadblocks. That was all it took. There were no bombings because there was hope.

By your joining us, you can help bring back hope.

RESISTING THE TOOL OF CONTROL
An interview with Ghassan Andoni
by Ghassan Andoni and bitterlemons.org, 7 October 2002

bitterlemons: You recently said at a lecture that "you can't build a mass movement with the current level of violence." What did you mean by that and do you think that it still holds true?

Andoni: I think that it is extremely difficult to accommodate civilian mass resistance with a high level of military clashes and violence because it affects dramatically the level of risk people are required to take by just stepping into the streets into a massive civil-based movement. But people who want to engage in the struggle against the Occupation cannot just wait for things to be suitable for them and by the book.

bitterlemons: Would you call yourself a supporter of non-violent resistance and why?

Andoni: From the start of this crisis, we have been organizing campaigns including Palestinians and Internationals in which we tried to remove roadblocks, defy check-points, demonstrate in occupied areas and reach families there. We have been engaged in front of tanks to prevent them from moving. We have been doing protection work by providing human shields for people who are threatened and constantly bombarded. We have people who are now living in homes that are scheduled for demolition by the Israeli army. We try to protect the homes and prevent punishment for the families and try to go with farmers to their fields when it is really risky and dangerous to do so.

bitterlemons: Why do you feel that these kinds of activities are important?

Andoni: We need to find a way for the Palestinian masses to join in, in an active way— not only in remaining steadfast throughout the hardship. We think that having Internationals with us will provide a better platform to defy the Occupation and to report the truth of what is happening here and to urge the international community to think more about the need to protect Palestinians when brutal war is being waged against them.

We also believe that civil-based resistance can indeed be effective in terms of cracking down on the tools of occupation, mainly the tool of control. We believe that if we grow more massive we can really affect this huge network of roadblocks and checkpoints and force the Occupation to rethink its policies in the Palestinian occupied territories.

bitterlemons: Does that mean that you do not think that armed resistance is valid?

Andoni: No, we state clearly that Palestinians have the full right to resist the Occupation with means that they think are suitable. We as the Palestinian Solidarity Movement have decided, however, that our tool for resisting the Occupation is non-violence.

bitterlemons: How might Israel practice non-violence?

Andoni: Occupation alone is a violent action that touches the lives of everybody who is under the control of the occupier. Recently, I think that the Occupation has taken on a new form and now includes direct killing of people, creating war zones and bombarding Palestinian areas. There is no question, however, that the Occupation is violent in using all its of its force to crack down on the will of Palestinians to be free and independent.

bitterlemons: What was your impression of the Common Ground poll that questions Israelis and Palestinians on their approaches to non-violent action?

Andoni: On the Palestinian side, I think that Palestinians stated clearly that we are willing to do whatever it takes to get out of this mess. There is a large majority that supports non-violence, but that same majority supports violence as well. That is my interpretation of the results.

On the Israeli side, I think that most of the questions asked were irrelevant. In my understanding, if we are to arrive at peace in this area, we must have an active Palestinian resistance and an active Israeli anti-war and anti-Occupation movement. This is the shortest way to conclude this conflict in a peaceful solution.

Therefore, on the Israeli side, I did not see questions such as "Do you support Palestinian non-violent resistance?" as relevant. The relevant question is, "Would you be engaged in non-violent direct action against your government's atrocities and violence in the occupied territories?" That is what I want to see the poll results for.

bitterlemons: You sometimes stage joint demonstrations with Israeli left-wing groups. How would you evaluate that experience?

Andoni: I am interested in trying to attract as many Israelis as possible to join in efforts towards ending the Israeli Occupation of the Palestinian territories. I consider this important and it has been important in all of the different historic examples where people were fighting against an occupier to liberate themselves on their land.

Secondly, in principle, we are willing to work with Israeli groups who are willing to join active civil-based resistance against the Israeli Occupation. In particular, the invitation to the Israeli groups must come from the Palestinian community in which the activity is happening. By doing things this way, we give priority to Palestinian unity over Israeli participation.

Now, this is sometimes problematic because some Israeli groups feel that they are not adequately included in the planning period. But we think our policy in this regard is right.

bitterlemons: How has the Israeli army responded to your joint activities?

Andoni: Evidently, the presence of Israelis and Internationals can defuse the ability of the Israeli army to use greater force against protestors and make soldiers think twice before starting to shoot or use force.

But this is not always the case. We have instances where Palestinians and Internationals and sometimes Israelis have been shot at or injured and treated brutally by the Israeli army. Soon, we will start a campaign of olive picking, in which Palestinians and Internationals and maybe some Israeli groups will join villagers as they work on olive groves that are close to settlements and in dangerous areas. In encounters with settlers, we will have to see how much "protection" Internationals and Israelis can provide.

THE TRUTH ABOUT OCCUPATION
Activists decry plight of Palestinians
by Gaelle Faure, 13 January 2003, UCSD Guardian

"The Truth About Occupation," a lecture that featured guest speakers Adam Shapiro and Huwaida Arraf from the International Solidarity Movement, took place on January 10 as the first event in a week of speakers presented by Students for Justice exploring the Israeli–Palestinian conflict.

Shapiro and Arraf, who are husband and wife, separately discussed their personal experiences living and working toward an end to occupation in Israeli-controlled territories. Both began their careers in the Middle East as mediators in conflict-resolution groups.

Arraf, whose Palestinian parents fled to the United States before her birth, worked in the Middle East with a group that brought together Israeli and Palestinian teenagers before co-founding the ISM in 2001. Her quickly growing organization adopted the mission of recruiting individuals from all over the world to join Palestinians in non-violent protests in Israeli-controlled areas.

"This is a Palestinian-led movement, but it needs Internationals," Arraf said, explaining that a Palestinian life is worth little to Israeli military, while the death of an International protester could cause a PR disaster, and that Internationals were there-fore protecting Palestinians from lethal violence.

"What I think promotes misunderstanding is that we were involved in a peace process from 1993 to 2000, but after that people assumed that Palestinians didn't really want peace. This is said without really knowing what went on during this time," Arraf said.

Arraf explained that while the peace accords were supposed to lead to the end of West Bank and Gaza Occupation, the number of Israeli settlers in these areas doubled, Palestinian land between settlements was confiscated, and roadblocks and checkpoints sprang up.

"Gaza was closed off. It's the largest prison in the world right now," Arraf said.

Arraf witnessed firsthand the first Intifada, and was inspired by the nonviolent protests she saw. When the military started instating 24-hour house arrests and regulating businesses' hours of operation, businesses protested by closing early, in response to which the military cut the stores' locks, said Arraf. Other Palestinians refused to pay taxes or burned their ID cards.

"Even children did creative things, like tying cans to cats' tails to put soldiers on edge after curfew when nobody was supposed to be on the streets," Arraf said.

Arraf described the daily difficulties of Palestinian life in occupied territory, including the routine of military checkpoints, which she had to pass regularly to go from one Palestinian town to another. According to Arraf, men are the most harassed, held at gunpoint with their hands in the air, made to lift their shirts and sometimes forced to drop their pants. The ensuing wait, she said, sometimes lasted from 7 a.m. until sunset, keeping men from going to work or the university.

One of the ISM's actions included escorting Palestinians to their olive fields during harvest season this fall. Arraf said that some days they succeeded, other days they were turned back, and that some Internationals were beaten by military in the process.

Shapiro, who lived for nearly four years on both sides of Jerusalem and who is now a Ph.D. student at the American University in Washington, D.C., went on to describe the life of victims on both sides of the conflict.

"I know what it was like, September 11, and it was very traumatic, but that was only one event, one day," he said, explaining the constant shadow of threat faced by Israeli citizens. However, he argued the Palestinian situation is much more difficult than the Israelis', who have the freedom to leave their houses every day.

"We should sympathize … but we should not be confused," Shapiro said, explaining that the Israeli situation is incomparable to the Palestinian situation.

He also pointed to difficulties in cracking into the average Israeli mindset, citing the media as biased.

"You don't hear the word 'Palestinian' in the Israeli media without the word 'terrorism' next to it," Shapiro said. "We are so free here in using the term 'terrorism.' But you cannot say that [the Israeli government killing civilians] is not terrorism."

As for his vision of the future, Shapiro said that he could not envision peace talks without an end to Israeli Occupation first.

"Peace has to be between two people who are free and equal," he said. "The Occupation hasn't generated stability for Israel …. Ending occupation is just about the only thing we haven't tried."

THE INTERNATIONAL INTIFADA
Foreigners stand in the line of fire in Palestine, Muslims and Christians united for the Holy Land
by Rhonda L. McCarty and Mazin B. Qumsiyeh, September 2001, Q News

Almost a year has passed since the latest Palestinian uprising against the Occupation started—600 Palestinians killed and 17,000 injured (a third of them children). Palestinians continue to struggle to survive and resist by means available to them. Heroic stories are so many that books are being written about the Occupation and its after-math. Here we wanted to shed some light on one aspect of the story, the international solidarity and non-violent resistance.

When Israel refused the presence of international monitors, civilian activists around the world recognized that they did not need to wait for their governments to take action. Mass non-violent action was initiated to support and defend Palestinian rights and shield them from the aggression by Israeli forces. Many Israeli peace groups struggled with identity and sense of purpose but a few true activists became more determined to join the Palestinian people in non-violent resistance.

The Palestinian Centre for Rapprochement, with the support of Italian activist and European Parliament member Luisa Morgantini, called for a week of non-violent direct action in mid-April with marches to Israeli military bases near peaceful Palestinian towns. Israeli Occupation Forces were not prepared initially for this kind of resistance. As time passed by, Israeli authorities intensified their aggression even on peaceful demonstrators.

Israeli activists like Neta Golan began acting as human shields, offering Palestinian farmers protection while doing their farming chores. Other key players in these early actions included Bat Shalom and the Women's Coalition for a Just Peace in Israel, Christian Peacemakers Team in Hebron, Gush Shalom, Rabbis for Human Rights, and Women in Black.

In the US activists began serious work to coordinate mass gatherings of Internationals for the purpose of providing tangible support to the Palestinians. Rev. Thom Saffold scheduled a delegation for August. The objectives of this mission were to offer protection, show solidarity, and draw attention to the realities on the ground. Israeli American activist Charles Lenchner gathered a delegation for an overlapping trip. The program, dubbed Olive Tree Summer, specifically recruited Jewish Americans. Both Thom and Charles voiced some concern initially that they might not be fully welcome in their pursuits. Palestinian activists and organizers such as Ghassan Andoni made it clear that they welcomed this support.

Jewish, Muslim, and Christian organizers carefully planned all aspects of the campaign: logistics, media coverage, training, and specific actions. Involved Palestinians, Israelis, and Americans discussed at length the needs of the community and the impact that each action would have on it. Organizers agreed on other important components such as a complete devotion to non-violence, a focus on ending the Occupation, that the campaign must be ongoing, clear messages to the media, and flexibility in planning and carrying out actions.

The umbrella framework for this ten days of action is the International Solidarity Movement and the Campaign Against the Occupation. The participants call on their respective governments to cease active support of Israel's aggression against Palestinian civilians and pressure Israel to comply with international law and UN resolutions.

Twenty-one Americans, eight Italians, four French, four British, and one Danish participant joined existing International, Israeli and Palestinian activists for the inauguration of the campaign. Additional activists joined the following week, including a group of twenty-five Italians and eight French delegates.

The group put all other plans on hold to address the closure of the Orient House [the administrative center of the Palestinian Authority in Jerusalem since 1993] by the Israeli Occupation Forces. For the next four days, the international, interfaith team of 30–40 in number would conduct non-violent protests. Holding signs calling for an end to the occupation of the Orient House, an end to violence and justice for all people, and Palestinian flags, each day they formed a line at the police barricade. Each day they were consistently true to their non-violent approach. Each day they were exposed to the violence of the Israeli police. Members of the International team, journalists, and other witnesses can only speculate about how severe the treatment of Palestinians is when they are not present. They see the treatment that they received as non-violent Americans, Israeli citizens and foreign visitors as a clear attempt to undermine any non-violent movement on behalf of peace in the region.

On Saturday, August 11, eleven were arrested, seven foreign civilians and four Palestinians. The Palestinians detained were observers and not participating in the International demonstration. The majority of those arrested were American, two of them Palestinian-American women. Two activists with remaining charges, Mahmoud Q. Mahmoud and Andy Clarno, are being defended by the Israeli human rights lawyer Lea Tsemel.

Thus, a Muslim, a Christian, and a Jew stand up to the racist legal and military Israeli system.

They will not be alone.

[…]

WHAT IS THE ISM?

The International Solidarity Movement is a Palestinian-led movement of Palestinian and International activists working to raise awareness of the struggle for Palestinian freedom and an end to Israeli occupation. We utilize nonviolent, direct-action methods of resistance to confront and challenge illegal Israeli occupation forces and policies.

As enshrined in international law and UN resolutions, we recognize the Palestinian right to resist Israeli violence and occupation[1] via legitimate[2] armed struggle. However, we believe that nonviolence can be a powerful weapon in fighting oppression and we are committed to the principles of nonviolent resistance.

- We support the Palestinian right to resist the Occupation, as provided for by International Law;

- We call for an immediate end to the Occupation and immediate compliance and implementation of all relevant UN resolutions;

- We call for immediate international intervention to protect the Palestinian people and ensure Israel's compliance with International Law.

---

1 UN General Assembly Resolution 37/43 affirms the right of an occupied people to resist foreign occupation by all available means, including armed struggle.

2 Abiding by the Fourth Geneva Convention and specifically to the definition of who is a combatant.

Due to the lack of respect for Palestinian human rights and human life by the Israeli government and occupation forces, an international presence is needed to support Palestinian nonviolent resistance. Palestinian activists trying to work or protest alone face harsh punishment from Israeli forces. This has included beatings, long-term arrests, serious injury and even death. International activists are thus a resource for Palestinians, both in terms of their presence and as witnesses to the daily humiliation and injustice of the Israeli Occupation. In addition to our ongoing actions on the ground in the Occupied Palestinian Territories, the ISM conducts campaigns of nonviolent direct action which international civilians are invited to join for a set period of time.

The first few days of the campaigns are reserved for orientation and non-violence training. Activists are equipped with practical, logistical and legal information. Also work structures and affinity groups are formed, responsibilities are assigned and strategies and methodology are discussed. With the highly sensitive and volatile nature of the situation in the Occupied Palestinian Territories, it is vital that activists are equipped with the knowledge and mental preparedness to be effective in achieving predetermined goals and aiding in the overall mission of bringing about an end to the Israeli Occupation of Palestine through the use of nonviolent methods and strategies.

2

FIRST AND SECOND CAMPAIGNS

TRYING NOT TO GO
Account of the first ISM campaign, August 2001
by Edward Mast, August 2001

I tried my best to find a reason not to go.

The call came over email in July of 2001, asking Internationals to come to the West Bank and join Palestinians and Israeli allies in nonviolent civil disobedience to resist the Occupation.

[...]

The United States is so complicit in the ongoing injustice that Linda and I felt strongly about the importance of working to change public and governmental opinion in this country. However, with the increasing violence against Palestinians, the ever more discouraging personal reports from friends both in Israel and the West Bank, and the escalating rhetoric and actions of Ariel Sharon, Linda hearkened back to our conversation about international bodies and aggressive tanks.

So when the call arrived, asking Internationals to come for the first two-week International Solidarity Movement campaign in August, I looked at my calendar,

Photograph by Goran Tomasevic. © Reuters, 2001. Reprinted with permission.

hoping that I had some prior commitment. My calendar let me down. We were newly married and pursuing adoption, but that paperwork could wait a few weeks. There wasn't even a party I'd have to miss. We had little information about the ISM or the campaign itself, but we'd both been there before and could certainly adapt. Generous relatives donated frequent flier miles to cover our airfare. The obstacles I'd hoped to pile up were failing to obstruct us.

[...]

We knew that there were people, both Palestinian and Israeli, who were standing and sitting and lying down in front of Israeli tanks and bulldozers to stop them from proceeding in their work of state terror. Linda, whose level of courage was somewhat higher than mine, seemed fully willing to join those lying down in front of tanks. I was dubious. But the work of going there and joining this movement was inarguable. The first Intifida had been largely nonviolent, and had been met with Israeli brutality. This second Intifada had a violent component, and was being met with unprecedented Israeli firepower, aimed at militants and civilians alike. Peaceful demonstrations were being met with live ammunition. Rocks were being met with bullets. Prison was no novelty to Palestinians under occupation, but the daily killings, maimings and assassi-nations were a sharp ramping-up of the stakes. Since Israel has always relied heavily on the good will of the world in general and the United States in particular, our pres-ence as US citizens could make a tangible difference. If we shared some of their danger, Palestinians could share some of our safety.

We had no illusions of ending the Occupation that summer, and we were firm in our commitment to avoid heroics or romantic notions. We were there not to show Palestinians how to be nonviolent; we were going to join as footsoldiers in a Palestinian nonviolent campaign. Perhaps one or both of us would lie down in front of a bull-dozer, but perhaps one or both of us would remain on the sidewalk as support. Our fundamental victory condition was simple and fairly assured: to arrive.

Best-laid plans

Compared to what has happened since, the summer of 2001 might seem almost placid. It did not seem so at the time. Almost as soon as we arrived in Bethlehem and began our nonviolence training, more assassinations of Palestinians took place and so a suicide bomber retaliated with an attack in Jerusalem.

The ISM coordinators had a carefully organized itinerary of events for the two-week August campaign: freedom rides through Israeli checkpoints, helping Palestinians remove Israeli roadblocks, working with Palestinian farmers in fields threatened by Israeli settler violence, and other actions. But sudden violence in Israel/Palestine always disrupts plans. Linda and I spent one night in Hebron as a protective presence in a Palestinian home often targeted for settler violence, and while we were there, a part of the threatened invasion took place.

The Israeli military invasion of Orient House was supposedly in retaliation for the suicide bombing, but in fact fit well with the apparent longterm plan to drive the Palestinian National Authority out of Jerusalem. Orient House, the longtime residence of the Husseini family in Jerusalem, had since 1993 become the administrative center of the Palestinian Authority. The Israeli assault was comparable to driving the US Senate out of the House of Congress.

We traveled with about thirty Internationals to Jerusalem to join the ongoing demonstrations against the assault.

[…]

ISRAELI POLICE "CARRY OUT ROUTINE, ORGANIZED CRUELTY"
by Robert Fisk, 14 August 2001, Independent

The Arabs called it a "day of rage" but the Israelis were the ones demonstrating their rage outside Orient House yesterday. The Palestinian youth who dared to hold up a Palestinian flag made of paper was seized by six border guards and plain-clothes police, kicked, beaten, punched in the face and back and then kneed in the groin in front of us all.

Many of the police had been brought down from Haifa, where a Palestinian suicide bomber had blown himself up a few hours earlier in a vain effort to murder Israelis in a café, and there was a tangible desire to inflict pain on some of the crowd.

A tall, thin young man with shaggy brown hair who tried to escape a policeman's grasp at the iron security barriers was dragged back into the police lines and set on by eight men. There must have been 20 television cameras and a score of photographers running level with the Shin Bet intelligence boys as they dragged the man screaming up the road towards Orient House, kicking him in the chest and forcing back his head until he choked. The moment he was in the back seat of a white police van, an Israeli plain-clothes man in a red shirt set upon him. As he was held down from the other side of the vehicle, the Israeli kicked him again and again between the legs until the young man was crying in a high, animal voice.

It was, as one of the foreign protesters muttered, enough to turn a Palestinian into a suicide-bomber. It was also very, very weird. Here we were, perhaps a hundred journalists watching a hundred "peace" demonstrators, European, American, Christian and Jew, and Palestinian, and every few minutes, on a signal from a fat policeman in a blue shirt, his colleagues would run amok.

After all the talk of Israel being a peace-loving state among the nations, founded upon the rule of law, the police would suddenly prove that those constant Palestinian complaints of beatings and brutality were true, right in front of us. A border guard became so fascinated by the beating of one man—he could not take his eyes off the fists that were hammering into the man's stomach and ribs—that he forgot to keep the press at bay and allowed me to walk up to the van as one of his colleagues viciously assaulted another man.

Every police force can lose its cool—we have our bad eggs in Britain—but this was calculated, routine, organized cruelty. A lot of the border guards were grinning when the Palestinians screamed. After a while it was obscene to watch.

I walked over to the Israeli mounted police. One of the officers was sitting in the saddle, smoking a cigarette and laughing as he talked on a mobile phone. A Shin Bet man patted the lead horse. "Most of these are Hannovers," he said of the breed. "We've got Hannovers and quarters. They take really good care of them."

Up the street, closer to Orient House, his colleagues were taking good care of their prisoners. In front of the horrified eyes of a group of humanitarian workers, one of them American, they beat the captured Palestinians all over again.

The crowd had no chance of seizing back Orient House, occupied by Israeli troops and police after Thursday's Jerusalem suicide bombing that massacred 15 Israelis.

They were kept all of a quarter of a mile from the building. But the horses were ridden into the crowd; a couple of stun grenades were fired into it. Just one officer realized, after more than an hour, that this piece of state bullying was a public relations disaster.

"Stop carrying them," he shouted as two Palestinians were dragged past the cameras under a rain of blows. "Let them walk."

But they could no longer stand upright. One of them had his shirt dragged over his head to reveal a back covered in red welts. A thought kept recurring in our minds: if this is what the Israeli police do to Palestinians in front of us, what do they do to them behind our backs?

Nor was it difficult to guess what these young men were thinking. Just a few hours before, they had heard that a 10 year old Palestinian girl had been shot dead by Israeli troops in Hebron, in another of those notorious "clashes", as the press likes to call them, and that, after a night of grieving, her 60 year old grandmother had died of a heart attack.

A little after midday yesterday, the little girl and her grandmother were buried together in the same grave.

INITIAL STATEMENT REGARDING ARREST AND DETENTION
by Andrew Clarno, 14 August 2001

On Saturday, August 11, 2001, at about 2:30 pm, Israeli police arrested me while I was standing on the sidewalk at the edge of the American Colony Hotel parking lot. I had arrived at the American Colony Hotel at around 2:15 pm along with twenty to twenty five other members of the International Solidarity Movement in order to peacefully demonstrate our opposition to the recent Israeli invasion and seizure of the Orient House. For about ten minutes, we witnessed clashes between Orthodox Jews and Palestinian youth and then we began our non-violent protest.

As we stood in a line on the sidewalk, holding signs and calling for justice and peace, we were attacked by the police. Without warning in either Arabic or English, the soldiers came towards us and began violently pushing and grabbing at Palestinians and then tearing the signs out of the hands of protesters. We began to chant "No Violence, No Violence"—calling on the police to recognize the non-violent nature of our protest and reinforcing our commitment not to respond violently to the violence used against us by the police. But the assault by the police continued. Soon police were pushing us all down the hill towards the American Colony. I saw several protesters knocked to the ground and kicked by the police while I was being pushed down the sidewalk in a group of protesters.

I had nearly reached the driveway of the American Colony Hotel when a police officer grabbed the beltloop in the back of my jeans with one hand and my right shoulder with his other hand. Although I did not resist, he forcefully dragged me into the street and put my head in a violent chokehold. His tight grip on my neck made breathing nearly impossible as he carried me nearly 100 meters up the hill towards Abu Obeidah street. We turned onto Abu Obeidah street, where the officer shoved me into the back seat of an SUV, then leaned into the front seat and reached around to punch me in the face twice with his left hand. In all, seven Internationals and four Palestinians were arrested at the protest that afternoon.

We were all taken to the Russian Compound, which is notorious for the torturous methods of interrogation and the violence perpetrated against prisoners by Israeli guards. One of the Palestinians was then released and the rest of us were charged with illegal assembly. In a seemingly random manner, a few of us were given the additional charge of assaulting a police officer. We were taken to our cells where we were held until 11:00 pm when a judge heard our case and gave the police twenty four-hours to complete their investigation. The following day, one Palestinian and one International were released without conditions and five Internationals were offered release on condition of not returning to the area of the Orient House.

The two Palestinians and I were brought before a judge and the police asked that we be held three days so that they could pursue their investigation of charges that the three of us had attacked police officers. The judge again offered the police twenty-four hours to produce enough evidence to bring charges against us, so we were returned to our cells and kept in prison another night. On Monday, August 13, 2001, the three of us were again brought before a judge.

The police released one of the Palestinians on similar condition as those offered to the Internationals the day before. Regarding the other Palestinian and I, however, the police argued that they had enough evidence to charge us with assaulting the police officers. They asked that we be detained for four days so that they could file charges against us and begin the trial process. The police have taken testimony from a police officer who states that he witnessed me push another police officer. They also presented testimony from the officer that arrested me—the one who grabbed, choked, and punched me. He states that I ignored his requests that I disperse and that I attempted to choke him.

Our attorney, Lea Tsemel, challenged all of this evidence. She highlighted the fact that the arresting officer did not mention this alleged attack in his initial arrest report and that his testimony was taken only AFTER the police had decided to charge me with assault.

Yesterday evening at 7:30 pm, the judge decided that there is enough evidence to charge the two of us with assaulting a police officer, but that there was not enough risk to keep us in prison pending further investigation. Therefore, Mahmoud Q. Mahmoud and I were released last night on condition that we not return to the immediate vicinity of the Orient House for forty days and that we agree to show up for further questioning and trial. The police were given forty eight hours to file charges against us—which they have promised to do.

I insist upon my innocence. I did not physically or in any other way assault or even threaten to assault a police officer or any other individual. I was never given orders to disperse and I did not resist arrest. I have always been a non-violent person and have supported struggles around the world for peace and justice. As part of the International Solidarity Movement Campaign to End the Occupation, I am committed to a program of non-violent actions in support of the Palestinian people in their struggle for national liberation and against the brutality of the Israeli Occupation.

The violence that day was perpetrated by the Israeli police—not by the protesters. The world has taken notice because the violence was directed against an American citizen and caught on film. But I guarantee that the charges are completely fabricated. I am convinced that they have been designed to undercut the non-violent campaign to end the Occupation. Please do not allow the Israeli police to portray and convict me as a violent offender. Please do not allow them to undermine our struggle for a just and non-violent resolution to this conflict.

STEPPING OFF THE SIDEWALK
by Edward Mast, August 2001

The campaign still had over a week to go, but the planned itinerary of events had been overturned by the escalating tension. Townships and communities became fearful of drawing attention to themselves and so becoming targets for random military reprisal. Still, we were able to complete several actions. Internationals formed a human chain to block soldiers from interfering while Palestinians tore down a military roadblock on the main road to the village of al-Khader. We went back the next day to play soccer with those same villagers on a field which had been declared off-limits, being too close to one of the Jewish-only settler roads. The local organizers were careful to monitor the mood of the many young boys and teenagers that tended to hang around us on these actions. We didn't want restless boys throwing rocks out of boredom.

[…]

The last action planned in that campaign was a nonviolent walk to break through the checkpoint between Bethlehem and Jerusalem. We practiced nonviolence in advance, making sure that we were not assaultive even in slow-motion. We had been joined by a larger delegation from Italy, and so about 150 of us marched late in the afternoon toward the checkpoint. About 40 Palestinians were with us. I was nervous about being arrested again: I didn't want to miss a flight home, and the chilling effect had done its work. I joined the march, but was planning to be vigilantly non-arrestable. This meant I would keep a flexible position, ready to step aside at the first sign of trouble, staying close to the sidewalk or on it. I was not alone.

We marched up the street toward the checkpoint, staffed by more of those bewildered young men in uniforms with automatic weapons. They called for backup, and police vehicles arrived fairly quickly. The march stopped and stood in place for quite some time while our organizers negotiated with the soldiers and police, suggesting that they let us pass through for a limited distance.

Our basic tactic throughout the campaign was to surround and shield Palestinians from police and soldier violence. On this march, the Palestinians were mainly grouped in the middle, with Internationals around them and scattered among them. All were linking arms, standing in place, sometimes chanting "No violence." As we approached the checkpoint, however, I saw a gap in the line of protection, leaving a line of several Palestinians extended to the edge of the march. Israeli police were starting to pace and lurk around, glaring and sometimes pointing at Palestinians they recognized. One officer had a video camera, panning across the crowd, getting all those faces on record. If the officers encountered a Palestinian on the edge, they could fairly easily grab him, and we could only protect him with a scuffle.

No one else seemed to notice, so I stepped off the sidewalk and took the arm of the young man on the edge. Sure enough, an officer came stalking past, and stopped next to me. He pointed at another Palestinian man a few feet away, and said "You. Come here." Our links got tighter, and I gently pivoted until my back was to the officer and he would have to get past me to reach the other man. The officer moved on.

Having stepped into the line, I realized, with some dismay, that I was part of the shield now, unless I wanted to make a sharp retreat. The officers kept circling like sharks or alligators, but nothing happened except more of the same intimidating behavior. We stood with linked arms for some time. I had not met the young man before, and we shared only a few odd words of English and Arabic.

The march was turned away, and the organizers led us back to the hotel which was our headquarters. The young man and I found a translator and were able to chat a little. We exchanged a handshake and a long look. I left the next day, so I didn't see him again.

Linda and I arrived home just in time for the disasters of September 11, 2001, and the sudden overwhelming need for education and action about Israel/Palestine and the Middle East has kept us busy ever since. There is much to do at home, but we keep encouraging Americans to step off the sidewalk and go to Palestine, because there is much to do there, as well. Getting arrested is one thing, of course, and attracts important attention. But more important still, I found, was walking the exercise yard with Palestinian prisoners, and linking arms with Palestinians on the street, shielding them for a passing moment from police violence and perhaps from their own despair. Nothing I did or have done was more valuable than being one of those to demonstrate with our bodies that these resilient, courageous, desperate people have not been and will not be forgotten. Giving them some measure of our safety, our hope, our possible future, is the quiet victory that we may count on for now, and will prepare us for that greater victory: when the Occupation ends.

MY MOTHER'S SON
by Trevor Baumgartner, 13 December 2001

As I write this from Jerusalem I still have no idea how he's doing. The 13 year old boy from Qalandia who Israeli soldiers shot in the face. Nor do I even know his name. We kneeled, shoulder to shoulder behind a parked car, while windows exploded like water balloons all around us. We had nowhere to go, and the instant he looked through the passenger side window it happened. The blast and his blood splattering on the ground with shards of glass.

And I've no idea how he's doing. Nor do I even know his name.

Just seconds earlier, as I stood completely alone and pinched between a car and a family bric-a-brac shop, one soldier trained his rifle on me. I ducked down behind this car and bullets whizzed past, dinging light poles and car doors and everything in their way. I picked a couple up and pocketed them—one rubber peg and one solid steel pellet.

Bullets are bullets. Whether rubber or rubbercoated steel or steel or "live".

When I raised my head and peered through the windshield I saw these soldiers bumble down the rocky hillside, straight for me. They hurled a tear-gas grenade at me, and as I stumbled away, onto the naked walkway I knew full well how exposed I was. I knew the soldiers were having their way with me—"smoking me out", like a rat or some other nuisance. That's all I was to them. Just something to be rid of. And as I stumbled through the poison gas he took my hand, this 13 year old boy from Qalandia, and led me to the sanctuary behind another parked car.

I had come to Qalandia to gather interviews from Palestinians (and Israeli soldiers) for a radio project, and to observe and document the abuses heaped on the West Bank residents by the Occupation Forces. Soldiers let no man with a West Bank ID into or out of Qalandia. Period. Regardless of who they are or where they work. Numerous men from the Palestinian National Authority Ministry of Education, armed with official Israeli permits granting them the freedom to leave the West Bank, were forced to wait in the holding area with all the other men. For hours. Of course this individual and collective detention of people violates quite directly the IV Geneva Convention and the UN Declaration of Human Rights, but when I asked the soldiers to explain their actions their response mirrored that of the international community: silence. "I don't want to talk," the only soldier who deigned to speak to me said. And neither do his words matter, for my concern is not his opinion, but whether or not he will let these men through.

Clearly this soldier wasn't moved by my presence, but a few Palestinian teenagers strolled up and were able to occupy his time, joking with him in Arabic. They diverted his attention long enough so that a few of the men from the Ministry of Education could slip through, the soldier more interested in returning insults than manning his post. And it was just when I started to think about this whole operation—how arbitrary the soldiers' attitudes are; how their point is not to stem wouldbe "terrorists" from entering Israel (the only people allowed into and out of the West Bank are men with Israeli ID), but to beat and humiliate the Palestinians into submitting to Israeli authority—that I noticed the three soldiers climbing over the "security" fence, toward the boys.

How do I navigate my way through this?

Moments of safety or sanctuary come infrequently in the West Bank. Near the checkpoints, you can be shot at any time by trigger-happy Israeli soldiers. (I don't mean to erase or downplay the reality of suicide bombings by focusing so much on Israeli Occupation Forces, but the fact is that bullets and grenades and rockets and missiles are fired with incredibly greater frequency by Israelis than by Palestinians. Of this there is no question.) I decided to walk into Qalandia so I could observe the three Israeli soldiers more closely. By the time I'd reached the string of shops (just a few hundred yards) the soldiers had already fired numerous shots, forcing the boys into the residential area.

Women and children hid behind cars and piles of rubble and scrap metal—whatever could provide them with some protection against the shooting—and traffic was in a confounded standstill. The shopkeepers began closing their metal doors, and none too soon, as rubber bullets slammed all around. It was in the midst of this chaos that

I found myself absolutely alone.

And the soldiers bumbled down the rocky hillside.

And they hurled a tear-gas grenade at me.

And they shot the boy kneeling down beside me.

And I still have no idea how he's doing.

Nor do I even know his name.

He staggered off, his hand over his bleeding face, falling into a cinderblock wall before a group of his friends scuttled him into a nearby van, at the frantic urgings of the driver. I just wanted to leave. To pretend I didn't just see all that. To pretend that this place called Palestine didn't exist. To pretend that war and bullets didn't live here. To pretend I didn't care.

I just wanted to leave.

But it hit me straight in my heart.

I am my mother's son.

And I filled myself with the courage she nursed me with, and I walked through the blood and across the street and up the rocky hillside straight in front of the soldiers. I stood there in between the guns and the grenades and the hailing stones. I stood there because there is no other place to stand here. There is no place for indecision or for the indecisive. In the middle of such irrational violence, there is no rational alternative but to stand between soldiers with guns and boys with stones. So I stood there and I belted out with all the strength of my mother:

"IN THE FACE—YOU SHOT HIM IN THE FACE—IT'S TIME FOR YOU TO GO—YOU SHOT HIM IN THE FACE."

One soldier looked at me and said, "Where? In the face? Yes!" and gave me the thumbs up. And another soldier grabbed my arm and crouched down behind me to protect himself from incoming stones. Was this really happening? Didn't this soldier, not even five minutes earlier, heave a tear-gas grenade at me? And now he would use me as his human shield? The stones were getting closer, and I pushed the soldier off of me and called him a coward and told them all that they were about to have an international incident on their hands if they didn't get out of Qalandia.

They expected me to go and tell the boys to stop throwing stones. The boys who just watched these same three men shoot their friend in the face. And I said I would.

And the soldiers crawled over the fence and tried to make their way to their jeep, which was getting pelted by stones. I called out to the boys, saying that the soldiers would leave if they let up for a couple minutes. And then I walked away, stones falling all around me. The soldiers, unable to reach their jeep, climbed back into Qalandia and the whole scene just kept deteriorating.

And where am I, anyway? Where am I that grown men are given guns to shoot at children? Where is this place called Palestine?

I left Qalandia, and by the time I reached Jerusalem my throat had swollen so badly that I couldn't swallow without much pain. And my stomach roiled in revolt of what it was seeing. And I thought, "I should be sick, here. I shouldn't be able to swallow this."

And I sat down to write out all that I just saw. And here it is.

A STRANGE TRIP
Account of the second ISM campaign, December 2001
by Trevor Baumgartner, December 2001

"This is a strange trip! Today it is nothing but a tragedy, and tomorrow we shall say it was an adventure."

The two-week International Solidarity Movement (ISM) campaign officially began on December 16, and after two full days of non-violence trainings and ad nauseam discussions about the legal ramifications of international civil disobedience, we were all ready to die.

So on the 18th we set out to do just that. After assembling in Ramallah, at Al-Manara, we marched through town and out past the Muqata'a in silence. The IDF had just stationed a tank, an armored personnel carrier (APC) a few hundred yards from Arafat's little compound, and as we approached them they made quite a fuss. One soldierboy fired a live round in the air, and once the APC revved its gigantic engine and started for us our "die-in" began.

We, all 60-odd of us, lay in the street, motionless, to deliver the message to the soldierboys and the world media (strategically gathered around the IDF war machines) that this Occupation kills people. Dead. Since Sharon's "visit" to Al-Haram Al-Sharif approximately 900 people have been killed. Shot dead in their homes. Blown up while talking on public phones. Shopping. 900 people.

Pizza with Arafat

And so we sent our message and then rose up and scuttled to the Muqata'a for a meeting with Palestinian National Authority President Yassir Arafat, who received us quite graciously. As he made his way around the room, shaking hands with each and every one of us, the media hawks swooped around him. I was surprised when he juked them and cut through an empty aisle to reach the last couple of solidarity delegates. Unfortunately, though, the media can only be avoided for so long, and as long as the entrances and exits are sealed there's no way Arafat can escape.

Watching Arafat dodge the hawks was a troubling microcosmic experience. There he was, totally penned in and having to use guile to get to where he wanted to go, and by the time he got there the hawks were already swarming. If you're Palestinian, you may get through Qalandia, but Al-Ram is only five minutes away. And then there are the "flying roadblocks" that the Israeli Police set up for you if you make it to Jerusalem. And then, of course, you have to go through it all again on your way back home.

Just to set the record straight, the ISM does not engage in Arafat apologetics. Quite a few of the delegates were uneasy as they walked into the conference room to meet a person with such a dubious past (and present). However, the overriding sentiment was that meeting with Arafat as an international delegation was a clear showing of support for all Palestinians in their legitimate struggle for independence. We all bear some responsibility in this ongoing illegal Occupation of historical Palestine, and if our governments refuse to work toward its end, then we must. If that means meeting with Arafat, so be it. The same for lying in front of APCs, or opening roadblocks.

And rain will fall and cleanse the streets.

Salfit region

The Salfit region is a beautifully complex geography of peaks and valleys, with olive trees breaking out and up through the rugged earth. We would be there five days and four nights, doing direct support work with the suffocated locals.

Our first action, in the driving rain, was to heave boxes and flats of essential fruits and vegetables from one flatbed truck, up and over a heap of deep Palestine mud, and into another truck on the other side of this roadblock. This truck would then deliver the goods to the people of Deir Istya. After we finished and the skies cleared a family brought us, all 60 of us, sweet sage and rosemary tea. We drank and talked and learned a bit about what rural life is like in these "B" areas.

Aside from being surrounded by mountaintop settlements, the Palestinian villages we worked in are all enclosed by roadblocks. No auto traffic in. No auto traffic out. These closures obviously have drastic impacts on the people who live in these villages, as the flow of goods and services (especially food and medical supplies) is severely restricted. As of now, there's only one 10-bed hospital in the entire Salfit region, for 70,000 people in 19 outlying villages. And this hospital is only available to the people who can reach it. According to the BBC, "homebirths have risen 26%" since Israel began digging up and blockading roads in the area.

So we set out to clear as many roadblocks as we could in our short stay. We opened Deir Istya for a day. Pulverized a double roadblock in Yasuf. And I must say, there's nothing like watching an ambulance drive through a roadblock you've just spent hours blistering your hands to clear. Each day people from the villages would come out with tea and piping hot flat bread and zaatar, to break bread and stones with us.

But like I said earlier, the Salfit region is a complex of peaks and valleys, and these roads only stayed open as long as we stayed out there. Sometimes they would be closed before we even made it back to Marda, the village we stayed in. We'd catch the news from the locals we stayed with, and we'd clench our jaws and fists and force the flood back behind our eyes. Few of us are used to being rendered irrelevant so quickly.

The Occupation is everywhere. And it doesn't sleep. To physically confront it each and every time it stands in the way is sure to drive one insane. And so critical thinking and clearly defined goals are essential tools for everybody who works here.

Though we may only be able to open a road for a few hours, the relationships that we make with the locals can't be buried. And this is a crucial piece of the ISM's work. Building relationships with people in both urban and rural areas throughout the year, so that there are mechanisms for evaluation and accountability. This is important in the context of building a movement that can be sustainable, as opposed to simple "activism," typified by large protests and short-term goals.

Bitter coffee in gold rimmed cups

After our three days clearing roadblocks we packed up and made tracks to Nablus. The plan was to go on solidarity visits with families of recent martyrs. The sharing of, and in, the 40 days and nights of grief is a cultural tradition in Palestine, and when we walked into Jawal Abdel Latif's home it had been less than two weeks since an undercover Israeli death squad forced him to lie face down in the red Salfit mud before assassinating him.

His father sat in the center of the room and tried to tell us about Jawal, the young man. The police officer. But he could only get a sentence out before his eyes broke and tears navigated his face. A relative poured out tiny cups of bitter coffee and passed them around to all of us, and we swallowed it hard.

He watered the earth; and in the earth he was buried

Next was the family of Diab Al-Sawari, who'd been assassinated just three days earlier. His wife had prepared a great meal because the tanks were pulling out of Nablus and Diab could return home after a week's absence. Just before sitting down they heard the unmistakable crushing of concrete outside. Tanks were pulverizing the road outside their home, and when Diab stepped out on his terrace to see what was going on, a sniper shot him cold. Three times in the head.

His cousins passed the disfigured bullets around the room, and I held in my hand what my taxes have paid for all these years. His wife, in her ninth month of pregnancy, called out to the Americans before we left her on the very terrace Diab died on, "What are you going to do about this? How come your people kill us? How come your people give Israel guns and tanks and Apache and F16 to kill us? What are you going to do about this? Does anybody see us?"

Her questions and her pain were more bitter than any coffee I've ever drunk. And harder to swallow. And in that moment all that ran through my head was a line from a June Jordan poem that says, simply, "How do I negotiate the implications of my shame?"

Indeed.

Diab Al-Sawari is survived by his wife and his five children.

X-mas in Bethlehem

Despite Arafat's promise to walk to Bethlehem, and Israeli claims that Bethlehem was "open," the city of Christ's birth remained seized. So on Christmas day over 1000 people marched from Beit Sahour to the Bethlehem checkpoint with the intention of going right through and on to Bethlehem. We were met by a line of soldierboys who pushed and shoved and trampled many of the frontline Internationals, and in the end successfully denied us the freedom to move. And all the 1000 people turned back.

This may not seem like much of a story, but there is something incredibly important that happened on that night. Namely, a basically unorganized march and confrontation did not explode. The scene was ripe for some, any, sort of violence; numerous marchers held huge candles, there were ample stones to be thrown, and of course the soldierboys were equipped with all sorts of weapons of destructive capabilities.

But the crowd held fast! And though we didn't push through into Bethlehem, we all went home planning for the BIG march on New Year's Eve.

"I am the sovereign power of this area"

Our next mission was a trip to Gaza with the French and Italian delegations of the Grassroots International Protection for the Palestinian People (GIPP). A full schedule had been arranged, including a tour of Khan Younis, more solidarity visits with families of martyrs, and general observation of the condition of human rights in this forsaken strip of land. A familiar refrain from many Palestinians in the goes like this, "It's bad here, but nowhere near as bad as Gaza." The night before, Apache helicopters launched missiles into residential areas, wounding two teenagers, which is getting to be a pretty common occurrence. So common that it barely broke the Arab news.

At any rate, we were all trying to prepare ourselves for this place called Gaza when we met Captain Joseph Levy at Erez Crossing. Levy is the head of the Israeli "International Organization Department," a dubious-sounding place that I'm not altogether sure even exists. He kindly told us, the US and UK delegation, that he couldn't let us in "for security reasons." The French/Italian bus was already through, and when we explained to him that we were together, he reunited us by escorting our European partners back to Erez.

After listening to Levy's half-hearted assertions that he was concerned about our safety, we decided to put his humanitarian good will to the test. So we walked away from Levy and toward the gates. What ensued was a surrealistic rampage. Indeed, no other word can describe how Levy stalked from woman to woman, choked and then threw them to the ground. It made no difference how old or young they were, as long as they were women Levy was after them.

I've seen this tactic before. In the US police generally single out women, under the false and misogynist belief that women are weaker and therefore should be subject to terror. But all the women bounced back up and we kept on, showing Levy and his bevy of soldierboys that we would not be moved. Until one soldier began shouting, "I'm going to shoot you in your leg," repeatedly, while Levy loaded his handgun and said, "You know what I'm thinking, so I'm not going to say it out loud," that we decided to stop, sit down and occupy the occupied crossing. And we did sit until Border Police dragged us off and into a bus and instructed the driver not to stop until we got to Jerusalem.

And so we saw up close how afraid Israel is of international human rights observers in the most densely populated area of the world.

They closed down a school and opened a prison

On December 29 we took over the Surda Checkpoint, allowing students to get to and from Bir Zeit University and the other schools in the area. This was our most highly coordinated action, as we teamed with local students as well as the GIPP to pull it off. For a solid three or four hours we body-blockaded the soldierboys in their big jeeps and APCs. All they could do was lob tear-gas in our direction, but we had roving teams of people whose sole job was to rid the area of that toxic gas.

When the soldiers did venture out of their armored vehicles to bother with us, we all held fast in our commitment to maintaining a safe passage for the students and others on their way to and from Bir Zeit. Similar to our time in the Salfit region, the long-term success of our actions in Surda really relies on strong local/international connections. The soldierboys, we knew, would intensify their pressure and brutality on the students after we left. We also knew that they would use our actions as justification for their apartheid. But in the end the power of right will win out over the power of might.

Turning back

By the time we were slated to go to Hebron everybody was beat. We all hoped to use the bus ride to gather up our energies so as not to be totally overrun by the children waiting for us there. Unfortunately the soldiers had other plans for us. So back into action mode, which is always preceded by meetings (yawn). From looking around the meeting it was difficult to tell who was there because they wanted to plan some kind of action or if they simply lacked the energy to get out of their seat.

By the time the meeting was half over, the only "action" that would've been appropriate, given the general energy level of the group, would've been a "nap-in." But nobody brought their pillows, so we turned back and agreed to take individual cabs back, which all went off without a hitch. Sometimes cooler (or sleepier) heads prevail.

We plant flowers while they fire bullets

The grand finale ISM event was slated to be a massive march from Bethlehem to Jerusalem. The whole thing was organized with the full support of the clergy, which if it wasn't the first time, it was certainly the first time the church was on board for any demonstration in a long time. And it showed.

There was to be no negotiation with the soldiers. Instead the plan was walk through the soldiers' line and toward Jerusalem, with the single demand that Jerusalem be opened and religious freedom be respected. But, unbeknownst to the 1500 marchers, the Patriarchate had negotiated with the Israeli "authorities" a limp compromise: we'd simply proceed to the checkpoint, pray, and go back home. Well, everybody was to go home except the Patriarchs, who all climbed into their sparkling Mercedes Benzes and were off to exercise their privileges. And it must be noted that these privileges come at the expense of the people of Bethlehem, Beit Sahour and Beit Jala. People who've been trying for years to organize a non-violent movement toward Palestinian independence saw the fruits of their labors spoil right there, in that street. For non-violence to be relevant, it has to have some clearly visible successes, even if they're limited. But what we saw on New Year's Eve was political cowardice and pacifism at their very worst.

And this is the situation we are in. The so-called leaders refuse to lead, and so the people take it upon themselves to determine their own destinies. This is no less true for the US delegates than it is for Palestinians living despite a brutal Occupation. The evidence abounds that any movement here will have to come from the ground up, and somewhere in the foundation non-violence will play a part. The sooner the better, for "bullets are not to be met with flowers. Nor is a tank to be met with a lily."

PART TWO: REOCCUPATION

3

SIEGE OF THE MUQATA'A

RAMALLAH UPDATE
International Solidarity Movement, 29 March 2002, 14:50

Into the evening Israeli forces continue their offensive on the Palestinian people:

— After heavy shelling of the Presidential compound all day Israeli forces entered the compound with tanks and ground troops. The Palestinian police have reported that no one has been taken but there has been office to office break ins and searches and resistance from the compound.

— Two Palestinian Red Crescent ambulances carrying a doctor and two foreign International volunteers American citizen Adam Shapiro and Irish national Caoimhe Butterly have been held up for over 3 hours trying to reach the injured in the compound

— Adam reported the ambulances being stopped and completely searched and everybody was being forced out of the ambulances.

— At the time of this writing one ambulance carrying the doctor and the two foreign civilian volunteers have been let in. One ambulance was turned back. Two injured are being removed from the compound now.

— Al-Jazeera satellite channel was showing people bleeding and lying dead on the

Photograph by Jamal Arouri, AFP/Al-Ayyam.

floor of the compound as the ambulances were held at the gate and the volunteers waiting to be let in to assist the injured could see smoke rising from the compound.

— Electricity throughout Ramallah has been cut in all neighborhoods and water tanks have been shot up causing them to leak precious water. Israeli forces have been shooting at anything moving in the streets as their tanks are positioned throughout Palestinian neighborhoods.

— The Shabak and Israeli police entered a hotel in Jerusalem where an international solidarity delegation of French and Swiss are staying. The Israeli forces demanded all the passports of the 50 Internationals. After the intervention of embassies and lawyers the passports were returned. It is unknown whether they will attempt to forcibly remove international witnesses in the area.

— Despite this form of intimidation by the Israeli authorities and army Internationals are intent on staying and expressing their solidarity with the Palestinian people.

We urge everyone again to please keep working to stop the continued atrocities being perpetrated by Sharon and his government.

GETTING THROUGH TO THE WOUNDED
An interview with Adam Shapiro
by Mark LeVine, July/August 2002, Tikkun Magazine

LeVine: To start with the obvious, what's a nice Jewish boy like you doing in a place like Ramallah?

Shapiro: I arrived in Jerusalem in September 1999 to work for Seeds of Peace, an American nonprofit organization dedicated to working with youth in regions of conflict to promote peaceful coexistence. I was director of their Center for Coexistence in Jerusalem. As the conflict escalated and Israel began using F-16s, I decided that as an American, I needed to start protesting the use of American weapons against Palestinians, so I got involved with the activities of the International Solidarity Movement (ISM)—especially humanitarian activities and protests against American involvement and support of the increasing Israeli escalation.

Last December, I left Seeds and became a full-time volunteer coordinator for ISM to work with Palestinians in struggling against the Occupation—removing roadblocks, replanting trees, rebuilding homes, marching through checkpoints.

When the invasion began we happened to have seventy to eighty international activists in Ramallah who had come for ISM's April Campaign Against Occupation. We were prepared to help in any way we could. We got calls from medical relief people saying they were being shot at by Israelis and they needed help to get through to the wounded, and I volunteered to go in one of the ambulances picking up wounded, delivering medicines, taking pregnant women to hospitals.

Towards the end of the day I received a phone call from the presidential compound in Ramallah that critically wounded people were inside and that any ambulance that came near was being shot at, so we found a Palestinian doctor and went over to the compound. We were shot at as we got there but I got on loudspeaker and spoke to the soldiers in English. After twenty minutes, I got out and stood in front of the tanks, and after another three hours I got access to the compound.

Inside there were two critically wounded people and we got them out, but I stayed behind to help the doctor treat wounded people, expecting the ambulance to come back and get me. However, a couple of hours later, my friend and colleague Caoimhe Butterly, an Irish citizen, came back inside and said that soldiers had arrested everyone in the ambulance and had impounded it—so we were stuck there.

LeVine: What happened inside the compound while you were there?

Shapiro: I was in the compound for twenty-four hours, from 7:00 pm Friday, March 29 until Saturday around 5:00 pm. The whole time the shelling of the compound and machine gun fire continued. The soldiers were getting closer, and everyone expected the Israelis to storm the compound. The Israelis knew we were in there ... but there was no communication with soldiers during this time. Our land line was cut around midnight, and our cell phones died by noon the next day.

I was downstairs on the ground floor while President Arafat was upstairs. He invited me up to join him for a light meal as a token of gratitude for helping his people. I left when a group of activists—this was on all the TV news programs—came with a few ambulances from the Red Crescent to bring humanitarian aid and they marched past the soldiers with Palestinian doctors. I left in exchange for one of the Palestinian doctors.

[...]

RAMALLAH UPDATE
International Solidarity Movement, 30 March 2002

As of 15.00 today, March 30, more than 50 foreign civilians accompanied physicians and Red Crescent personnel in a civilian mission to get urgent medical aid into the Presidential compound.

Medics and civilians left from an area under total siege and marched past tanks deployed in the Manara. Shortly before reaching the President's compound they were stopped and Israeli forces refused to allow them to proceed. The group protested that the Israeli military were in flagrant contravention of the Geneva convention, as well as international humanitarian law, by choosing not to allow medical assistance to the injured. The delegation insisted that they would take medical personnel and supplies in. Finally it was agreed that two doctors, two ambulances and four foreign observers would be allowed access inside the Presidential compound.

The two Internationals who were inside the compound expressed their great relief to see that eventually pressure had succeeded and that medical aid was eventually allowed in. One body has been removed and the injured inside have now received medical attention.

The international delegation who accompanied the medical group comprised of Huwaida Arraf, Jose Bove a French national and an Italian member of Parliament. They all expressed their solidarity with the Palestinians struggle for freedom and voiced their condemnation of the war policies of Sharon's government.

The foreign civilian's who entered the compound went in as a symbol of the international outcry over the brutal attacks on the Palestinian people and as a symbol of the intervention that is immediately sought from the international community.

Adam Shapiro has now left the compound in exchange for one doctor and one medic. Caoimhe Butterly has remained due to her concern that medics are not being allowed free access and that her continued presence may help facilitate further assistance.

Inside the Presidential compound the foreign civilian delegation met with President Arafat. Both the President and the other Palestinians inside are in good spirits and expressed their heartfelt gratitude for the international solidarity. President Arafat stated that "Occupation is the real terrorism, and the Palestinian people will continue to struggle for their freedom. Our people will be free." The foreign delegation supported the President's statement.

INTERNATIONALS IN WITH ARAFAT CALL FOR THEIR AMBASSADORS

International Solidarity Movement, 31 March 2002, 15:11

FOR IMMEDIATE RELEASE

[RAMALLAH] 50 International civilians entered Yasser Arafat's Presidential Compound today, which is under continuous siege by the Israeli Forces. The group of Internationals is comprised of civilian volunteers from France, Brazil, Canada, Belgium, Britain, Ireland, Germany, and Israel who are here on a humanitarian mission. Thirty-four (34) international civilians remain inside. The group has stated that they will remain inside of the Presidential Compound until the siege is lifted; they remain in solidarity with all Palestinian people who are now under occupation and extend their demands to include the end of Israel's Occupation of the entire West Bank and Gaza Strip. The Israeli's have cut power, phone lines and water supply to the compound. Food is also in short supply.

The 34 foreign civilians are asking for their respective ambassadors to urgently come to President Arafat's compound.

The city of Ramallah, where the group of Internationals is currently based, is under closure and violent occupation by Israeli Forces. Power has been cut in most neighborhoods of Ramallah and water and food is in short supply in many homes, hospitals have had to resort to back-up generators and the transport of medicine and medical supplies has been disrupted. International witnesses have reported Israeli forces breaking in doors of homes and conducting mass arrests, where Palestinian's have been bound and placed in torturous positions for extended periods, there have also been at least 14 extra-judicial executions performed by the Israeli Forces in the last 2 days. Medical personnel have been arrested by the Israeli's and several ambulances have been confiscated, Israeli Forces also attempted to enter Ramallah Hospital earlier today but were kept out by a human blockade of Palestinian doctors and Internationals.

For more information call:
Adam [number withheld]
Huwaida [number withheld]

ENDS

PEACE ADVOCATES IN ARAFAT COMPOUND HOPE TO DETER ISRAELI TROOPS

by Joel Greenberg, 3 April 2002, New York Times

JERUSALEM—Declaring that they want to protect him from the Israelis, more than 30 foreign activists holed up with Yasir Arafat at his besieged office in Ramallah have become a complicating factor in Israeli calculations of how to proceed against the Palestinian leader.

The foreigners, mostly Europeans, are part of an ad hoc group that arrived several days ago for a series of actions in the West Bank and Gaza Strip in support of the Palestinians and in protest against the Israeli military presence there.

Their televised walk through a ring of tanks into the compound on Sunday caught Israeli soldiers by surprise, and they have effectively become human shields. Their continued presence in Mr. Arafat's offices has flustered the Israelis, complicating their self-declared mission of isolating the Palestinian leader.

The gunfire around the building has died down, supplies have been allowed in, and Palestinian concerns about an imminent Israeli assault have receded.

"We thought that as long as there were Internationals here, there would be no vicious Israeli attack," said Claude Leostic, from Brest, France, in a telephone interview from the besieged office. "And we've been right so far. We're here as a deterrent against shelling and missile attacks."

Neta Golan, an Israeli peace advocate who is with the foreigners at Mr. Arafat's office, said she believed that the group's presence was having a restraining effect on Israeli troops.

"We're hoping that our presence on the front line with the Palestinians will make the soldiers more cautious about shooting without reason," Ms. Golan said. "The death of Europeans or an Israeli would cause a stir that Palestinian deaths are not causing."

The overall operation had been going on for months, attracting modest media attention and serving as a mild irritant to the army. However, when the Israelis launched their broad offensive into West Bank towns this week, the protests gained sudden prominence.

The foreigners in the compound, many from Italy and France, came on a visit organized by two West Bank groups that have organized nonviolent action against Israeli forces there: the International Solidarity Movement and Grass-roots International Protection for the Palestinian People.

During the 18-month Palestinian uprising, the actions have included removing roadblocks, planting trees in place of those uprooted by the Israelis, demonstrating in front of Israeli tanks and trying to walk through army checkpoints that restrict Palestinian movement.

However, the march into Mr. Arafat's office by more than 40 foreigners took the protests to a new level, because it broke a tightening Israeli ring of armor and gunfire that appeared perilously close to reaching Mr. Arafat himself.

The Israelis responded by banning foreigners, including journalists, from Ramallah, and by arresting and deporting a group of French protesters who had left the compound, among them José Bové, the union leader and antiglobalization protester.

Like the rest of Ramallah, Mr. Arafat's offices have been hit by power blackouts and disruption of water supply after electric cables and water pipes were damaged by the Israeli tanks, and the foreigners have been rationing food supplies with the office staff and guards.

A shipment of food, water and medicine was allowed in today by the Israelis. An army statement said the food included 66 containers of yellow cheese, 600 pieces of pita bread, 40 cans of halva, 23 cans of tuna, 13 cans of hummus, 34 crates of mineral water, more than 140 pounds of coffee and 55 cans of sardines.

Caoimhe Butterly, an activist from Ireland who helped collect the supplies, said Israeli soldiers filmed her and Ms. Leostic as they stepped out of the office, and called them over for a chat in an area where there were waiting police vehicles, an apparent attempt to lure them into arrest. The two women refused to go.

Ms. Butterly said that despite the persistent tension and siege, morale at Mr. Arafat's offices had improved greatly and the Israeli assault had abated after the arrival of the international group on Sunday.

On Saturday night, she said, Palestinians in the building were readying themselves to die in an Israeli attack after they refused an ultimatum to surrender.

The foreigners have also appeared in other West Bank locations that are targets of the Israelis. One group defied an Israeli checkpoint and walked into Bethlehem on Saturday; another marched through the neighboring town of Beit Jala on Monday after it had been invaded by Israeli troops, drawing gunfire that wounded seven demonstrators. Other foreigners have gone to homes of Palestinians in neighboring refugee camps in an effort to offer protection and support.

At Mr. Arafat's compound, the foreigners say they will stay as long as it takes for the Israelis to withdraw.

"It makes a difference," said Miriam Ferrier, from Paris. "We are a voice for the Palestinian people."

THE WORLD IS WATCHING
An interview with Neta Golan by telephone from the compound on 8 April
by Neta Golan and Ian Urbina, 13 May 2002, In These Times

On March 29, Israel Defense Forces surrounded the compound of Palestinian leader Yasser Arafat. In hopes of forestalling an attack, 40 international peace observers took up residence in the besieged building. Among them is Neta Golan, an Israeli-Canadian activist with the International Solidarity Movement. She gave this interview to Ian Urbina by phone from the compound on April 8.

Can you describe the scene there?
Things are pretty bad. The Israeli army has let in food but no medicine. We have a lot of people with diabetes and hypertension. There is also no water, so sanitary conditions are deteriorating. But really, the thing that's hitting the Palestinians in here the worst is the unknown. All of them have family in Jenin and Nablus where huge massacres are taking place. No one knows if their children and parents are alive. My husband is in Jenin, and he may be dead.

Who is in the compound with you?
There are 450 people total in the building. Roughly 40 of them are Internationals. In a lot of ways, it's more diverse in here than outside. There are French, Italian, Canadian and German. Many are with the anti-globalization movement. We take shifts and try to keep spread out and moving at all times. The last time the soldiers came to deliver food, they were sure to take as many photos as possible of the inside. Obviously, they want to know where people are for the purposes of storming the place. Some Internationals are near President Arafat around the clock.

Do you think your presence is making a difference?
Sure, our presence helps. For Sharon, foreign blood costs more than Arab blood, but we definitely aren't a 100 percent deterrent. Even after we occupied the building, [Israeli Gen. Shaul] Mofaz was caught on a camera he didn't know was rolling, telling Sharon that they had to get rid of Arafat right away. We watched it here on CNN.

Are they going to storm the compound?
It's hard to say. It would be pretty stupid, but just two days ago they started firing machine guns at the building. This isn't all that unusual, and everyone knows to stay away from windows and thin walls. But then the tank fired and hit the building. That really surprised us. I think the Israelis were testing the waters to see how the international community and press would react.

Were there casualties?
Yes. Two Internationals were hurt and four Palestinians got it pretty bad, one lost his eye and was in critical condition.

Where is he now?
Well, he was taken out of the compound by medics, but apparently Israeli soldiers stopped the ambulance and removed him. No one has heard anything since, so we're not sure if he's gone.

What needs to happen before the Internationals will leave the building?
The Israeli troops need to get all the way out of Ramallah.

Do you think Colin Powell's trip will help matters?
Yes and no. Assuming he comes to the compound, which he hasn't yet committed to, he will probably get the Israeli troops to move back a little. But the problem is the Occupation. Until he gets the troops to pull all the way back to the UN-recognized 1967 borders, nothing will really change here.

Is the international community helping?
Again, yes and no. The United Nations keeps getting measures vetoed by the United States. Some aid organizations are doing really important work on the ground. But to slow the bloodshed, we desperately need more international peace shields to come to the Occupied Territories. There also need to be efforts abroad like what was done to bring down apartheid. Rhetoric from foreign governments and citizens isn't going to change anything. There will have to be sanctions and popular boycott efforts.

When it comes to advocating solutions, is there political debate among those on the inside?
I can't speak for Arafat's inner circle. I'm sure there is discussion all the time there. With the Internationals, there are some differing views on tactics but not much else. Basically, everyone here thinks that the Occupation is wrong and Israel needs to pull back to the 1967 borders for there to be real peace. Most in here are not hard-core ideologues, it's just that circumstances got so bad that we thought it was time to do something.

"THIS IS THE OCCUPATION"
by Jeff Guntzel, 10 April 2002

We left for Ramallah yesterday morning. In order to enter the city, our little group had to avoid the Israeli checkpoint by walking (and sometimes running) through the brush just south of the checkpoint. Once we were safely inside the military zone, a taxi driver with whom we had made advance arrangements drove us about a mile into Ramallah and stopped.

He would not go any further for fear of Israeli snipers who were situated in many of the city's tall buildings. A Red Crescent ambulance driver offered to take us to the Sheik Zayed hospital where we had arranged to meet two organizers with the International Solidarity Movement (ISM), Huwaida Arraf and her fiancé, Adam Shapiro. We had heard that tanks and troops surrounding the hospital might block our passage.

Those of you who have been following the news carefully might remember the Sheik Zayed hospital as the site of a mass grave dug, several days earlier, in the parking lot as a temporary burial ground for 29 Palestinians, including one American citizen. The morgue at the hospital was full, and there was nowhere else to put the bodies. Coming down a steep hill about three miles from the hospital, we spotted a tank and an armored personnel carrier (APC). These days, in Ramallah, the only vehicles on the streets are tanks, APCs, and ambulances (I guess you could also count the mangled cars peppering the roadside that tanks had rolled over during the invasion). Suddenly a soldier appeared. He crouched on one knee, aimed his M-16 directly at us, and fixed his eye to his gun's sight. We stopped. The driver began slowly backing up the hill and several more soldiers appeared, some of them taking aim and some motioning us to come closer. We all held our passports up to let them know there were Internationals in the car.

Israeli troops had been harassing, arresting, and even shooting ambulance drivers since the start of the invasion. We had no idea what to expect. When we got to the soldiers at the bottom of the hill we stopped again. Eight M-16s and a tank were aimed at us. The soldier directly to my right looked tired and scared. That scared me. Our driver was ordered out of the car and asked a few questions in Arabic. Then we were ordered out, with all of our bags. We laid our bags out on the ground and opened them. After a not-so-thorough search several soldiers asked us a few questions while others encircled us. The soldier who at first struck me as tired and scared now just looked cautiously curious.

"Why are you here?" he asked, not quite meeting our eyes.

"We came to bring medicine and food to people under curfew," said one member of our group.

"Don't you know there are terrorists here, it is dangerous," he replied, "do you think you can bring peace?" "We don't know," we said, almost in unison.

Then Kathy, my roommate and co-worker, stepped in: "We are here because we know that our government pays for much of what is going on here and we feel a responsibility to intervene nonviolently in this terrible situation."

"We did not ask for this, it is the Palestinian leadership, bad leaders, they are responsible for this," replied the soldier.

"But over half of the people here are children," Kathy said, "and children can't be bad leaders, they can only be children!"

"I know there are children here," he replied solemnly, looking off into the distance, "but there are also terrorists. You cannot drive to the hospital," said the soldier.

"Then we will walk," replied Greg, another member of our group, who then began walking towards the tank and APC that partially blocked our path.

"Stop! You cannot walk either," demanded the soldier, who then paused and looked around. Directly in front of us was a soldier on one knee, holding each of us briefly in his cross-hairs, one person at a time.

"Don't you understand that you make the terrorists happy when you come here to help them?" the soldier continued.

"We are here to help the innocent people in Ramallah who are being terrorized and killed every day," replied Kathy.

"We do not kill innocent people."

"We read *Ha'Aretz* [an Israeli paper, printed in Hebrew and English] every day and we know innocent people are being killed," Kathy said.

"Do you think I like this?" the soldier demanded, "I don't want to be here."

At that moment there was an enormous explosion and sustained machine gun fire. It was coming from directly behind us, and it was really loud. Two members of our group stepped away to smoke, and the others drifted back towards the ambulance. Kathy and I remained with the soldier.

"Do you know what Arafat wants, he wants murder, why do you want to help a murderer?" he asked.

"Maybe there is another way to look at our presence here," I replied. "We are here operating beneath the level of the leaders who we believe do not want real peace. I think you and I have more in common than you have with Sharon, or than I have with Arafat, wouldn't you agree?"

"Yes, I agree."

"So let us go to the hospital," Kathy responded. Silence.

Then the soldier spoke again, "You know, it is not just the Palestinians who are suffering."

"We want a just peace for both sides," we responded. "We want an end to *all* of the violence."

"It is too late," insisted the soldier, "there can be no peace now."

"It is difficult to see a way out, but … why don't you work on behalf of the Jews, why can't you be objective?" At that moment, another soldier came up to us and began speaking in Hebrew. Then, suddenly, we were told we could get back into the ambulance and push ahead towards the hospital.

The hospital is actually two buildings separated by a road. It was in that road, just yards from the hospital, that an elderly woman with a walker was shot dead by an Israeli sniper just weeks ago. In the parking lot we saw the mass grave we had all read about. It was empty; the killing was less frequent 11 days into the siege, giving hospital workers the window they needed to dispose of the bodies properly.

For our second day in Ramallah, we agreed to divide our efforts. Some of us could accompany ambulances making house calls while the rest would defy the curfew by walking to the office of the Union of Palestinian Medical Relief Committees (UPMRC) to assist in deliveries of food and medicine to families. We had walked about one block when we spotted an armored personnel carrier (APC) at the intersection three blocks ahead of us. On top of the APC were a mounted machine gun and a soldier; another soldier, bearing an M-16, crouched in front of the APC. Both were aiming at us.

We stopped.

A soldier yelled something. Adam yelled out, "I'm sorry I can't hear you." One of the soldiers fired.

"I hear your bullets," Adam replied, "we're going to deliver food, we are all foreigners."

We waited. There were shots in the distance. The soldiers ahead of us seemed to be engaged in some sort of operation that drew them out of the APC. They were moving around. We were a distraction. We began walking very slowly, then stopped, and again called out our intent to deliver food. Adam asked to speak to the commander, with whom he has spoken before. Then he asked for some signal that we could pass. Nothing.

We resumed our slow march, white flag held high. We heard a dynamite explosion nearby. The soldiers were blowing their way into a building. We stopped again and Adam continued, "Soldiers, we wish to proceed, may we approach to speak to you?" After a long silence we decided to turn back and try again later. We worried that the soldiers would do something stupid to deal with their "distraction". Turning around, we walked back slowly, in the direction of yesterday's snipers.

While we were engaged in our sort-of-stand-off, Alexandra had ducked into a refugee camp and returned with a heart medicine prescription for a middle-aged woman who couldn't reach the hospital to fill it because of the snipers and the soldiers. The hospital was one block away. We returned to the hospital, got the heart medication, and decided to head back to the refugee camp, which was just in view of our friends with the APC.

We began again, white flag waving, and arrived at the entrance to the camp (really indistinguishable from the rest of the neighborhood) and were pleased to see that the soldiers had moved on. We decided to again attempt making our way to the UPMRC offices. Just as we were getting ready to walk on, a man approached us to ask if we could get an ambulance to take his feverish son to the hospital. We decided to escort the boy to the hospital since it was so close. While we were regrouping in the parking lot, two ambulances sped into the driveway. Inside one was the body of 28 year old Manel Sami Ibrahim, who was standing near her window when an Israeli sniper shot her through the heart. Her husband and three children were in the apartment.

"This," as one Palestinian relief worker said to me, "is the Occupation."

We started off again for the UPMRC offices. I felt a small sense of victory as we passed the location of the soldiers we had confronted just an hour earlier. We turned left and headed up a hill. The streets of Ramallah were empty and ruined. Bullet casings of all varieties littered the streets. The Israelis had shot up banks, internet cafes, bars, clothing stores, medical relief offices, civil service organizations, and homes. Tanks had bulldozed power lines, dumpsters, and street signs. But the houses were full. Every once in awhile, somebody would lean out of an upper window to say hello or just look at us, wondering. A woman from Los Angeles came down for a quick visit. A man planting a tree in his garden showed us the bullet casings he had collected around his yard. It was surreal.

Occasionally, an APC would rumble by us on a nearby street, but we didn't encounter any soldiers until the very end of our walk. It was right out of a war movie. Two young men in fatigues with a lazy grip on their M-16s. Clearly bored out of their minds and blasting Bob Marley's "I Shot the Sheriff", they made us open our bags and barely even looked into them. Soon we were on our way.

At the UPRMC offices, workers took us on a tour of the damaged building. Two family apartments were heavily hit with damage to the ceilings, walls and floors, which were covered with debris and broken glass. The clinic's reception room and examining room were similarly damaged, but had also been ransacked. A ruined copy machine had crashed to the floor. All of the patient files had been stolen. And every window was shattered. After seeing the damage, I was assigned to an ambulance and given a UPMRC/Red Crescent vest to identify me as a medical relief worker. Alexandra and I accompanied a doctor and two UPMRC volunteers on food and medicine deliveries to various homes that had requested help. The trip through Ramallah neighborhoods was successful and without incident.

Returning to the Sheik Zayed Hospital, we learned that IDF soldiers had shot Arduf Mussa Khandil, a 23 year-old mentally retarded man whom we had seen on the hospital grounds just hours earlier. Apparently he had wandered out into a street behind the hospital. Witnesses saw 11 Israeli soldiers chasing him. They speculated that the young man ran because he was scared when he saw armed soldiers. He was unarmed. They shot him dead.

Scott, a member of our group, visited the morgue to confirm the details of the day's deaths. A third body was delivered to the morgue while we were out. It was the body of Mahmoud Farid Bawatma, who had been dead 7–15 days, his body only recently discovered. He was shot, but the details of his death are unclear except that the bullet had entered through his buttocks and exited through his head. The morgue was full again and the doctors were talking about a second mass grave.

As we were leaving the hospital to attempt a return to Jerusalem, two APCs rolled up the street and parked at the intersection nearest the hospital. It was the same army unit that had stopped us on our way in. Now they were telling us we couldn't leave. After five minutes of talking and ten minutes of waiting while they struck war poses, we were allowed to leave.

Now I am back in Jerusalem, working on getting to Jenin with Kathy and several others. They say there has been a massacre there.

INTERNATIONALS ENTER PRESIDENTIAL COMPOUND IN RAMALLAH—SEEK TO PREEMPT ISRAELI RAID
International Solidarity Movement, 21 April 2002

FOR IMMEDIATE RELEASE

Under threat of an Israeli commando raid on the Presidential Compound in Ramallah —where over 300 Palestinians are holed up with 26 Internationals—six more Internationals entered the compound. Earlier in the day, Israel announced that it was planning an assault on the compound. Additionally, the French consulate sent in three cars to try to remove the French nationals who had been in the compound since March 31, the first such effort by the French and a further indication of the intent of the Israelis to take action.

The mission to get the Internationals—including 2 Americans, 2 British, 1 French and 1 Danish citizen—inside safely involved two teams totaling over 30 foreign nationals. As one team approached the main gate of the compound on Irsal Street, the second "entry team" approached from the rear of the compound.

The first team entered the main gate and immediately drew the attention of the Israeli soldiers located at the front of the compound. Internationals, including Scottish MP Lloyd Quinan and Nobel Peace Prize nominee Kathy Kelly, were met with force by Israeli soldiers, including stun grenades and live ammunition fired in their direction. One American was slapped in the face by an Israeli soldier, while another Scottish citizen had his camera taken, broken and his film confiscated. Two Scottish flags were taken and torn by Israeli soldiers. The Internationals were then forcefully pushed out, being violently shoved even as they were trying to retreat and having stun grenades thrown at them as they exited the compound and walked towards the city center of Ramallah.

Meanwhile, the "entry team" approached the rear entrance of the compound and was met by a single Israeli tank. Soldiers from inside the tank threw tear-gas and stun grenades, but the Internationals were undeterred. The tank then moved into position and started firing live ammunition in the direction of the Internationals. Moving forward with their hands raised toward the door of the building in which the Palestinians are staying with the other Internationals, the group encountered Israeli soldiers deployed on the ground. At this point the team of 6 was able to hop over the barbed wire cordon and enter the building. The remaining Internationals were escorted off the grounds of the compound by Israeli troops.

The names and nationalities of the 6 foreign civilians that entered the presidential compound:
Ms. Rebecca Murray—New York, USA can be reached at [number withheld]
Mr. Kevin Skvorak—New York, USA
Mr. Peter Brachenridge—London, UK
Mr. Nikilai Hanselt—Copenhagen, Denmark
Mr. James Matthews—London, England

Other numbers inside the presidential compound: [numbers withheld]
For more information, please call Huwaida at [number withheld]
(Please note that my [number withheld] number is no longer available as Israeli soldiers snatched and threw that phone. I wasn't able to retrieve it.)

ENDS

FOR ACTIVISTS WITH ARAFAT, A WHIFF OF RELIEF
Deal to end siege is hailed as success for their tactics
by Doug Struck, 1 May 2002, Washington Post

JERUSALEM, April 30—Inside Yasser Arafat's gloomy, airless offices, a band of rumpled activists are ready to celebrate the end of their self-appointed role as body-guards to the Palestinian leader.

Since March 29, when the Israeli army began its siege of the Palestinian Authority's West Bank headquarters in Ramallah, the group has camped out in Arafat's offices, enduring what one member called "a big, gigantic, stinky slumber party." They make odd housemates for an Arab politician: a collection of European, American and even Israeli peace activists who moved in uninvited to share quarters with the Palestinian chief.

The activists, who operate under the name International Solidarity Movement, say they believe that by putting themselves in the line of fire, they will cause Israel to use more restraint than it would if dealing only with Palestinians. So they have slept in Arafat's offices, even posting a few people to curl up on blankets outside his room at night.

They are convinced they have succeeded—that their presence helped moderate Israeli Prime Minister Ariel Sharon's actions and added to the international pressure that resulted in an agreement Sunday to lift the siege.

"I have no doubt that Sharon was planning to come in here and deport or exile the president [Arafat]," Neta Golan, 30, a Canadian Israeli who has been in the compound for 29 days, said by cell phone from inside the compound. "We made the operation complicated for him, if not impossible."

It is difficult to determine what weight their presence had on Israeli or international considerations. But to the activists, the vigil has been a validation of their get-in-the-middle style of intervention.

"I think there is a likelihood that it would have been different without us," Golan said.

The activists put their bodies where their politics are. They ride in Palestinian ambulances that are often stopped and sometimes shot at by Israelis. They sleep in Palestinian villages they suspect are vulnerable to attack. They challenge Israeli check-points and police lines to join Palestinians under siege.

Two members were at Arafat's compound when the siege began. Three days later, a group of 60 arrived. Some have left; others have braved Israeli warning shots to join those inside. About 30 are in the compound now, sleeping in two crowded rooms, grumbling over the dwindling food supplies and giving interviews to reporters when their cell phones are not being jammed.

The announcement Sunday that Israel had accepted a US plan to end the siege in Ramallah brought cheers from the group, though the days needed to work out the details have been a difficult addendum, according to Kevin Skvorak, 39, a New York freelance film technician who said he came to Ramallah because "the injustice and the inequities are so clear."

In the last few days, those inside have watched as the Israeli army stepped up the destruction of property within the compound. They said the army has gutted nearby offices of the Palestinian Authority with explosives, and used a bulldozer to ram dozens of official cars outside the compound and scrape them into a huge pile.

"The cars are now a totally surrealistic picture of siege," Golan said. "These are new cars, shiny red and blue cars, all in a pile. Salvador Dali would like this scene."

The army seized control of all of Arafat's compound except part of one building. The foreign activists have shared the cramped quarters with Arafat, his aides and dozens of Palestinian guards and office workers trapped there. The Palestinian leader sleeps and works upstairs, and his guards and the foreigners sleep on blankets or rumpled sheets downstairs.

For the first 17 days, there was no water and little electricity. There was "a particular smell," said one diplomat who visited.

"We stank," Golan said.

Everyone complained about the shared toilet. The chain-smoking Palestinians shared their dwindling cigarettes—three persons to each cigarette, according to peace activists and diplomats who have been inside.

"It's pretty close to unlivable," said another diplomatic visitor.

The group persuaded Palestinian negotiator Saeb Erekat to smuggle in fresh women's underwear in his briefcase when he visited the compound, and bargained with the Israeli army for 25 bars of soap.

In Bethlehem, where Palestinians are besieged at the Church of the Nativity, the

Israeli army has played a deafening audiotape of screeching, screaming and metallic scraping in a form of psychological warfare. The foreigners in Ramallah say they think their presence has dissuaded the army from such tactics.

"I think we have made it easier for the people here, and provided some comedy relief," Skvorak said.

With the end of the siege in sight, "everyone is jumping around and joking and dancing. All the Europeans are happy," he said.

"I hope to be going back to New York soon," he added. "We hope to be out within 24 hours, eat some good food, breathe some fresh air, have a little party, and then think about what we do from here."

4

SIEGE OF THE CHURCH OF THE NATIVITY

HOW I WISH THAT EVERYTHING WAS AN APRIL FOOL'S JOKE

by Nancy Stohlman, 1 April 2002

Each night I think to myself this is the most terrifying night of my life and each night it gets worse.

All night I counted my life in hours. I just have to stay alive until 6 o'clock. Until 7 o'clock. Until 8 o'clock. Each passing moment a new gray hair on my head.

We waited all night to be invaded and the birds twittering in the morning were like water to parched lips.

I opted to stay in the Aida Refugee Camp with eight other Internationals and come morning the other eleven Internationals returned to Bethlehem for supplies.

Our cell phones were dangerously low of charge and time. The sun came out for a while and I actually began to feel calm. International Solidarity Movement (ISM) organizers called to say that the remainder of the international group was going to march to Beit Jala and try to visit with the Palestinian families under threat. Three of our nine in Aida Refugee Camp went to the Beit Jala march, the other six of us stayed.

The kids in the refugee camp scrounged up a guitar. We taught them yoga out back on the concrete. They set up another game of volleyball and begged me to play while I looked at email. In the middle of a phone conversation Sean (from the US) comes to me with fear in his eyes. Four Internationals were shot during the march! Internationals shot?! Real bullets, not rubber bullets.

The six of us gather and the first thing that comes out of my mouth is, "I want to go back to the hotel." A "me too" pipes up on either side of me. The others raised the question, "What about the people here?" All I can think of is that our nonviolent weapons, and purpose in the refugee camp, was to protect the Palestinians with our international status.

We all clearly now see that the Israeli military is unconcerned with our international status and our lives in the refugee camp feel like more logs on the fire. I want to get out. Four of us decide to go, two to stay. Put on layers and bright colors, I advised. The Palestinian mothers, the doctor—they tried to be understanding, but under their wan smiles is a layer of disappointment, under that layer is fear. I start crying and hugging them feeling like a rat fleeing from a sinking ship.

I call the ISM to coordinate. I'm told there are seven shot, not four. They insist that we walk and not drive. The two that are staying are crying. I am crying and ashamed. But I desperately need to get back to the hotel in Bethlehem, that's all I can think about.

I yell "tomorrow" to the group of boys halted in their tracks holding a volleyball. The thin wire stretched across the alley looks like a deserted IV tube. Six or seven of the refugees escort us to the end of the camp and point the way.

My son is ever present in my mind. We hear gun shots, the roads are deserted, not even a scrap of paper floats by. More shots. We curse under our breath. "Oh Fuck!" It seems like we're walking right towards the shots but it seems like the only way back to the hotel. All around us I imagine Israeli snipers taking aim. Different kinds of shots are going off, some booming, some single rifle shots, some rat-a-tat-tat.

Under my breath I'm whispering, "almost there, almost there." Sky is the color of oatmeal. Mysterious flakes of white are falling like snow in the cool humidity. I can only think about putting one foot in front of the other, constantly scouting for a place to hide with every step.

We round the corner on the main street of Bethlehem and the road is completely littered with bombs the size of small TVs, wired one to the next. I can't be sure when they're going to go off, but we have to cross that street. Ahead I see a group of boys frantically motioning to us. I want to run as fast as I can. Then I hear another International, Rory, reminding us not to run, imagining snipers looking for panicked targets.

We cross the booby-trapped street. The next hurdle is the tower (tall narrow building), it looms above the town of Bethlehem and we're sure that snipers will be there. And for one complete stretch of road we're completely unprotected from it.

I keep saying "almost there, almost there" like a mantra. Roosters are crowing from all directions. "I wonder why the roosters are crowing," one of us asks. "The rooster crows three time because we've betrayed our friends," comes a solemn answer behind me. My heart sinks.

We turn off the sniper street and step behind the wall of Bethlehem University, where the giant white stone walls only give a small sense of security if you forgive the tank shell marks – big holes the size of a grapefruit, with charred black rings, but I know we're only 100 feet from the hotel, round a few more corners, and we spill into the lobby.

The lobby of the Bethlehem Star Hotel is chaos with press and medics and bandages adorning the bodies of my International friends. I try to relay what just happened to us but everyone is preoccupied with his or her own trauma and the horrifying truth is that no one has suffered any less than anyone else.

I run up to my hotel room and lie down on the floor. The explosions sound like a 4th of July fireworks show gone terribly wrong. I call Ben from CCMEP on the phone and proceed to freak out. He's able to calm me down and I'm able to get off the phone.

One of the other people who just walked through hell finds me in my room. At this point everyone who isn't sobbing has eyes caught in a perpetual flash bulb. I feel like I finally calm down and I go downstairs to where I see Issa's injured leg, a piece of shrapnel is still embedded and they've only bandaged her—she was one of the Internationals shot by the IDF at the Beit Jala march.

I'm envisioning a long night of fending off her infection. Then I notice that I'm shivering and my mind feels sluggish. In retrospect I'm pretty sure it was post-traumatic shock. The Israeli invasion lasted until the wee hours of the morning. I slept on the floor with my cell phone in one hand and my passport in my other.

UNDER FIRE IN BETHLEHEM
by Nicholas Blincoe, 3 April 2002, Guardian

I was unlucky to be in Bethlehem when history was being made. Anyone coming fresh to the Israeli occupation of the Palestinian territories must feel bewildered by competing versions of events. It is useful to have facts. This is one: on Monday, live ammunition was used against international protesters for the first time by Israel's armed forces.

I was climbing to the summit of Beit Jala, a small Christian Arab town stretched across two hillsides, overlooking Bethlehem. The illegal settlement of Gilo is visible everywhere here. Because of its position, Beit Jala was the favoured route when Israeli forces invaded Bethlehem last month. No house in the town is without its bullet holes or shell holes.

The reason I was climbing Beit Jala, among 150 foreign protesters, is that Israeli tanks had taken up position there again, signalling their imminent invasion. Our non-violent action was intended to show that Bethlehem was filled with peaceful foreign nationals. A second aim was to visit families cut off by the Israeli advance.

When we reached the first of two Israeli armoured personnel vehicles, we stopped and our negotiators stepped forward. Both are British nationals: the writer Lilian Pizzichini and a Glaswegian technology consultant named Kunle Ibidun. They were unable to state our intentions because the soldier in the vehicle's turret opened fire with his rifle.

His shots were aimed in front of us. They could be called warning shots. But the bullets fractured on impact and his first five bullets injured four people: Kunle himself, a young Japanese woman from Bradford, an Australian woman from Hebden Bridge and Chris Dunham, a Londoner. As we backed down the hill, an elderly Englishman received shrapnel fragments in his face and an American was wounded in the leg. As I write, the Australian is still in hospital and the Japanese woman is returning home for treatment.

I came to Bethlehem to accompany my wife as she made a documentary about the West Bank-based International Solidarity Movement. The ISM has become well known in recent days, after the Canadian Jewish activist Neta Golan and others succeeded in entering Yasser Arafat's compound in Ramallah. But its purpose is to support non-violent direct action in the occupied territories. Palestinians face extreme violence when they demonstrate. It comes not just from Israeli soldiers, who are fairly disciplined and can be expected to operate under direct orders (the soldier who fired at us appeared to be listening to instructions on his radio headset). There are also the notoriously violent Israeli Border Police and the settlers' movement. This is why Internationals are needed: to increase the chances of successful non-violent actions and lessen the risk of violence against the Palestinians.

It would be preferable if the Palestinians could pursue non-violent direct action. In whose interest is an increase in violence? I write this, listening to the Israeli tanks shelling the D'heisha refugee camp 400m away, watching news reports of the burning mosque in Manger Square and an attack on a local priest. I am unable to leave the house. My fellow protesters are split between two refugee camps and a local hotel. The hotel has had its power cut off: presumably an attempt to drive away the foreign media, who are also there. The press and TV are banned from Ramallah and my wife's cameraman and a BBC crew received the worst of the live fire in yesterday's demonstration (although none, fortunately, was wounded). The overwhelming impression is that the Israeli army wishes to behave in any way it chooses, unseen by outsiders.

I was in Bethlehem once before when history was being made: Christmas 1995, when Yasser Arafat gave a speech from the roof of the Nativity Church in Manger Square. The agreement he had signed with Yitzhak Rabin was then termed the "peace of the brave". At that time, Ariel Sharon was already on record as saying he would rip up this agreement.

The Palestinians long ago recognised Israel's right to exist within the international borders it had in 1949. The Likud party, now led by Sharon, has never made a reciprocal statement. The Palestinians believe Sharon will do everything in his power to make sure that the door is left open for an Israel that stretches to the Jordan River. I now believe this, too. Members of his coalition argue openly for the forcible expulsion of the Palestinians. Perhaps the first candidate will be Arafat himself.

Reprinted with permission.

FOUR DAYS IN HELL
by Jeremy Hardy, 15 April 2003, Guardian

Last April, I had occasion to be evacuated from Bethlehem by the British Consulate. It wasn't the first evacuation I had experienced that week—an Israeli tank muzzle outside your hotel bedroom window is an excellent purgative.

The invasion of the city began two nights earlier, on Easter Monday. As it progressed, the various consulates decided to remove as many of their nationals as were prepared to leave, and I was one. We were trapped in the hotel and the consul told me if we didn't leave now, it might be weeks before he could get another car into Bethlehem.

So I was relieved when two Range Rovers pulled up. I was further relieved not to be an American. The US consulate sent the CIA in armoured limousines, and their agents had helmets, flak jackets and guns. Our man had driving gloves. And travel sweets.

I had arrived on Good Friday to make a documentary about the International Solidarity Movement. I was on the plane when Ariel Sharon announced his intention to reoccupy the entire West Bank. Leila Sansour, the producer, had said I would not be put in any danger. The look on her face when she met me at the Bethlehem check-point told me she knew it had been a rash promise.

The idea was that I should join the ISM and take part in its usual activities. But with tanks at the edge of the city, our options were limited. On previous trips, actions had involved demonstrations but also practical help.

The presence of Internationals affords locals some protection. Activists ride in Red Crescent ambulances. They help farmers who try to labour in the shadow of Israeli settlements and their violent occupants. They remove roadblocks so that people can go about their business. They run playgroups. They bear witness.

And they take a fair amount of verbal and physical abuse from settlers, police and soldiers. The group I was with was the first to sustain bullet wounds, as we marched cheerfully to Beit Jala that Easter Monday. Fortunately, none of us was killed … although several were injured. An Australian friend is still carrying bits of a bullet in her stomach. And if you have ever heard that stuff about nervous soldiers panicking under pressure, I particularly urge you to see this film.

You will never see a soldier under less pressure than the man who decided to open up on us. You will see Kunle and Lilian, our designated negotiators, walk forward with arms outstretched to approach the armoured personnel carrier. Kunle was hit in three places.

That night, we knew the Israelis were going to take the city. Most activists volunteered to stay in the refugee camps, which, I firmly believe, prevented a massacre. The rest of us did media work in the hotel and, on Wednesday night, some of us took the chance to escape with our consulates. My premature departure made one thing certain: I would have to go back to Palestine to finish the film.

When I returned in July, the wrecking of Leila's hometown, and the destruction of the whole fabric of Palestinian life, had turned the completion of the film into a mission for her. I didn't want to disappoint her. She has a way of getting people to do things. She fixes you with pained and hopeful eyes, and although she doesn't actually use the words, "the suffering of my people", you know she will if you don't agree.

We were based in Jerusalem, from where ISM activity was directed. Bethlehem was under curfew like most of the West Bank. But Leila is an ingenious planner and managed to find a Russian-speaking cabbie who knew a Russian soldier at the checkpoint. She is fluent in the language, and her Russian mother lives in Beit Jala, so she was able to blag our way through the checkpoint on the basis of a family visit.

The contrast with Easter was stunning. For all the menace in the air before the incursion, there had been a frenzy of human activity. Now everyone seemed to have vanished and nothing moved but armoured cars. Except, that is, in the refugee camps.

Despite being besieged in the camps, the residents were able to move about. We visited D'heisha, a camp that had seen its fair share of suffering (including the shooting of a young stonethrower the previous week), but still seemed to have some kind of life.

We stayed the night with a Palestinian family. I began with perhaps the most stupid question I could have mustered: "Have you ever been to England?" Palestinian women have a way of looking at you that says: "Are you uniquely stupid, or is it a male thing?" But I think I redeemed myself when the baby took a shine to me. Apparently they sometimes ask after Mr Jeremy.

We visited Leila's mum, an elegant and gracious widow living alone in Beit Jala, hospitable as ever and remarkably serene considering the chaos of her adopted country. It seemed fatuous to ask Leila what it's like to have to break curfew to pop in on your mum and see that she's OK.

In fact, it was hard through all of this not to feel quite useless—which is why I was glad that, back in Jerusalem, I was able to join in with a successful action. I was also heartened that it was organised by Israelis, the Ta'ayush peace group, who booked a convoy of coaches to take medical supplies into the West Bank town of Salfit.

This is my favourite part of the film, probably because we did something helpful and practical that involved a direct challenge to the military occupation. Having said that, I am gratingly chirpy at this point in the film. Perhaps, being a middle-aged man on a coach trip, I was impelled to make a daft joke every few seconds. That is tangential to the wider issues, obviously, but I want to make clear that I'm aware of it before anyone sees the film.

My four days were up, so I headed home. I had no idea what the film would look like but, having seen it, I'm proud. Not of myself—except as an intriguing study in bewilderment—but of Leila, and of the activists the film shamelessly champions. I'm sure no broadcaster will touch it. I just hope it doesn't spawn the idea for a series called I'm a Celebrity—Evacuate Me.

Reprinted with permission.

NOTE FROM THE EDITORS: At the time of writing, 'Jeremy Hardy vs the Israeli Army' has been shown in New York, Tel Aviv and Beirut and in towns and cities across the UK, having secured a general release there, a rare achievement for a documentary.

BETHLEHEM DIARY
by Georgina Reeves, 16 April 2002

Tuesday 16th April, 2002 19.00

It appears that a preliminary assault is being made on the Church of the Nativity. As the Israeli army took over the Star Hotel earlier today, the only vantage point from which one can see Manger Square, there will be precious little footage or reporting available. I spoke to friends around the area, plus a call to those inside, and the situation sounds very grim. There was a sustained attack for about 20 minutes or so, many loud explosions and a lot of gunfire.

The sounds of attack have been interspersed by the sounds of fireworks from neighbouring Gilo, built on land stolen from Beit Jala and now masquerading as a suburb of West Jerusalem. The Israelis are celebrating what they call 'independence day'. I wonder how many of them think, or even realize, the tragic cost to other people's freedom and lives their 'independence' has brought? Judging by the things I have seen and heard these last few weeks, nowhere near enough.

INTERNATIONAL ACTIVISTS REACH DOOR OF CHURCH OF THE NATIVITY
by Larry Hales, 28 April 2002

We walked right in to Manger Square—"right through the front door." The writer in me wants to create some suspense, but I am ecstatic—my heart continues to beat at the rate it was when we were walking through.

We were planning the night before and were planning around another demonstration led by clergy. Our plan was to walk to the checkpoint before Bethlehem and protest. This morning we decided to participate in this action but to also continue on if the participants of it were stopped.

Well, we were stopped and the clergy weren't so much interested in pushing through as they were in just challenging the checkpoint.

After this action, which lasted only about 30 minutes, we decided to take a route through a monastery. No one expected us to get through this way either because the soldiers were very close, and if they were looking, would be able to see us. But they didn't and we continued on into Bethlehem.

The city was a ghost town, it was on curfew and it was almost completely quiet— at first. As we walked on, people began appearing at their windows and cheering us on. It was very powerful to see these people, children and elderly people, looking out and throwing up peace signs. Our presence gave them hope and as we continued we began to see more and more people, mostly children coming out of their homes. They wouldn't come out on the streets but they were coming out.

We stopped after having walked for quite a while, and we began to plan for the march on the Church of the Nativity. No one thought that we would have gotten as far as we did. We planned and planned and waited and planned; finally, some of us decided to talk to some families that had gathered just in front of their homes; a few of them were fluent in English.

They were entirely full of gratitude—they let us into their homes and served us coffee—these people are resilient. Their lives are being put on hold by an occupying force; they can't go to work; their children can't go to school, yet they were so willing to share with us. Some even invited me to stay with them.

Time began to get short, so we had to go with the plan we had, which was for five of us to cross the barricade with water and food but we didn't think that we would get through; and so we were considering that the action would be symbolic at best. We waited some more and finally set on our way with a box of water and a bag of rice—meant to be symbolic of course because in the church there is barely any water, let alone a way of cooking the rice.

People began coming out more. I guess the word had gotten out. There was a group of Palestinians just before the barricade and some walked to it with us, holding down the barbed wire so that we could walk over it.

When we saw Manger Square we thought the siege had ended. It was empty except for an M1 Abrams tank. We walked on and at the halfway point Israelis began yelling for us to stop. These soldiers doing the yelling didn't have on their Kevlar helmets or their rifles—they were caught off guard.

We continued on through the yelling and made it to the door of the Church. When there we were instructed to sit by Huwaida. We did and the soldiers threw smoke canisters to block the press from seeing us. We knocked at the door and yelled that we had food; the soldiers looked on, the smoke rising. The tank moved so as to scare us. The media began moving so the smoke wouldn't block their view. We held our hands up while yelling at the people inside to open the door, then the soldiers moved towards us and started pulling us up and throwing the food away from the door.

They were attempting to hold us but we were leading them more than them us. They tried to confiscate cameras, but we refused and they capitulated. However, they did drag some people. The soldier holding me was telling me how he didn't agree with what was going on but that it was his job. He seemed to be a good man.

We were put in one area and Ted Koppel [ABC news reporter] came over and interviewed Huwaida. He got the entire incident, all the cameras did despite the smoke. When he finished we came to the conclusion to walk out. The soldiers weren't prepared for this. They tried to stop us but we defied them and kept on walking 'til we were clear of them.

The action was one of the most spectacular things I have ever seen, and the people I was with are some of the most brave people I have ever known. Tomorrow we will begin to try and get some people into Hebron and the Gaza Strip. I will be going to Hebron. More to come.

BETHLEHEM DIARY
by Georgina Reeves, 29 April–2 May 2002

Monday 29th April, 2002
Nothing has changed here in the last 4 weeks. Actually, that's not true, it has, and it has been for the worse. The whole district is still imprisoned; curfew is constant bar a few hours here and there. Sometimes Beit Jala and Beit Sahour are given a few hours of freedom, but as Bethlehem separates them people cannot visit friends who don't live nearby. Never is the whole district given 'freedom' at the same time. It is wearing people out, me included. Even though I have the 'luxury' of being able to break curfew, as a foreigner who they assume is a journalist, it is still a little nerve-wracking. Tanks thundering past a few feet away, soldiers in APCs pointing their guns, snipers who knows where.

Thursday 2nd May, 2002
Overnight has been awful. Shooting and bombing around and at the Church. Two fires were started by flares, although those inside did manage to extinguish them. Still more shooting this morning. A man has been shot, about half an hour ago. The Israelis keep saying they are not shooting on or into the Church. So how come people are

being injured and killed? The siege of Arafat has now ended, so the Church remains the last 'problem'. I have a horrible feeling that there will be more deaths in the Church and the Israelis are certainly getting very anxious to end it. There are now 2 cranes in the Square; one has a radio-controlled sniper rifle mounted on it, and from the other hangs a massive speaker through which they have been playing ear-splitting noises.

In response to our last attempt to get to the Church the army has put up a hand-written sign in English, at the press barricade. It says 'No entry, closed military area'— as if we would take notice of it! We are determined to get through.

INTERNATIONAL PEACEMAKERS ENTER BETHLEHEM CHURCH OF THE NATIVITY
by Dennis B. Warner, Jerusalem, 2 May 2002

At 17:40 hours this afternoon a group of international peace activists of the International Solidarity Movement (ISM) successfully evaded Israeli military patrols and entered the Church of the Nativity in Bethlehem. This was the second time in four days that the ISM attempted to breach the Israeli military siege of the church to bring sorely needed food supplies to the 100+ people taking refuge in this holiest of Christian shrines.

On Monday, 29 April, members of the ISM reached the door of the church before they were forcefully pulled away before they could enter. This afternoon they not only reached the interior of the church with supplies of rice, flour, salt and sweets but left ten of their party in the church to share the confinement with the resident monks who oversee the operations of the church and a large number of Palestinians who had fled to the church for protection during the Israeli invasion a month ago. A journalist for the *Los Angeles Times* also joined with the group and remained in the church with the ISM members.

On this second penetration of the military cordon around the church, a primary purpose was to put international peace activists in the structure to underscore to the international community the severity of the conditions there and the illegality of the Israeli military occupation of the city of Bethlehem.

The ten ISM activists included five Americans, one Briton, one Dane, one Swede, one Irish and one Canadian. Three of these are women.

The entry to the church began at 17:40 hours when three ISM groups totaling 23 activists approached the structure from three directions. Crossing Manger Square at a steady but rapid walk, they reached the door of the church which was briefly opened at their arrival. The Israeli troops stationed around the church and Manger Square appeared to be taken by surprise and were unable to intercept the activists before they had successfully crossed the square. Fortunately, no shots were fired and no tear-gas or stun grenades were used by the Israeli troops.

Thirteen ISM members remained outside the church where they were immediately detained and arrested by the military. This group included eight [sic] Americans, three Britons and two Swedes. Again, five members of the detained group were women. A number of mobile telephone calls by the detained activists indicated that they were not mistreated but being held by Israeli authorities for questioning. As of this report, no word has been given of the fate of the detainees. ISM organizers believe that the detainees may face deportation from Israel.

The ten ISM activists intend to remain in the church until the military siege is lifted. Before beginning this action, ISM organizer Ms Huwaida Arraf, one of the current detainees, expressed the hope that the presence of international observers in the church will help deter the Israeli military from firing into the structure. Over the past several weeks, several Israeli assaults against the church have been attempted. The most recent attack occurred last night and resulted in two fires in the church and, according to the Mayor of Bethlehem, one Palestinian killed and two wounded.

Following the breach of the military cordon, a group of ISM members who had remained at the barricades compiled lists of activists in the church and in Israeli military custody. Names and passport numbers were reported to the consulates and embassies of the countries from which the activists came. In addition, information was given to the score or more of international press corps present at the scene.

This action occurred on the same day that the military siege of the Presidential Compound at Ramallah was lifted.

The International Solidarity Movement is a Palestinian-based organization dedicated to non-violent resistance to Israeli occupation. Founded two years ago, it encourages international peace activists to come to Palestine to provide non-violent support to the Palestinian resistance.

    —Dennis B. Warner of Falls Church, Virginia, representing Pax Christi USA in support of ISM.

NOTE FROM THE EDITORS: The detained Internationals were Jeff Kingham (USA), Kate Thomas (UK), Marcia Tubbs (UK), John Caruso (USA), Nathan Musselman (USA), Nathan Mauger (USA), Trevor Baumgartner (USA), Jo Harrison (UK), Johannes Walilstram (Sweden), James Hanna (USA), Thomas Koutsoukos (USA), Ida Fasten (Sweden). Huwaida Arraf was also detained.

BETHLEHEM DIARY
Georgina Reeves, 3 May 2002

Friday 3rd May, 2002

Yesterday saw our third, successful 'assault' on Nativity Church. With full coordination with Palestinians inside the church we decided to get food and medicine in, as well as people. I have to stress that they welcomed our attempt and were happy for Internationals to go in with them. Having been in touch with people inside, I got a list of the foodstuffs they needed. With a friend, we collected as much of the food that they had asked for in the morning, then waited for a group of Internationals to arrive from Jerusalem and then we made our plans....

    17.45: Following a briefing the group split into 3 to cause diversions, and made their way in to Manger Square. The soldiers were, again, caught totally off guard. Snipers in the windows were yelling at us, "Stop! Go back" but noone took any notice. There was a final dash for the door, which was opened for those going in, and 10 people went through (there were supposed to be 5!). The group received a rapturous welcome. Although we didn't get a huge amount of supplies in, it was better than nothing. Also, one of the group is a nurse, something they so desperately needed.

    The others had a less hospitable welcome. As they made their way back across the square they were detained and dragged in to the Peace Centre. They were then held for 7 hours before being carted off in jeeps. The men were taken to Kiryat Arba police station and held overnight—illegally detained in an illegal settlement. The 5 women fared much worse. They were tied up, physically abused then dumped in the middle of the night near a settlement north of Bethlehem.

Since yesterday afternoon I have been on the phones non-stop with media, legal advisors, consular staff and goodness knows who else. The majority of today was spent trying to track down the whereabouts of those who were illegally detained. I have finally succeeded, more or less. The response from everyone, except the Israelis, has been phenomenal though. The locals all thought it was wonderful and really welcomed what we did. They don't see anyone else making much effort to help them so a group of Internationals prepared to try is a real boost for their morale.

INSIDE THE CHURCH OF THE NATIVITY
Phone conversation with Larry Hales, 4 May, 20:00
by Colorado Campaign for Middle East Peace, 4 May 2002

CCMEP: Larry! How are you?

Larry Hales: We're doing good! Our spirits are up. Our spirits had been down, they killed a man today.

CCMEP: A Palestinian man?

LH: Yeah. He was hanging some clothes up to dry that he had washed (the water here comes from a well), and they shot him in the back—from the side.

CCMEP: So he was outside of the church?

LH: Yeah.

CCMEP: Have you been able to get the body out?

LH: Yeah, we got him out. They patched him up, made him comfortable. It took forty-five minutes to get him out. You could kind of tell that he was going to die because he started turning really, really pale. It was crazy. He was really brave, he didn't make a sound.

CCMEP: Did the Internationals take him out?

LH: The monks here—the priests—they took him out. These guys are really something.

CCMEP: How is everybody in there? How are the Internationals?

LH: We keep it light—we joke with people. We try to keep it as light as possible. Even the Palestinian guys, they don't walk around with sour faces. They laugh, we joke with the ones who speak English.

CCMEP: How is the food situation?

LH: Well, there is no food. We ate the last of it today. (Muffled voices.) Oh, I guess there's something, a little bit of something. Most of it is light—like there are grape leaves, so people cook the grape leaves.

CCMEP: How are everyone's spirits?

LH: We feel really good, we just wish that from the start we had told someone that we were going to be distributing food. We couldn't bring all that much because we paid for it ourselves …. We're a good group—with each other we just sort of keep it going. If anyone gets down, other people try to lift them up.

CCMEP: Have you been able to contact anyone from the outside, other Internationals or organizations?

LH: There are a couple people who didn't get arrested—they contacted us. They're hanging around in Bethlehem. We've been talking to a lot of media.

CCMEP: What are people's speculations about what's going to happen?

LH: A far as I know, it's coming to a close. I guess Sharon is going to the States, and I guess one of his bargaining chips is that he's going to pull out of here, so I'm thinking tonight or early tomorrow morning. I think within a matter of hours, actually.

CCMEP: What are the Internationals planning on doing then?

LH: We're going to wait behind, we're not going to go out with the other people.
CCMEP: Are you getting any sleep?

LH: Yeah, they're actually letting us sleep in the place where Jesus was supposedly born!

CCMEP: Are there any messages you want to send back home?

LH: Just tell everybody thank you for helping me get here, and for taking care of my girlfriend.

CCMEP: Anything else you want to say?

LH: Most of the people in here are civilians. They were people who were defending their homes. What they are fighting for is just—their cause is just. They're not a bunch of suicide bombers, they were just defending their homes. I'm really disappointed and mad at the same time. It's just not fair.

ISRAELI ARMY ARRESTS TEN PEACE ACTIVISTS IN NATIVITY CHURCH
Illegally detained, activists join hunger strike
International Solidarity Movement, 10 May 2002

FOR IMMEDIATE RELEASE

BETHLEHEM—Today at 2:40 pm (ME time), the Israeli army stormed the Church of the Nativity and arrested ten international peace activists, after ending their 38-day siege on the holy site. The activists risked their lives to bring food, medical supplies, and the protection of their international status to the Palestinian citizens and clergy trapped inside the Church of the Nativity. They had been maintaining their vigil in the church for just over one week.

Earlier today, the Israeli army exiled 13 Palestinian men wanted by the Israeli government, and escorted 100 some other Palestinians to the Gaza Strip to be interrogated before being allowed to return home. All of the Internationals have been detained in a Jerusalem prison. Yet none of them have been charged. The activists did not leave the church of their own choosing. They requested legal counsel and a guarantee from the Israeli army that they would not be arrested or deported. They received neither.

"Israel continues to try to remove any independent witness or humanitarian peace activists from helping or working with the Palestinian people. This is part of its effort to maintain global silence and total control over information on its unjust war on the Palestinian people," said Adam Shapiro, a coordinator with the International Solidarity Movement, which has organized groups of peace workers to travel to the West Bank. Shapiro spent time inside Yasser Arafat's compound.

When the Internationals arrived in the Church of the Nativity just over a week ago, they brought rice, lentils, salt and other essential foodstuffs. The besieged Palestinians and clergy had eaten nothing but boiled grass and lemon leaves for three days prior to their arrival. One of the Internationals, Mary Kelly, a trained nurse, was able to treat the injured and sick who had been denied access to medical treatment.

All 10 activists have joined the hunger strike that Seattle native Trevor Baumgartner and three other detained US citizens began a week ago. They are demanding to be able to leave Israel of their own free will, so they can continue their peace activism. Trevor is now on his 9th day without food. As of Thursday, Nathan Mauger and Thomas Koutsoukos have refused to take either water or food.

The list of the detained Internationals is as follows:

1. Nauman Zaidi, USA
2. Robert O'Neill, USA
3. Larry Hales, USA
4. Kristen Schurr, USA
5. Alister Hillman, UK
6. Allan Lindgaard, Denmark
7. Stefan Coster, Sweden
8. Erik Alger, Sweden
9. Mary Kelly, Ireland
10. Jacqueline Soohen, Canada

ENDS

BETHLEHEM DIARY
by Georgina Reeves, 13 May 2002

Monday 13th May, 2002

At the moment my time is spent trying to support the guys in prison. There were, in total, 22 Internationals held. Those from the church have been arrested, the others who helped them are detained without arrest. None are charged. So far, 10 have been illegally deported, the remaining people will be deported in the following 24 hours. That is really rough for them as they have paid a very high price for their belief in justice and freedom as they will probably never be allowed back in to the country.

I find it incredible that Israel can be allowed to do this; they were carrying food for God's sake. The people in the Church needed help and no government was prepared to stand up and do the right thing—someone had to do something. Today I had so many local people come up to me to thank us for everything we tried to do to help them. Before all the shit happened the guys wrote a statement, which I have never issued. It is a shame as it told of the jubiliation over their arrival. When they arrived they were greeted with such enthusiasm and gratitude. "Now we know that everyone has not forgotten the Palestinian people." That is what one young man said after they arrived.

It was a very emotional and warm welcome, the departure was even more emotional but full of sadness, disbelief and some anger. Despite the reports of the withdrawal of Israeli forces from the district, they have not gone. They are out of the centre but they are still close. A CNN report I watched this morning had some excitable woman driving around Bethlehem, talking about how everything is getting "back to normal". Does she not understand that nothing is normal here; occupation is not normal.

5

INVASION

COURAGE UNDER FIRE
by Katie Barlow, 27 November 2002, Guardian

On Friday, Iain Hook, a British UN volunteer, was shot and killed in Jenin. Caoimhe Butterly, a 23-year-old Irish activist, was also shot, but survived. In October, I spent two weeks filming Caoimhe for a documentary.

[…]

In April, she received international attention when she smuggled her way into Arafat's Ramallah compound, at that time under siege by IDF soldiers. She went in to give basic medical aid to a Palestinian friend who had been shot in the leg, and had called her for help after the IDF denied him access to the Red Crescent ambulances. She managed to get help to him, but couldn't get herself out again.

"The Israeli army announced officially that any International trying to leave the compound would be immediately deported and arrested, if not shot at," says Caoimhe. "By day three, it became glaringly obvious that I had made a huge mistake. We were just beginning to get the news that the tanks were on their way to Jenin. I spent the next 12 days in there as the stories of Jenin got worse and worse, and I knew I had

Photograph by Jennifer Midberry.

friends who were bleeding to death."

She escaped by luck, when the IDF forgot to shut a gate surrounding the compound, and ran for her life past tanks and soldiers. She got back to Jenin camp towards the end of the invasion. "It was the smell of rotting human flesh that first hit me. There were still soldiers in the camp, but a lot of people chose to violate the curfew, to bury their dead and to drag in the wounded. One man had been shot at close range, and his body was rolled over by tanks until he was nothing but bones and a sheath of flesh. There was no machinery to dig up the dead, so I helped to dig up the bodies by hand. Very few intact: burnt, broken body parts, a little girl's plait and the foot of a baby. In clearing away the rubble I picked up what remained of a head. There was the body of a little girl who was curled up with her teddy bear. She had suffocated when her house was demolished."

For a while, after April, she felt a numb fearlessness that allowed her to walk up to tanks and into the line of fire, to confront soldiers and withstand beatings at checkpoints. She emphasises that atrocities occur daily—and, indeed, in the two weeks I was with her, 19 civilians were shot, six fatally. Seven of the victims were children on their way to school, shot as tanks opened fire in the middle of the town. One market stallholder was shot in the head in an erratic spray of bullets from an invading tank as he was setting out his vegetables.

Friday was a very close call. Caoimhe was shot in the left thigh as she stood in between a firing IDF tank and three young boys in the street. I spoke to her on the phone shortly after the attack as she lay in her hospital bed. She explained that she had been trying to persuade the IDF, after they shot dead a nine-year-old boy, to stop shooting at the children. They had told her to get out of their way or they would shoot her. It was while she was clearing the children off the streets that she was shot. She is sure she was a direct target; the tank was close by, the soldier pointed his gun at her and fired, and continued to do so as she crawled to an alleyway for shelter.

[...]

Caoimhe tells me she is OK. A chunk of her thigh is missing but she is grateful that the bullet passed through her leg. Tragically, her friend Iain Hook was shot through the stomach and died. Earlier that day, they had been negotiating with the army to get a sick child to hospital, but the IDF refused to let an ambulance through. When Hook was shot, the ambulance was detained again.

Will she now leave? "I'm going nowhere. I am staying until this Occupation ends. I have the right to be here, a responsibility to be here. So does anyone who knows what is going on here."

THE BOY WHO KISSED THE SOLDIER
by Starhawk, 1 June 2002

"What source can you believe in order to create peace there?" a friend writes when I come back from Palestine. I have no answer, only this story:

June 1, 2002: I am in Balata refugee camp in occupied Palestine, where the Israeli Defense Forces have rounded up four thousand men, leaving the camp to women and children. The men have offered no resistance, no battle. The camp is deathly quiet. All the shops are shuttered, all the windows closed. Women, children and a few old men hide in their homes.

The quiet is shattered by sporadic bursts of gunfire, bangs and explosions. All day we have been encountering soldiers who all look like my brother or cousins or the sons I never had, so young they are barely more than boys armed with big guns. We've been standing with the terrified inhabitants as the soldiers search their houses, walking patients who are afraid to be alone on the streets to the UN Clinic. Earlier in the evening, eight of our friends were arrested, and we know that we could be caught at any moment. It is nearly dark, and Jessica and Melissa and I are looking for a place to spend the night. Jessica, with her pale, narrow face, dark eyes and curly hair, could be my sister or my daughter. Melissa is a bit more punk, androgynous in her dyed-blond ducktail.

We are hurrying through the streets, worried. We need to be indoors before true dark, and curfew. "Go into any house," we've been told. "Anyone will be glad to take you in." But we feel a bit shy. From a narrow, metal staircase, Samar, a young woman with a wide, beautiful smile, beckons us up.

"Welcome, welcome!" We are given refuge in the three small rooms that house her family: her mother, big bodied and sad, her small nieces and nephews, her brother's wife Hanin, round-faced and pale and six months pregnant.

We sit down on big, overstuffed couches. The women serve us tea. I look around at the pine wood paneling that adds soft curves and warmth to the concrete, at the porcelain birds and artificial flowers that decorate a ledge. The ceilings are carefully painted in simple geometric designs. They have poured love and care into their home, and it feels like a sanctuary.

Outside we can hear sporadic shooting, the deep "boom" of houses being blown up by the soldiers. But here in these rooms, we are safe, in the tentative sense that word can be used in this place. "Inshallah", "God willing", follows every statement of good here or every commitment to a plan.

"Yahoud!" the women say when we hear explosions. It is the Arabic word for Jew, the word used for the soldiers of the invading army. It is a word of warning and alarm: don't go down that alley, out into that street. "Yahoud!" But no one invades our refuge this night. We talk and laugh with the women. I have a pocket-sized packet of Tarot cards, and we read for what the next day will bring. Samar wants a reading, and then Hanin. I don't much like what I see in their cards: death, betrayal, sleepless nights of sorrow and regret. But I can't explain that in Arabic anyway, so I focus on what I see that is good.

"Baby?" Hanin asks.

"Babies, yes."

"Boy? Son?"

The card of the Sun comes up, with a small boy-child riding on a white horse. "Yes, I think it is a boy," I say.

She shows me the picture of her first baby, who died at a year and a half. Around us young men are prowling with guns, houses are exploding, lives are being shattered. And we are in an intimate world of women. Hanin brushes my hair, ties it back in a band to control its wildness. We try to talk about our lives. We can write down our ages on paper. I am fifty, Hanin is twenty-three. Jessica and Melissa are twenty-two: all of them older than most of the soldiers. Samar is seventeen, the children are eight and ten and the baby is four. I show them pictures of my family, my garden, my step-granddaughter. I think they understand that my husband has four daughters but I have none of my own, and that I am his third wife. I'm not sure they understand that those wives are sequential, not concurrent; but maybe they do. The women of this camp are educated, sophisticated; many we have met throughout the day are professionals, teachers, nurses, students when the Occupation allows them to go to school.

"Are you Christian?" Hanin finally asks us at the end of the night. Melissa, Jessica and I look at each other. All of us are Jewish, and we're not sure what the reaction will be if we admit it. Jessica speaks for us.

"Jewish," she says. The women don't understand the word. We try several variations, but finally are forced to the blunt and dreaded "Yahoud."

"Yahoud!" Hanin says. She gives a little surprised laugh, looks at the other women. "Beautiful!"

And that is all. Her welcome to us is undiminished. She shows me the shower, dresses me in her own flowered nightgown and robe, and puts me to bed in the empty side of the double bed she shares with her husband, who has been arrested by the Yahoud. Mats are brought out for the others. Two of the children sleep with us. Ahmed, the little four year old boy, snuggles next to me. He sleeps fiercely, kicking and thrashing in his dreams, and each time an explosion comes, hurls himself into my arms.

I can't sleep at all. How have I come here, at an age when I should be home making plum jam and doll's clothes for grandchildren, to be cradling a little Palestinian boy whose sleep is already shattered by gunshots and shells? I am thinking about the summer I spent in Israel when I was fifteen, learning Hebrew, working on a kibbutz, touring every memorial to the Holocaust and every site of a battle in what we called the War of Independence. I am thinking of one day when we were brought to the Israel/Lebanon border. The Israeli side was green, the other side barren and brown.

"You see what we have made of this land," we were told. "And that; that's what they've done in two thousand years. Nothing."

I am old enough now to question the world of assumptions behind that statement, to recognize one of the prime justifications the colonizers have always used against the colonized. "They weren't doing anything with the land: they weren't using it." They are not, somehow, as deserving as we are, as fully human. They are animals, they hate us.

All of that is shattered by the sound of Hanin's laugh, called into question by a small boy squirming and twisting in his sleep. I lie there in awe at the trust that has been given me, one of the people of the enemy, put to bed to sleep with the children. It seems to me, at that moment, that there are indeed powers greater than the guns I can hear all around me: the power of Hanin's trust, the power that creates sanctuary, the great surging compassionate power that overcomes prejudice and hate.

One night later, we again go back to our family just as dark is falling, together with Linda and Neta, two other volunteers. We have narrowly escaped a party of soldiers, but no sooner do we arrive than a troop comes to the door. At least they have come to the door: we are grateful for that for all day they have been breaking through people's walls, knocking out the concrete with sledgehammers, bursting through into rooms of terrified people to search or, worse, use the house as a thoroughfare, a safe route that allows them to move through the camp without venturing into the streets. We have been in houses turned into surreal passageways, with directions spray-painted on their walls, where there is no sanctuary because all night long soldiers are passing back and forth.

We come forward to meet these soldiers, to talk with them and witness what they will do. One of the men, with owlish glasses, knows Jessica and Melissa: they have had a long conversation with him standing beside his tank. He is uncomfortable with his role.

Ahmed, the little boy, is terrified of the soldiers. He cries and screams and points at them, and we try to comfort him, to carry him away into another room. But he won't go. He is terrified, but he can't bear to be out of their sight. He runs toward them crying.

"Take off your helmet," Jessica tells the soldiers. "Shake hands with him, show him you're a human being. Help him to be not so afraid."

The owlish soldier takes off his helmet, holds out his hand. Ahmed's sobs subside. The soldiers file out to search the upstairs. Samar and Ahmed follow them. Samar holds the little boy up to the owlish soldier's face, tells him to give the soldier a kiss. She doesn't want Ahmed to be afraid, to hate. The little boy kisses the soldier, and the soldier kisses him back, and hands him a small Palestinian flag.

This is the moment to end this story, on a high note of hope, to let it be a story of how simple human warmth, a child's kiss, can for a moment overcome oppression and hate. But it is a characteristic of the relentless quality of this Occupation that the story doesn't end here. The soldiers order us all into one room. They close the door, and begin to search the house. We can hear banging and crashing and loud thuds against the walls. I am trying to think of something to sing, to do to distract us, to keep the spirits of the children up. I cannot think of anything that makes sense. My voice won't work. But Neta teaches us a silly children's song in Arabic. To me, it sounds like:

"Babouli raizh, raizh, babouli jai, Babouli ham melo sucar o shai."

"The train comes, the train goes, the train is full of sugar and tea."

The children are delighted, and begin to sing. Hanin and I drum on the tables. The soldiers are throwing things around in the other room and the children are singing and Ahmed begins to dance. We put him up on the table and he smiles and swings his hips and makes us all laugh.

When the soldiers finally leave, we emerge to examine the damage. Every single object has been pulled off the walls, out of the closets, thrown in huge piles on the floor. The couches have been overturned and their bottoms ripped off. The wood paneling is full of holes knocked into every curve and corner. Bags of grain have been emptied into the sink. Broken glass and china cover the floor.

We begin to clean up. Melissa sweeps: Jessica tries to corral the barefoot children until we can get the glass off the floor. I help Hanin clear a path in the bedroom, folding the clothes of her absent husband, hanging up her own things, finding the secret sexy underwear the soldiers have obviously examined. By the time it is done, I know every intimate object of her life.

We are a houseful of women: we know how to clean and restore order. When the house is back together, Hanin and Samar and the sister cook. The grandmother is having a high blood pressure attack: we lay her down on the couch, I bring her a pillow. She rests. I sit down, utterly exhausted, as Hanin and the women serve us up a meal. A few china birds are back on the ledge. The artificial flowers have reappeared. Some of the loose boards of the paneling have been pushed back. Somehow once again the house feels like a sanctuary.

"You are amazing," I tell Hanin. "I am completely exhausted: you're six months pregnant, it's your house that has just been trashed, and you're able to stand there cooking for all of us." Hanin shrugs. "For us, this is normal," she says.

And this is where I would like to end this story, celebrating the resilience of these women, full of faith in their power to renew their lives again and again.

But the story doesn't end here.

The third night: Melissa and Jessica go back to stay with our family. I am staying with another family who has asked for support. The soldiers have searched their house three times, and have promised that they will continue to come back every night. We are sleeping in our clothes, boots ready. We get a call.

The soldiers have come back to Hanin's house. Again, they lock everyone in one room. Again, they search. This time, the soldier who kissed the baby is not with them. They have some secret intelligence report that tells them there is something to find, although they have not found it. They rip the paneling off the walls. They knock holes in the tiles and the concrete beneath. They smash and destroy, and when they are done, they piss on the mess they have left.

Nothing has been found, but something is lost. The sanctuary is destroyed, the house turned into a wrecking yard. No one kisses these soldiers: no one sings.

When Hanin emerges and sees what they have done, she goes into shock. She is resilient and strong, but this assault has gone beyond "normal", and she breaks. She is hyperventilating, her pulse is racing and thready. She could lose the baby, or even die.

Jessica, who is trained as a Street Medic for actions, informs the soldiers that Hanin needs immediate medical care. The soldiers are reluctant. "We'll be done soon," they say. But one is a paramedic, and Melissa and Jessica are able to make him see the seriousness of the situation. They allow the two of them to violate curfew, to run through the dark streets to the clinic, come back with two nurses who somehow get Hanin and the family into an ambulance and taken to the hospital.

This story could be worse. Because Jessica and Melissa were there, Hanin and the baby survive. That is, after all, why we've come: to make things not quite as bad as they would be otherwise.

But there is no happy ending to this story, no cheerful resolution. When the soldiers pull out, I go back to say goodbye to Hanin, who has come back from the hospital. She is looking dull, depressed: something is broken. I don't know if it can be repaired, if she will ever be the same. Her resilience is gone; her eyes have lost their light. She writes her name and phone number for me, writes "Hanin love you." I don't know how the story will ultimately end for her. I still see in the cards destruction, sleepless nights of anguish, death.

This is not a story of some grand atrocity. It is a story about "normal", about what it's like to be under an everyday, relentless assault on any sense of safety or sanctuary.

"What was that song about the train?" I ask Neta after the soldiers are gone.

"Didn't you hear?" she asks me. "The soldiers came and got the old woman, at one o'clock in the morning, and made her sing the song. I don't think I'll ever be able to sing it again."

"What source can you believe in order to create peace there?" a friend writes. I have no answer. Every song is tainted; every story goes on too long and turns nasty. A boy whose baby dreams are disturbed by gunfire kisses a soldier. A soldier kisses a boy, and then destroys his home. Or maybe he simply stands by as others do the destruction, in silence, that same silence too many of us have kept for too long.

And if there are forces that can nurture peace they must first create an uproar, a vast breaking of silence, a refusal to stand by as the boot stomps down.

TULKAREM: A WEEK OF EXTREME VIOLENCE
by Rebecca Murray, 14 August 2002

I have just spent the past week in Tulkarem. Tulkarem straddles the line of the West Bank and Israel, where you can see the lights of Netanya and the sea in the distance. But the city is completely isolated, and this imprisonment heavily enforced by the surrounding Israeli military.

This is a city where extreme violence carried out by the Israeli military on all Palestinian citizens is hushed up. Journalists are strictly forbidden from this "military zone".

Apaches this past week have been flying low over the city day and night, firing into Tulkarem camp and city with routine frequency. Tanks have occupied the center and outskirts of the city, also firing often. And the soldiers in jeeps, many of them Druze, drive around constantly, shouting that if they see anyone on the street they will shoot. The military is very busy arresting and shooting at civilians, on many occasions children as young as seven years old. Journalists have been threatened with arrest unless they get out of town immediately, their film confiscated on site. This week *Ha'Aretz* reporter Gideon Levy's car was fired upon with no provocation (a bullet straight in the center of the windshield), the only thing saving his life being the bullet-proof glass.

Cold-blooded executions

On Tuesday, August 7th, the military executed one of the men on their "wanted list", Ziad D'ayas, 28 years old, in cold blood. They also murdered two Palestinian civilians in the vicinity, afterwards claiming they too were "wanted". This official military statement is an absolute untruth.

One, Mahair Jesmawi, 17 years old, was a student who had learnt moments before he had just passed his end of the year school examinations. Elated, he stepped out briefly onto the street and was killed. The other was Mohammed Saidz, 24 years old, a mechanic working in his shop who had the bad luck to be happened upon by soldiers going after Ziad. He was shot and died a slow death after ambulances were prevented from retrieving him.

This military action was conducted in a particularly gruesome way. According to eyewitnesses in neighboring buildings, it started around nine that morning. Snipers and soldiers, many in plain clothes, surrounded the area of the mechanic's roof where Ziad was sleeping. They proceeded to aim and shoot, hitting Ziad in his leg and neck. Ziad fell off the roof into the shop, breaking his limbs but still alive. They then proceeded to bash him all over his body with their guns, before firing nine dum dum bullets directly into his head, killing him instantly. Their dogs were set on the body, and acid was poured on his arms, legs, and stomach.

Ambulances were prevented from moving for five hours that morning. One tried to retrieve the three bodies that the military held in a small field outside the mechanic's house, but the ambulance was fired upon and had to turn back. Finally, a civilian car rushed the bodies to the government hospital as soon as the soldiers left the the vicinity.

I viewed the bodies as they came in. Ziad's body was grotesquely tortured, limbs broken, and his skin peeled off in huge sections from the acid. His head was half blown off. Mahair, the 17 year old student, was shot in the head. And Mohammed, the mechanic, had a bullet in his torso.

Meanwhile, the houses in the area of the murders were emptied of families, as the soldiers went through each one, damaging furniture, stealing money on two occasions.

A group of roughly thirty men were arrested and taken to Israel, including two wounded by live ammunition.

The hospital and ambulances under siege

The ambulance dispatch center is next to Tulkarem's government hospital. On three occasions this past week both the hospital and ambulance entrance have been blocked by tanks and jeeps. Apparently this is quite normal.

On these occasions, soldiers scream at the hospital gate keepers to close the gates. Once, to punctuate their point, the soldiers fired live ammunition through the gaps in the gate, towards the emergency room entrance, hitting a car in the process. Thankfully, the car had no occupants at the time.

On these three occasions the Red Cross has been informed by the military that the ambulances cannot move AT ALL. Shooting at moving ambulances is unfortunately not uncommon in Tulkarem.

[...]

Summer camp for kids continues under fire

The summer camp for children is popular, but often caught up in the violence. The kids have been in the downtown camp on numerous occasions when the tanks come in to the downtown area and start firing.

The kids who attend (roughly 7–10 years old) are from both the city and the camp. Every morning the kids, escorted by the teachers, run single file along the sides of buildings to reach the summer camp. The same routine happens upon their return home.

Running to the homes of the kids one afternoon we came across a tank and had to duck into a nearby house. The kids were terrified, one 8 year old girl sobbing with fear uncontrollaby. The tank opened fire outside the house as we cowered on the floor.

Thankfully, there was a small kitten lounging on the floor. We used it to divert the kids' attention from the blasts outside, playfully pulling the kitten's tail and saying "Look, look." They focused on the kitten and the small girl stopped crying. We left when when the street fell silent again, and ran to their houses.

To sum up
It is hard to conclude this essay of what was witnessed this bloody week in Tulkarem. The violence was so strong, and details brutal. For more information please call: Rebecca @ [number withheld]

SWEPT CLEAN
by Annie Higgins, 18 January 2003

The idea of Sharon with broom in hand is comical enough, but the suggestion that he sweep the rooms of the Islamic Center that his soldiers left in shambles made me laugh. My friend, who conducts Qur'anic study sessions, always manages to find humor in the midst of the bleakest conditions. Her laughter itself is a resistance against the gravity of oppression. The Center's rooms have chairs, a cabinet with copies of the Qur'an, and floors full of dust.

The Army appropriated the computers that had been donated for the advancement of the Refugee Camp community. Still the ladies come to learn, to consider new ideas, compare interpretations, and especially to address issues relating to martyrdom, remarriage of young widows, visiting graves, handling grief, and pondering heaven. I take my turn with an infant who is energetically doing callisthenics on my lap, and I comment on his strength. "That's because he is from the Camp," beams his mother, articulating the resiliency of Camp identity.

At home, the Qur'an teacher laughs as a sock attacks us when a coil of wire it is caught in springs out of reach. "Sharon doesn't want us to go visiting on the holiday, Eid; he just wants us to work at home." Later, neighbors chide me for not visiting during the three-day holiday of Eid Al-Fitr, but how could I abandon my friend whose house was raided as soldiers searched for a "wanted" family member?

Instead of holiday baking, we face oil in the salt and sugar, and the pantry's many treasures mixed with pots, pans, lamps and implements. The kitchen is picture-perfect compared with the bedrooms knee deep in clothes, clothespins, dismembered notebook pages, shoes, jewelry, framed pictures, manicure sets, and artificial flowers all swirled together in heaps. We concentrate on the kitchen, with her daughter Maryam expelling us to do the final clean sweep, swooshing plenty of water with a fan-shaped hand-held broom.

Sweeping is part of the rhythm of home life. After a meal you gather the fragments of bread, just as Jesus' disciples did following the post-sermon meal on the hillside, and then you sweep up the crumbs. Dry sweeping, wet sweeping, inside sweeping, outside sweeping seem almost like reflexes, and assure a constant orderliness in the home and on the street. The Israeli soldiers are acquainted with the manners and methods of the people whose lands they occupy. The incredible messes they so frequently produce, for no security reason, seem to be a physical and spiritual attack on hearth and home.

But sometimes they too fall into the rhythm of local order and orderliness. A family in Jenin city tells that when soldiers left a building they had been occupying, they disposed of their garbage and then swept all of the apartments in the building. During that period, one of the homeowners had passed by an alley after the evening/maghrib call to prayer, and saw an Ethiopian soldier in uniform clearing the ground to pray. He confided to the local Jenin resident, "Shhh, I am Muslim. Don't tell."

[…]

Another day brings more tanks on a street nearby. Amidst the detritus the tank has sucked into the street is a broom which has become part of the clutter it might clear away. I restore its mission, walking toward the tank and sweeping the street with ritual, rather than practical, motions. This has little effect on the rubble in the steet, but delights the children who cheer this gentle defiance of the tank's bullying. I hope that the tank's soldiers will not burst a bullet hole in my bubble of whimsy, but there is no guarantee of their sense of humor.

Very soon the boys, who have been fearlessly lobbing stones and trash at the tanks, call me back with uncharacteristic urgency. They report excitedly that an international friend has been wounded. I think they are joking but they insist that some of the boys carried her to safety on a home-made stretcher. She was getting a few small children off a street when a tank sniper shot her. A local journalist confirms the news, and we find her in the Emergency Room at the hospital. Minutes later, another foreigner is wheeled in, and we learn that UNRWA's Jenin Refugee Camp director, Iain Hook, has been killed.

[…]

Clean sweeps and holiness are related in Semitic tongues. In Arabic, a church is called "kanisa/swept place," just as a Jewish holy place is called in Hebrew "bayt kaneset."

The same word is found, with modified transliteration, in the familiar name for the Israeli Parliament, the Knesset.

The morning prayer on the Eid Al-Fitr holiday closing the month of Ramadan was held on the barren ground of the former Hawashin neighborhood, alarmingly obliterated in the April invasion. When I heard of the prayer plans, I realized that the boys I had seen collecting stones were not resupplying their munitions, but making a clean-swept place for this holy day.

The image of Sharon sweeping an Islamic center in a Refugee Camp is still comical. But elections are coming up. Perhaps the Knesset could use sweeping.

ABU MUHAMMAD SAID TO ME ...
by ISM volunteers in Nablus, 20 July 2002

"I left Haifa in 1948 without carrying anything with me. I was 12 years old. I came to this refugee camp, I lived in a tent for few years, and restarted my life once again. I could build this house by working for more than 50 years. And now I see it all destroyed in front of my eyes. How I will like Israel? How I will accept what is not acceptable for anybody in the world? I could not even take my picture album. I and all my family members left our house by force in our pyjamas. This reminds me exactly of 1948. And now I see that the 50 years of my life were lost once again, I am homeless once again. I am refugee to the refugee camp's dwellers, who will host me for few days, but not for ever. Who can host me and my married sons and their families? Why I have to be refugee?"

6

DEFYING CURFEW

**ISRAELI ARMY OPENS FIRE ON CIVILIANS
IN THE STREETS OF JENIN**
International Solidarity Movement, 21 June 2002, 12:50 pm

FOR IMMEDIATE RELEASE

[JENIN] The curfew in Jenin was lifted mid-morning today. Two hours later, with no warning the army returned to the main city. The streets were still full of people trying to buy supplies before curfew was reimposed. Israeli soldiers opened fire on the crowd of people in the market and in the streets. Al-Razi Hospital has a dead 6 year old girl, Sujoud Mohammad Turki—shot in the head, and several more wounded, including Sujoud's 12 year old brother and 2 ½ year old sister, who went out with their father to buy food from the market.

The streets are still blocked by tanks, preventing people from moving back to places of safety. There are several Internationals in the city. Some are trying to get to other hospitals in the area.

Photograph by Jennifer Midberry.

Contacts in Jenin: Tobias [number withheld], Jim [number withheld], Rick [number withheld], Rebecca [number withheld], Dr. Ali Jabareen (Al Razi Hospital) [number withheld]

Dead: Sujoud Mohammad Turki—6 yrs old
Injuries: Nael Mohammad Turki—12 years old, Sheva Ahmed Turki Fahmawi—2.5 years old, Hassan Amin Al-Tamimi—16 years old (bullet in head), Khaled Taha Ahmed—42 years, Diab Mahmoud Al-Staty—20 years, Hassan Abu-Zaid (serious condition/shot in chest)—27 years old

ENDS

ARMY TANK SHELLS KILL THREE IN JENIN
International Solidarity Movement, 21 June 2002 1:17 pm

FOR IMMEDIATE RELEASE

[JENIN] Two brothers, Ahmed Abu Aziz (6 years) and Jamil Abu Aziz (12 years) were just killed and a third brother injured when the Israeli army fired tank shells into the street where they were playing during an army-announced lifting of curfew. A third man, Hilal Shidah (52 years) was also killed in the same incident.

Ahmed Abu Aziz's arm was blown off and both his legs severly ripped into. He died instantly. Jamil was taken into the emergency operating room, but died after 15 minutes. The boys' father is an ambulance driver at the Jenin Government Hospital.

The Israeli army is announcing to the residents of Jenin that the curfew is lifted until 6pm tonight, and they can come out of their homes.

Dead: Ahmed Yousef Abu Aziz—6 years old, Jamil Yousef Abu Aziz—12 years old
Hilal Mustafa Mahmoud Shidah—50 years old
Injured: Tarek Yousef Abu Aziz—age unknown: massive injuries to chest, liver and stomach; currently in surgery and in critical condition, but expected to live.

For more information: Jenin Government Hospital [number withheld]
Internationals in Jenin: Tobias [number withheld], Jim [number withheld], Rick [number withheld], Rebecca [number withheld]

ENDS

THE CONSTANT CONFUSION OF CURFEW
by ISM volunteers in Jenin, 21 July 2002

One of the daily deadly perils in Jenin is the constant confusion over curfew. Although curfews here are usually announced on television and radio late the night before, the Israeli army is notorious for changing its mind with little or no warning. This has proven deadly because the military has a habit of declaring curfew in Jenin by means of driving through the town and camp using loudspeakers punctuated by heavy fire aimed directly at civilians.

For example, last night after 8pm multiple tanks rolled into the camp and then the city to impose night curfew. There was heavy firing aimed directly into homes in the camp. This was clearly visible to us due to the use of night tracers on the bullets and flares in the sky. At approximately 1am the television announced that the curfew would be lifted the following day from 8am to 8pm. Jenin's population went to sleep believing that they would go to work, shops would be open, and their children could attend summer camp in the morning. Few people heard the jeeps, with their limited-range loudspeakers, drive through random neighborhoods at 6am to say that indeed, there would be curfew this day.

At 8am Jenin became a bustling city of shops, cars and pedestrians. Although UNRWA was informed of the curfew at 9am, it was 10:30am before a local summer camp was told to send all its children home immediately as the tanks and jeeps were on their way in. Within a half hour vendors in the open air market were scuttling for cover and people rushed to get to their homes as the tanks rolled in to town.

Thankfully no one has been killed in the past 24 hours. However, this curfew confusion is exactly what precipitated the deaths of three children and an elderly man, shot dead by Israeli tank fire in the marketplace, when we arrived in this city a month ago.

DEFYING CURFEW IN NABLUS
by Rae Levine, 29 June 2002

Yesterday was incredible. We had a great demonstration of about 100 people—30 Internationals and 70 Palestinians. We walked through the Old City of Nablus on the main street, and in the main square in defiance of curfew. It was covered on CNN, BBC, and Al-Jazeera and by local paper and TV. Everyone here was so pleased … it was completely non-violent (young boys marched with us but did not throw stones) and we were not confronted by soldiers at any point, so it was a complete victory of breaking curfew.

Later in the day we went to an apartment building that has been taken over by Israeli soldiers. They have evicted the residents of the roof flat to use it as their headquarters, have put an Israeli flag on the roof, and are holding 6 families with 25 children and 18 adults in house arrest … We are trying to help them negotiate basic things with the soldiers, but their main concern is to get the soldiers out. We need to see about launching a campaign in support of this building and about 9 others like it in Nablus.

Please let everyone know that we are doing fine. The warmth and hospitality of the people here is beyond anything I have ever experienced. It will be difficult to leave here in a few days. People here are very appreciative of our efforts and say that our involvement is helping to boost their spirits and solidarity with one another.

Can't write more now. Rae

NABLUS RESIDENTS BREAK CURFEW AND DELIVER APPEAL TO KOFI ANNAN
International Solidarity Movement, 5 July 2002

FOR IMMEDIATE RELEASE

[NABLUS] On Friday, July 5 over 100 Palestinians and Internationals marched through Nablus, challenging and effectively breaking the curfew, or house arrest, imposed on the civilians of the city. The march was led by the strong voices of Palestinian women calling for an end to the rape of their cities, the torture of their men and the killing of their children. The protesters marched from the center of Nablus to the UN office, delivering a message for Secretary General, Kofi Annan. The march ended at the Union of Palestinian Medical Relief offices.

For more information on the march, please contact: Anan [number withheld]
For an international perspective on participating in this resistance: Neta [number withheld]

Text of the letter to UN General Secretary Kofi Annan below:

His Excellency Mr. Kofi Annan
General Secretary, United Nations

Your Excellency

As you are aware it has been 15 days since the Israeli army re-invaded the city of Nablus and its four refugee camps. Two hundred thousand residents of Nablus and suburbs have been imprisoned in their houses, as the military has imposed a strict 24-hour curfew

Moreover, the Israeli Occupation has launched a campaign of mass arrests, through which hundreds of Palestinians have been detained and arrested. Residential buildings have been occupied by the soldiers and turned into permanent military posts. More than 25 houses have been subjected to this sort of atrocity.

Education, healthcare and social systems have been brought to a standstill. Women, children and men have been deprived a normal human life, as the Israeli army has vandalized the streets of the city, terrorizing people and dehumanizing them. Economic and social life of the population of the city has been severely disrupted and Palestinian infrastructure has been badly damaged.

We believe that the Israeli government, through such measures, is destroying the last hope for peace in the region. We ask the United Nations to stand up to its responsibility and act immediately to pressure Israel to abide with international law. Unless this happens, our suffering will continue and the stability and security in the whole region will be jeopardized.

We urge you to act immediately to pressure the Israeli government to withdraw its troops from all Palestinian areas and lift the closure, which has been imposed over Palestinian towns and villages since September 2000.

The situation in our country is catastrophic. The level of suffering and deprivation is dramatically deepening. The need for international protection for Palestinian civilians represents a necessary step to be taken by the United Nations as soon as possible.

Residents of Nablus
5th July 2002

ENDS

NOTE FROM THE EDITORS: Nablus remained under more or less continuous curfew until February 2003.

ISRAELI ARMY FIRES ON CROWDS IN JENIN
International Solidarity Movement, 11 July 2002

FOR IMMEDIATE RELEASE

[JENIN] Israeli soldiers have reentered Jenin city with tanks and armoured personnel carriers (APCs) during a lift in curfew.

At approximately 1600 one APC deliberately hit an electrical pole, knocking it down and crushing it. The electric wires fell on the APC trapping the soldiers inside and preventing further movement. The army immediately moved in with two more tanks and several jeeps and opened fire indiscriminately on the crowds of Palestinian civilians in the area. The army shot out windows of buildings and showed no restraint in this attack.

International witnesses report that one journalist, Emad Abdel Aziz, has been shot. He was clearly marked on his vest with the word PRESS in white lettering. He was shot from a tank with an 800mm round at a distance of 8 to 10 feet. When he arrived at the hospital he had [unmeasurable] blood pressure. He is currently in a critical condition.

A ten year old boy was also injured. Activists are at the hospitals now assessing further injuries or deaths.

A Reuters cameraman was on the scene and footage is available via the Reuters office in Jerusalem.

For more information contact: Tobias [number withheld], Caoimhe [number withheld]

ENDS

US GUNS USED ON US AND PALESTINIAN CIVILIANS IN RAMALLAH
International Solidarity Movement, 17 July 2002

FOR IMMEDIATE RELEASE

[RAMALLAH] Over 150 Palestinians and locals came under live fire from the Israeli Army this afternoon in an attempt to break the house arrest that has been imposed on the whole city.

At approximately 4:45pm the people singing, chanting and carrying signs saying 'We will decide when we go home' and 'Freedom' arrived at the city center, AlManara circle. One hour past the time curfew was re-imposed jeeps and armoured personnel carriers swarmed towards the group from all surrounding access roads, and cutting them off from escape routes. Immediately international activists lay across the roads leading to the circle to protect the Palestinian civilians in the center.

The Israeli soldiers reacted violently to this peaceful demonstration by opening fire with live ammunition, throwing concussion grenades and dragging Internationals from the roads. Palestinian women and children were able to get out of the center and we have no injuries reported yet.

Three Internationals including one Scot and two Swedes were forced into an armoured personnel carrier and have been taken to an unknown location.

Two Americans were forced onto their knees and handcuffed to each other and a pipe. Looking up at the soldier standing over them with an M16 they could see clearly stamped on the gun 'Property of US Government.'

ENDS

PEACE, YES—OCCUPATION, NO!
by Conor, 26 August 2002

The game of cat-and-mouse with the army intensifies .... We're not exactly sure what is going on here, but the army has become much more aggressive towards the Internationals in Nablus. A few days ago three Internationals were arrested after trying to bring food to an occupied house. These are homes that the army rolls in and takes over, usually keeping the family in one room in the basement or first floor and locking them in while they trash the house (we've seen campfires built in stairwells and toys and clothes strewn about). Because of the illegal curfew the family are not allowed out of the room and are sometimes locked up for weeks at a time.

The checkpoints have become much more intense and impenetrable. When a group of Internationals tried to enter through the main checkpoint at Huwara village they were told that "No Internationals, no Palestinians, not even press may enter Nablus. Not even that donkey there may enter."

[…]

On Saturday a group of about 30 Internationals from GIPP (Grassroots International Protection for Palestinians—a largely European group) and ISM traveled to Huwara, the village right outside Nablus and next to the main checkpoint, for a joint Ta'ayush (Israeli Peace Group)–Palestinian–International demonstration against the Occupation and curfew.

Huwara, being right next to the main military base in Nablus, thus bears the full brunt of the Occupation. The town has been under almost continuous curfew for

TWO YEARS and has had food shortages for about two months. Virtually nothing has been allowed in or out of the town since the beginning of the intifada in 2000. Can you imagine being threatened by a foreign army with injury/arrest/death (snipers) if you left your house for two years?

Apparently there was a TV announcement of the demonstration and the last one ended with the arrest and injury of several activists, so were were nervous already when we found out that no one was even being allowed OUT of Nablus today. We then took a route that included three separate legs of taxi drives (one by my friend Ibrahim who is proving ever resourceful) to get around the roadblocks and checkpoints (without crazy/genius taxi drivers and cellphones this movement would not be possible) and a 2 kilometer walk along a settler road—not a very safe route to take.

When we made it into Huwara we found the march ready to start and, sure enough, it did 3 minutes after we arrived. There were dozens of Palestinians with banners and flags chanting and moving through the streets and we didn't really have time to prepare or get in position. Military police (the most brutal of the military we deal with) showed up immediately, so we tried to position ourselves between the police and the Palestinians, holding up our hands and shouting that this was a peaceful demonstration.

There were no rocks thrown or any weapons anywhere in the crowd, but the police jumped out of their jeeps and tossed several bright orange concussion grenades at us (also known as flash-bang grenades—they explode with a loud flash and a boom and it disorients and shocks you—like a mild concussion) and shot several tear-gas mortars into the crowd, including the long-range kind meant to be fired in an arc but they shot many straight into the crowd—two whizzed by my head and legs. I had not had time to take my contacts out, and you can be blinded with the gas the army uses if you leave them in so I ducked down an alleyway coughing and choking and frantically pulled out my contacts.

I couldn't see for a few minutes but soon there were arms helping me to my feet and someone shoved an onion under my nose—it cuts the gas quite effectively—and as I regained my senses I found it was a small crowd of Palestinian children helping me, looking quite concerned for this foreigner.

We ran back into the street where the army continued tear-gassing and tossing concussion grenades while driving their jeeps through the crowds at intimidating speeds. Once close enough they would toss tear-gas grenades out the back of the jeeps, which was bad because those things just explode in a cloud of gas that's very hard to escape. All the while we tried to stay within and in front of the crowd and document the whole thing. I suspect the presence of Internationals at the rally kept things from getting quite nasty. As it was it only generated a paragraph in a story buried deep within CNN.com. They know if Internationals were killed then it would be a huge story, and in solidarity with the Palestinians we used that privilege to protect them.

We retreated from the main street, regrouped with the Palestinians, and then heard the chanting of the few hundred Israeli peace activists who had bussed down for the demonstration and dodged their way through the tanks of their own army with trucks of food for the village. We joyously joined together and Palestinian embraced Israeli embraced International. Together we turned to the army and began to chant in Hebrew and Arabic "Peace, yes! Occupation, no!"

The Israelis and Internationals linked arms and surrounded the crowd to protect the Palestinians as a long train of APCs and tanks entered the village and people were laughing, crying, and hugging while the Palestinian children banged together the cans of baby formula the Israelis had brought with them. It was one of the most beautiful things I have been blessed to witness.

[...]

LOOKING FOR WORDS
by Susan Barclay, 2 October 2002

Why do I not find words for the realities that lie before my very eyes?

Witnessing life in Nablus these past few days has been particularly difficult, infuriating, and heart breaking, for the situation is the worst it has ever been. Today marks 104 days of curfew; 104 days during which 200,000 people have been imprisoned in their homes—over three months, over 2020 hours inside (curfew has been lifted for about 70 hours total).

The inhabitants of Nablus have been breaking the curfew en masse, especially since the beginning of the school year, refusing to abide by this truly inhumane Israeli Army practice that punishes and oppresses the entire civilian population. In response, the Army has been using more violence (physical and psychological) to impose the curfew, attempting to keep the population caged in their homes like animals through the use of terror and excessive military force.

[...]

In spite of the ever present tanks, tear-gas, injuries, bullets, tank shells, humiliation, jeeps and checkpoints, Nablus residents are determined to continue to live. This struggle to survive has been met by an incredibly aggressive Israeli Army assault specifically targeting the students and schools. Three days ago when school was let out, Internationals witnessed as tanks chased and shot at over 150 young students (5–15 years old) who were trying to pass in front of the government building (the muqata'a) to go home.

The tank began by opening fire on the muqata'a itself in order "to scare the people", as one soldier said bluntly. It then proceeded to literally chase the students at high speed shooting continuous rounds of live ammunition in the air, as the children ran in all directions. I watched as young girls and boys ran, some in tears and all in fear, their faces seized by terror, crinkled in panic. The tank came and went a number of times, doing circles and leaving for just long enough to allow another stream of children to begin passing, before opening fire again. The tank was followed by a jeep carrying four soldiers who habitually stopped, got out, and fired M-16s at everything in the street.

This went on for over 30 minutes in front of the government building and continued throughout the day. I watched in horror, in complete and utter disbelief, knowing that it was only a matter of time until someone was injured. I was however anything but prepared for it to be two children, one 2 years old and one 3, shot in the head and arm hours later by this indiscriminate, furious firing.

[...]

I remember one 14–15 year old girl with tears rolling down her cheeks, her face filled with fear, screaming, as her friend tried to calm her while running away. One tank gone mad that manages to make 150 children run in every direction and one soldier anything but humane who terrorizes the innocent, but who nonetheless couldn't keep them from coming back.

[...]

I thought of how convenient it was that all the press was in Ramallah covering Arafat and the reality that I was going to be one of the only witnesses of these terror tactics. Schools have been tear-gassed every single day this week; tanks arrive in front of the various refugee camps and schools in the city center by 6:30 a.m. when they begin firing endless rounds of ammunition, frequently large caliber rounds (250, 500). This is what we wake up to in Nablus. This is what children hear as they eat their breakfast, filling their bellies with bread, olive oil, and fear as they begin thinking about the treacherous journey to school.

[…]

What do I hold fast in my heart during these difficult days to carry me on? The image of a father walking to school with his two young boys at 7 o'clock in the morning among dozens of others, making me almost believe that life is normal for a few seconds … I know too well however that the tears I feel blistering below the surface are because he is risking his life just to get his children to the school entrance, and that this bravery is anything but mundane.

I hold onto the photo of hundreds of thousands at the demonstration in London against the imminent war with Iraq, to the audacious actions of two Israeli women who recently came to Nablus to confront their own army, to the face of an old woman at the hospital who told me "There is still hope", and to the laughter of the little children that rings in my ears with resilience.

I cannot capture in words how greatly I admire the people of Nablus. Previously, people attempted to hide and avoid the Israeli Army but currently the people of Nablus cannot be stopped. They refuse to be imprisoned in their houses any longer, they refuse to starve, they refuse to go without work, they refuse to allow their children to be robbed of an education, and they refuse to resign.

Truly horrifying plans are being talked of and created currently and as the US moves ever closer to a war with Iraq, the possibility of a mass transfer of the Palestinian population becomes more and more terrifying and likely. May the world not wait too long, may we not let massive war crimes occur yet again, only to say sorry after the fact, "If only we had known".

May we instead learn from the people in Nablus who have so very much to teach us. They know that there is power in numbers, that there is great strength in organizing, that you can effectively resist, that hope is a magical force, and that you can beat the world's fourth largest army with your head and your heart.

SOLDIERS BATTLING THE WILL OF THE PEOPLE
Violently trying to impose curfew in Nablus
International Solidarity Movement, 7 November 2002

FOR IMMEDIATE RELEASE

[Nablus City] The people of Nablus are out en mass as Israeli soldiers are using their artillery to try to impose a curfew on the east side of the city

"Tanks are blocking over a hundred cars, students on their way to school have had tear thrown at them, and soldiers are firing sporadically" said ISM activist Susan Barclay. A UN team has been waiting with a medical team for over 45 minutes. 150 school girls have been trying to pass a checkpoint set up between east and west Nablus, to have gas and sound bombs lobbed at them.

At least two high school girls were down on the ground, suffering from the tear-gas inhalation, one school girl fainted from the shock of the sound bombs, and many are crying. Two Japanese activists, Aisa Kiyosue and Noda Ryosuke were slightly injured by shrapnel and Susan had bullets fired over her head when she tried to approach the soldiers.

For more information: Susan [number withheld] or [number withheld]

ENDS

CHILDREN BREAKING CURFEW IN RAMALLAH
by Erica for John R, 28 November 2002

"… two boys with backpacks and their school stuff, walking to school today. They can't be more than 5 or 6 years old. Walking by themselves with soldiers all over the place trying to harrass them. Little kids. Not even 10 years old. Just trying to get to school. Having to break curfew and walk through tear-gas to get there."

This was part of the call I got from Seattle activist John R just now from Ramallah in Palestine. He asked me to send out something to let people here in the US know about what people are doing today to defy the curfew in Ramallah on the Second Anniversary of the start of the second Intifada.

John has been in Ramallah for about a week (since Israeli Occupation Forces destroyed all but one building in the Muqata'a (Arafat's headquarters)) and he reports about the beginning of a very big day of planned events there. Indeed, the day is just beginning there. It is about 8:30 am (ok close to 9 am by now). Hundreds of children are walking—some alone, some escorted by family members—to school. The children just want to get to school to learn, to see their friends and teachers, and to have a chance at a normal life.

Today is not a normal day. Normally the children cannot leave their homes because of the curfew. Normally they can't go to school because of the curfew. But today, in defiance of the curfew and resistance to the Occupation, the children are going to go to school. There are hundreds of children taking part in the act of resistance and strength. They are having to walk past soldiers and APC (armored personnel carriers). The soldiers are from the fourth largest army in the world. The Israeli soldiers are taunting the kids. And soldiers are setting off tear-gas and sound bombs around the children. And so "the war on the children continues …"

The children's will is as strong as that of their parents, many of whom are expected to gather at cemeteries around Ramallah to honor the dead (beginning at 1 pm Ramallah time) and then to join a march in the evening to celebrate this anniversary.

That is all for now. Perhaps we here in the US can find inspiration from the children of Ramallah.

BEGINNING TO UNDERSTAND?
by David Redmon, 10 January 2003

Tonight at 9:00 p.m. in Beit Sahour, Palestine, an Israeli soldier aimed and shook his M-16 rifle at me and my Palestinian friends. What did we violate to receive such deviant treatment? We were standing outside, talking to each other in front of our hotel, otherwise known as "breaking curfew." "Get back inside! Get back inside!" the Israeli soldier yelled as he walked towards us with his American-funded gun aimed at my body.

For an American who walks the streets of Boston with my friends and loved ones, the experience with the Israeli soldier was confusing and scary. For Palestinians who live in the cities where the Israeli military occupy their land with tanks and F-16s, patrol the streets 24 hours a day, kill Palestinian civilians on a daily basis, and terrorize Palestinian families while sleeping in their homes, this abnormal situation is common. I follow the soldier's orders and go inside the empty hotel that caters to the non-existing tourists. Hussein, an eleven year old boy who lives next door to the hotel, looks at me and says, "I speak French, English, and Arabic. What do you speak?" I respond in the singular, "English." Hussein smiles and says, "We cannot be Palestinians in our land. We cannot exist if the Israeli military continues to patrol our streets and enforce curfew."

"Elevenished" by his eleven year old intellect, I inquire with a seemingly naive question, "What is curfew?" Hussein ponders for a few seconds and carefully explains curfew to me as if I am an eleven year old. "It is house arrest. It means I can't go to school, I can't go outside to play. I can't go see my friends, buy food with my family, or go for a walk." I continue, "What will happen if you go outside?" Hussein chuckles at my question. In an adult-like manner he shrugs his shoulders, raises his hands in frustration, and says, "If the soldiers catch me, they will arrest me."

Two Israeli military jeeps slowly driving through the Palestinian streets immediately interrupt my lesson from eleven year old Hussein. The men inside the jeep are holding M-16s and repeatedly announce, "It is forbidden to be outside! It is forbidden to move!"

Epiphany: I am a prisoner inside this hotel. I cannot leave. I cannot talk with the neighbors, buy a fresh pineapple, or go for a walk with Hussein. For a brief moment, I am Palestinian. Hussein looks at me, projects a frustrated smile, shrugs his shoulders and expresses his frustration, "See what I mean? Do you understand our situation?"

Epiphany: I am an American, imprisoned by pro-Israeli propaganda everywhere in the USA. What can I do but respond to him with honest, sincere ignorance? "No, but I'm beginning to understand. I'm trying to understand."

In 10 days I will return to the privilege, expensive rent, and gross inequalities in Boston. I will hold the hand of the woman I love as we walk the streets together, passing the homeless who use Starbucks coffee cups to request spare change. During this walk I will wonder, "Do the hundreds of other people in the streets around us understand the situation in Palestine?" If not, I hope they are beginning to understand; I hope they are trying to understand.

It's too bad Hussein will not be there to explain it to us like an eleven year old.

TODAY WE HAVE MADE THIS DEMONSTRATION BECAUSE WE WANT FREEDOM
What the children said to the occupation forces in occupied Beit Furiq
by Emily, 24 July 2003

We asked the children "If you could say anything to the soldiers, what would you say?" Using the children's words, we composed a poignant speech to be read to the Israeli Occupation Forces.

On the afternoon of July 24th, the ISM accompanied about 20 children in a peaceful march to the Beit Furiq checkpoint. The children faced the soldiers, held their posters, sang songs and chanted "Free, Free Palestine" while one of us read their speech to the soldiers.

The demonstration lasted about a half-hour. It ended peacefully with the children marching back home.

Here now are the words of the children. I hope you will read them carefully and take them to heart.

Today, we have made this demonstration because we need freedom
We need to pass freely with no problems
We need to live under democratic conditions
We want to go to Nablus with no delay
Do not catch our fathers and brothers and put them underneath the hot sun,
When they come back to the village, do not make bomb sounds
Let emergency cases pass freely to the hospital
Do not stop ambulances

Treat men and women equally as human beings
Do not shoot Palestinian children
We need to live under peace
Move the roadblocks
It should not be up to you when we can and cannot cross

Do not put our people in prison
Do not destroy our homes
Do not search us
Treat us like human beings
Do not destroy our farms
Do not put young people in prison
Do not come at night and scare the people

Give us our freedom
Do not search our houses at night and scare us
Do not detain people in the cold night
Do not destroy our land and make new settlements
Do not cut down our trees to extend settlements

Stop letting people shoot at farmers
Do not cut down our trees
Do not destroy our olive trees to make roadblocks
We are against the wall
Do not occupy our houses
Do not point lasers at our houses—it hurts our eyes
Do not light flares—it is dangerous and can start fire

Stop assassinating our people
Leave our land
Stop killing and scaring children
Stop destroying our roads with your tanks
Leave Palestine
We want a free state.

7

CHECKPOINTS AND FREEDOM OF MOVEMENT

ISRAEL'S PALESTINIAN BINGO POLICY
by Linda Bevis, 25 December 2002

On Dec. 23, several ISM members visited the area where the Israeli forces (IDF) had blocked the road joining the city of Nablus with three outlying villages: Azmut, Salem, and Deir Al-Khatab. Besides blocking at least two access roads to Nablus, the army has dug a large, steep moat to keep people from crossing fields to reach the Nablus access road. We had heard that the villagers were suffering from being cut off from jobs and food and hospitals in Nablus, as well as suffering from pollution coming from the chemical plant of the Israeli colony/settlement called Alon Moreh, which sits on two hills overlooking the three villages.

The roadblock is intermittently staffed by the IDF. Usually there is one Armored Personnel Carrier (APC) (looks like a tank, except it doesn't have a large gun), with 3–4 soldiers at the wall of red earth that is the roadblock. Every time a Palestinian approaches the roadblock, slipping and sliding on the steep muddy paths approaching it from either side, the soldiers take his or her ID card. Then the Palestinian must wait in the rain and cold until the ID is returned. (These IDs are issued by the Israelis and

Photograph by Jennifer Midberry.

are necessary to move around the country and to enter hospitals, etc.)

When we ISM Internationals first arrived on the afternoon of Dec. 23, about 20 Palestinian men were crouching in the rain, forced to face one direction and not to move. The soldiers, meanwhile, were taking their time checking every ID by telephone. They seemed to wait 'til 10 or 15 IDs had been checked before allowing any of the 10 or 15 people to leave.

Occasionally, the soldiers would allow one or two people who approached the roadblock to pass directly on through. Unfortunately, this had the effect of convincing more Palestinians to try to pass through. In our three days of roadblock watch so far, we have found that the vast majority of Palestinians who have tried to pass through the roadblock have been stopped and held for 2–7 hours. Those stopped have included men, women, and the occasional donkey. Usually, younger children, very old people, and people so sick that they are on stretchers, have been allowed through with minimal (though not the absence of) hassle.

During negotiations, the soldiers explained their behavior to us in the following way: "This is a game of Palestinian Bingo: we gather all the IDs and sometimes we have a 'bingo' and find a terrorist." Thus, I understand Palestinian Bingo to be a strategy of not only criminalizing but actually arresting an entire population, in hopes of sifting through them to shake out likely suspects. The soldiers insist that this harassment and collective punishment is "justified by the end result" of occasionally catching someone they believe might be trying to bomb children in Tel Aviv. Clearly they are fearful, often making men bare their bellies (to show no explosives) before allowing them to approach the soldiers.

Unfortunately, on the night of Dec. 23, the "bingo" was our friend Omar Al-Titi, who has been helping the nonviolent International Solidarity Movement and who had led us down to the roadblock, thinking that any security check on himself would reveal that he was not "wanted". That night, however, after making Omar squat with the men for three hours, the IDF said that he was a "wanted" man and arrested him (true? or just trumped up charges to punish the ISM?). Although Internationals tried to block the APC's exit, Omar was taken away. His whereabouts are currently unknown.

The ISM has been successful at the roadblock in ensuring that no one was beaten or shot while we were there. The people tell us that our presence helps prevent this, as well as preventing some of the more egregious humiliations such as being made to kneel in muddy rainwater (in plentiful supply). However, the people also tell us that sometimes their punishment is doubled after we leave, thereby emphasizing that we cannot afford to ignore places that we begin to help.

At the roadblock, we witness various levels of power games. One captain admits he's been reprimanded for hitting soldiers and indeed he is the most rigid about making the detained men squat and face a certain direction—handcuffing any who attempt to speak to him. In another power trip, a young soldier with round glasses constantly aims his machine gun up the hill at little boys shouting far in the distance. When I stand before the rifle saying "I hope you aren't going to shoot anyone", he replies, "they're throwing stones", though they aren't. He keeps aiming and I keep standing in front of the muzzle 'til my partner helps me realize that this is his power game with me. So I distract with another request to let the detainees go.

Later, in the rain and dark, only one detainee is left, but the Captain will not let him go. At first, he says it's because the man refused to call neighbors over to this Venus Flytrap of a roadblock when ordered to do so. Finally, the Captain tells us "because of you. You push too much. If not for you, this man would be gone." We realize then that we have pushed our political discussion too far, and this last detainee has paid the price. We ask if it would help if we step back. He nods and we step away, out of the shimmer of APC headlights. Minutes later, this last detainee is freed.

We have learned all kinds of lessons about power today.

DEIR IBZI'E CHILDREN'S SUMMER CAMP
by ISM volunteers in Deir Ibzi'e, 1 July 2002

Two hundred and thirty children excitedly clamor around a dozen adults in anticipation of their third day of summer camp in the Palestinian village of Deir Ibzi'e. Their numbers had grown from one hundred and fifty on the first day, which was already straining the capacity of the house and materials.

The summer day camp was the vision of Deeb, a Palestinian man who had left his home in Deir Ibzi'e at the age of 19 to be educated in Germany. He returned to

Palestine during the optimistic atmosphere surrounding the Oslo Accords in 1993. Two years ago Deeb and his family decided to move to Deir Ibzi'e, then only a seven-minute drive from the city of Ramallah. Soon after their move the Israeli Occupation Forces installed a military checkpoint on the road between the village and the city, making transportation difficult and often impossible. Later the military rendered the road completely impassable, cutting off Deir Ibzi'e and thirty-one other Palestinian villages from the central West Bank.

At the summer camp children learn environmental science, English, art, drama and sports. In the environmental science class children are focusing on water and its ecological as well as political significance. Teaching English is woven into all of the camp's activities and Leila, Deeb's 17 year old daughter, is teaching an additional English class.

The noisiest room in the house is where the art classes are taught. Children exuberantly express themselves with crayons, markers and clay. At the same time the English instruction continues and children enjoy learning the words for the colors and images they create. These images range from flowers and butterflies to Palestinian flags and Apache helicopters as well as Israeli soldiers shooting Palestinian villagers. In the back yard girls, Muslim and Christian, compete with the noise of the art class as they enjoy an enthusiastic made up game of football.

The International Solidarity Movement team that has been working with the camp is leaving on Friday, July 5th. The camp will continue for another two weeks. Internationals are desperately needed to replace them. The camp is already understaffed and Deeb is concerned about interference from the Israeli military once the Internationals leave.

This truly creative form of nonviolent resistance is a powerful message, and help, financial and physical, is needed to keep it flourishing.

NOT ALLOWED TO LIVE
by ISM and CPT volunteers in Hebron, 2 July 2002

On the morning of July 2, 2002, a group of seven Internationals, working with the International Solidarity Movement (ISM) and the Christian Peacemaker Teams (CPT), accompanied a group of Palestinian farmers from the village of Halhoul, outside Hebron, to harvest their fields. The fields are close to the settlement of Karme Tzur, and the farmers have been routinely denied access to their lands by soldiers and attacked by settlers when they attempt to work there.

As we approached the first roadblock, a family came climbing over. An elderly woman was crying and shouting, clutching her head in pain. The family had been working on their land when settlers attacked, throwing stones. The woman had been hit in the head and had a laceration as well as a lemon-sized lump over her left eye. She was very upset and frightened, and in a lot of pain. As we tried to comfort her and call an ambulance, the soldiers came. They pulled up in an APC, three soldiers sticking their heads up out of the hatch.

The farmers began to tell the soldiers that the woman had been attacked and needed medical attention. One soldier repeated, "I don't care. This road is closed. You have to get off." The other two kept their rifles trained on us.

The farmers we were escorting had written permission from the police to work their land, and we showed this to the soldiers. They didn't care; they just kept getting angrier, shouting at us to get off the road and firing in the air. One woman from CPT got the chief of police on the phone and convinced the soldier doing most of the yelling to talk to him. A few moments of quiet while they talk, just the sound of the woman crying. He handed the phone back. "They cannot be on this road. There is a curfew on this road and these fields."

There was no curfew in Hebron or in Halhoul, but there suddenly was a "curfew" in the exact place where we needed to be. We argued some more, and the soldiers began firing again, first in the air and then at us, over our heads. They threw a sound bomb, and we retreated down the road a short distance. At this point the APC turned around and headed down the newly closed road. An ambulance arrived to take the injured woman to the hospital, and we waited for several hours by the side of the road while the farmers discussed what to do.

Finally we approached the roadblock again. A jeep pulled up, and we attempted to reason with the soldiers again; we were again unsuccessful. This time, the soldier in charge physically pushed us away from the roadblock, and gave us a vague promise that we could come back "later." Most of us headed back to the home of one of the farmers for lunch and rest, while two of us headed back to Hebron. When we reached the bridge between Hebron and Halhoul, however, we found out it was closed; snipers shot at us when we tried to cross. There was a large group of Palestinians waiting for the shooting to stop so that they could get through to Hebron.

We returned to the farmer's house and spent the afternoon there. Around 4:30 p.m. we put in a call to TIPH (Temporary International Presence in Hebron), who told us they hadn't heard any shooting at the bridge for half an hour, so we made our way across. We are all back in Hebron now, and plan to try again in the morning.

ILLEGALLY DETAINED BY THE ISRAELI DEFENCE FORCE: COMPLAINT TO THE US CONSULATE
by Eric Levine, 4 July 2002

Between July 1st and July 3rd, 2002, I was abducted and held captive by the Israeli Defense Force along with one American man, one British man and two Palestinian men. Throughout the duration of our detention we were denied access to telephone usage, refused explanation as to the reason for our detention and kept in inhumane conditions under armed guard. We were threatened on several occasions that we would be shot if we attempted to leave the area.

Background
At about 1:00 PM on July 1st, 2002, I left Jerusalem in a taxi for Nablus in the West Bank. I was in the company of Brian Dominick, an American paramedic, and Peter Blacker, a British volunteer medical worker.

[…]

On July 1st, Nablus was under strict 24-hour curfew, and on the recommendation of friends in Nablus, our taxi took us along the back road through the village of Borin in the direction of Tell village. Our taxi driver drove until we encountered several large ditches (8–10 feet long, 4–5 feet deep and as wide as the entire dirt road) dug by Israeli Defense Force (IDF) bulldozers as part of operations that have sealed off all exit and entry points to Nablus and the surrounding villages for motorized transport (a common practice in all major cities in the West Bank). We proceeded from that point on foot and were soon joined by two Palestinian men, Akhmed and Mejdi, headed along the same route.

We walked about five (5) kilometers around the twists and turns of the dirt road. During this time, I telephoned my mother and Mejdi telephoned his wife (both in Nablus) to inform them of our status and that we expected to arrive shortly. At around 3:30 PM, while we were taking a short rest in the shade offered by a large rock at the side of the road, an army jeep coming from the direction of Nablus approached and stopped in front of us. Mejdi spoke briefly with the soldier in the passenger seat of the jeep in Hebrew. The soldier, without requesting any identification, instructed us to continue on to Nablus.

We continued along the same road for approximately another 200 meters, rounding the last bend in the road before descending into Nablus and were stopped by the voice of an Israeli sniper positioned in the third story window of the first building on our left (at this point we were standing in the entry/exit intersection above the Nablus neighborhood of "Matfiya"—not sure of spelling). The soldier, holding an M-16, pointed down to the road in front of us, instructed us to stop (which we did), and called an armored personnel carrier (APC), which arrived quickly. The APC appeared from the road to our left and two soldiers emerged … with M-16s at shoulder level pointed at us.

We were instructed to line up on the side of the road and the lieutenant called each of us over one at a time, examining our passports and searching our bags, while the private guarded the rest of the group.

[…]

After this initial examination, the lieutenant called the two Palestinian men over one by one, berated them in a loud angry tone, and instructed them to continue down the road into Nablus, which they did. I was then called over by the lieutenant and was told that we (Peter, Brian, and me) needed to come with the soldiers to "answer a few questions". At this point, the lieutenant motioned for Brian and Peter to join me next to the APC, and produced plastic handcuffs (commonly used by IDF soldiers and stored in the handles of M-16 rifles). We were handcuffed behind our backs, and instructed to enter the rear door of the APC. When asked why we were being detained and handcuffed, the lieutenant gestured up the hill and said, "everything will be okay". Being stopped by soldiers is very common in the West Bank. As we had not expected to be handcuffed without justification or explanation, we had not telephoned anyone to explain our whereabouts or our abduction. Once handcuffed we were unable to contact anyone for obvious reasons.

Abduction

At approximately 4:00 PM, we were transported in the APC to one of the buildings occupied by IDF soldiers in the most recent incursion which overlooks Nablus from the southern hill above Matfiya. We were placed, still handcuffed behind the back, in a stairway leading down from the ground and guarded by a soldier with an M-16 in his lap. We were instructed to sit and wait. The soldiers refused to answer all questions regarding the reason for our abduction and treatment as well as what was going to happen.

We waited in this position for about an hour, observing soldiers unload food and beverage supplies from an APC outside, and we could distinctly hear Palestinian children speaking in Arabic from behind the closed door at the bottom of the stairs. We assumed that these were the children who lived in the building, as it is IDF common practice to lock residents in buildings that have been occupied by soldiers, presumably as human shields preventing any attack. After an hour in this position, with no answer regarding what we were being held for or what was going to happen next, a different lieutenant ... approached us and inquired where we were from. After hearing that we were American and British, he cut off our handcuffs, refused to answer any of our questions and instructed us not to use our telephones or cameras.

After another 30 minutes, we were put back in the APC with our bags and driven to another occupied building. This one was still under construction, with power lines strung from a neighboring house, also occupied by soldiers with residents kept captive on the premises. We were led to a senior officer .... While this officer refused to give us his name upon request, he was later referred to by younger soldiers as the "big commander of Nablus". Sitting handcuffed on the steps in front of the senior officer and three other soldiers were Mejdi and Akhmed, who we had last seen walking down the road into Nablus. Mejdi informed us that they had been detained and abducted by a patrol of soldiers about 100 meters into Nablus.

The senior officer examined our passports, handed to him by the first lieutenant, and asked us if we were press reporters. We responded that we were not …. He asked us three or four times what we were intending to do in Nablus, to which we responded repeatedly that we intended to assist the ambulance services in the delivery of medical services and supplies. Brian had been doing this kind of work with the Red Crescent for six weeks in Ramallah, and Peter and I had been doing so with the Union of Palestinian Medical Relief Committees in Nablus the previous week. The senior officer then took our mobile phones and all film from our cameras and bags (all of which was blank) and placed them in a plastic bag along with our passports.

[…]

We were led to an outdoor patio area, six paces by six paces, and told that we would spend the night there. The patio area led to a two-sided door of metal bars locked from the inside by a wooden beam rigged up with steel reebar. A soldier armed with an M-16 rifle guarded us from this position at all times. We were instructed not to leave the patio area for any reason. After inquiring what would happen if we left the patio area, we were told that we would be shot. We were held captive in this area until approximately 2:30 PM on July 3rd.

[…]

We were forced to remain outside on the patio for the entirety of our illegal detention, baking under the sun during the day and freezing in the cold wind at night. We were occasionally allowed to sit under the small roof by the guarded door (which provided the only shade during the day) depending on which soldier was on guard. This space only provided shade for 2 people at a time. On one occasion a soldier chambered a round into his M-16 rifle and shoved it through the bars at my chest in a threatening manner, because I was too close to the gate. On the second day, after more than 24 hours of requests for telephone usage and explanation of the reason of our illegal detention, I picked up my bag and informed the soldiers that I was leaving. I walked around the corner of the building (approximately 20 feet) at which point I was surrounded by 5 soldiers pointing M-16 rifles and threatening to shoot me if I did not return to the patio. I returned to the patio.

We were not allowed access to toilet facilities. We were, on request allowed to relieve ourselves on the other side of the wall of our patio location. No inquiries were made as to our need for medical aid. We were given one meal a day, consisting of several cans of IDF supplies (corn and beans) and shortbread. We were given limited quantities of water after exhausting the supplies from our bags. Requests for cigarettes were also denied.

[…]

On one occasion, an Israeli ambulance (a white van marked only with a red Star of David inside a red circle) arrived at the other occupied building on the hill below our position. Six armed IDF soldiers exited the rear of the ambulance, stopping before entering the house to unchamber bullets from their M-16 rifles (indicating that they had been loaded and chambered while in the ambulance). To my knowledge, it is a violation of several international agreements to use ambulances to transport military troops.

At about 2:30 PM on July 3rd, we were handcuffed and blindfolded and led into an APC. The blindfolds were removed after entering the APC. We were then driven down to the IDF Huwara base, and sat in the sun for about a half an hour before our handcuffs were cut off. Shortly after this, Sergeant Amos Yamin instructed us to follow him to the entry gate of the base where he handed us our passports and mobile phones in a plastic bag. Peter's 11 blank DVD tapes were not returned, estimated at approximately $100US. No explanation was given for our release, just as no explanation was ever given for our detention. We walked free from Huwara base at approximately 4:00 PM on July 3rd, 48 hours after our initial abduction.

Throughout the entirety of the illegal abduction and detention mentioned above, I was in the company of Brian, Peter, Mejdi and Akhmed. Huwaida Arraf of the International Solidarity Movement has taken testimony from both Brian Dominick and Peter Blacker, and can be contacted at [number withheld] for further information and/or to corroborate this testimony.

I can be reached at [number withheld] in New Haven, Connecticut.

NOTE FROM THE EDITORS: Both US and UK consulates made formal complaints on behalf of Eric, Brian and Pete.

IF I DON'T WRITE NOW ...

by Susan Barclay, I August 2002

[…]

The morning begins with laughter as a friend tells me that he likes to watch *Tom and Jerry* because it makes him smile. "Why do people watch *Rambo*? We see that everyday—here it is not TV, it is real." When Internationals first arrive they are often baffled by the military machinery waging this war, but the novelty wears off so very quickly; loss of appreciation frequently goes hand in hand with habit, routine and repetition. Today alone, I saw over 15 tanks, 7 APCs, a number of jeeps, 30+ soldiers armed with M-16s and a Land Rover full of commandos. This is life here. Children 2–3 years old know the words for soldier, tank, shooting, prison, and death; slowly and surely war creeps into their beings.

The children play "war" frequently. One mother told me the other day—"The terribly sad thing is that they always want to be the Israelis, no one wants to be Palestinian, to be controlled, to be the victim. These little children know who has power."

[…]

We have been doing a lot of roadblock removals during the last few days. The Israeli army has closed every single village repeatedly and the Internationals staying in Iraq Bureen heeded the locals' call to remove these roadblocks. A group of nearly 40 of us headed out to Tell, Iraq Bureen and New Nablus and removed three roadblocks one morning. It was incredibly beautiful to watch this simple success—working for a few hours and then watching as water trucks, vegetables and taxis begin to pass— encouraged by the sound of our clapping and the smiles of resistance.

Palestinians at the Iraq Bureen roadblock then asked us to come to Salim village, where we helped remove three other roadblocks. We left a few people in the village who called an hour or two later to say that an APC and tank had come and a bull-dozer was reported to be on its way. We moved quickly and had Internationals there in time to block the bulldozer. Five people sat on the ground and the bulldozer was unable to re-do the roadblock; the jeeps however did come and the soldiers began threatening arrest. After 30 minutes they begin taking the men, one by one, quick cuffing each one (with plastic handcuffs) and blindfolding them. They were put in the back of an APC and taken to Huwara military base (released hours later from Huwara after refusing to say anything).

We stayed in the area until they left, knowing they would bulldoze during the night. The day after we came again to remove the roadblock and will continue this resistance as long as the Palestinians want to do so.

JUSTICE FLOWS LIKE WATER
by Adam Stumacher, 13 August 2002

The town of Beit Furiq lies a mere seven kilometers from the West Bank city of Nablus, but under military curfew they might just as well be separated by an ocean. According to Atef Hanini, the town's mayor, not a single resident of this town has been to Nablus for two months now. As a farming community, Beit Furiq is dependent on access to the nearby city in order to sell produce, and most of the town's working population is employed there (though of course were they by some miracle able to get to Nablus, they would find all shops and businesses closed due to 56 consecutive days of military curfew). However, the real crisis in Beit Furiq is not unemployment, but water.

Every ounce of water for this town of 12,000 residents must be brought by truck from Nablus. The Israeli authorities have refused to tap into the water pipeline that passes less than 500 meters from the city limits. But perhaps more significantly, there is a spring close enough to this town that the residents can hear its gurgling (when their ears are not filled with the sound of M16 rounds). This spring has enough water to meet the needs of all the town's residents, plus the residents of the nearby community of Beit Dajan, which faces the same water shortage. But 100 percent of the water from this spring is diverted to illegal Israeli settlements in the Jordan Valley. So the water tanker truck has become the tenuous lifeline for this whole community.

The town owns a total of five water tankers. The trouble is, these trucks are sporadically held at the army checkpoint on the Nablus access road. In theory, the trucks have permission to pass back and forth to Nablus between the hours of 10 a.m. and 2 p.m. But soldiers often detain the trucks so long at the checkpoint that even completing one run per day can be a challenge. Sometimes, when unable to pass through the checkpoint, desperate truck drivers fill up from non-sanitary water sources, which has contributed to an outbreak of amoebic dysentery in the town (which has almost no access to medical care, again due to the curfew).

Beit Furiq has been averaging eight tankers of water per day since April, while Hanini assesses the community's basic survival need at 20–26 tankers per day. But when I visited the town today, extremely strict enforcement at the checkpoint for the past couple of days meant that only one water truck had arrived in the town over the last 48 hours. Hanini asserted that this was a fairly typical pattern, and the military would most likely ease up enforcement at the checkpoint in the next day or two.

Some town residents have been without water in their homes for over 40 days now. The only way this community survives is by sharing whatever limited resources they have with their neighbors. Lack of water has severely damaged the town's agricultural output. Farmers have stopped watering their crops, and most of the town's livestock has been slaughtered because there is insufficient water to keep both animals and humans alive. In short, the people of Beit Furiq are being murdered, very slowly and system-atically, by the conditions under Israeli occupation.

[…]

Dr. Martin Luther King once said that we should not rest until justice flows like water. But for the people of Beit Furiq, the tankers are still detained at the closest checkpoint.

SUCCESSFUL ACTION AT THE IRON GATE TODAY
by Dave, 19 December 2002

There was a march organised by many committees and groups from the local Palestinians supported by 18 Internationals. There were probably 150 people with banners and placards, accompanied by ambulances. Also a lot of local people just joined in as we marched, so there was a good crowd by the time we arrived at the gate. The traffic came to a complete stop and snarled up for a considerable distance in all directions.

Spanners were brought and the hinges were removed. The gate is immensely heavy and it took some time to get organized enough to lift it and then carry it away to great cheering. It now lies at the bottom of a nearby ravine. There was no interference from the IDF, but they were undoubtedly watching from the overlooking fort. We now have to monitor what they do in case of retaliation.

Till then, peace and bright moments, Dave

THE WAR AGAINST TEAPARTIES
by Robin Horsell, 14 February 2003

As I stepped onto the hill leading down from the Refugee Camp, I saw him crouch down, aim his gun in my direction, and take aim. The sound of the shot echoed round the valley.

I took my mobile out of my pocket and rang the Consulate, explained that I was trying to get to Salim Village to have tea and celebrate Eid with a friend, and that despite the fact I was wearing my high visibility jacket, and had been wearing it around this soldier for a month, he was shooting at me.

Further down the hill and another shot. I yell "International" at the top of my voice and continue down. The Consulate talks to me as I pick my way across the impossibly muddy mess that is Azmout Checkpoint (or not as the case may be). At the other side he comes running up to me and pokes me hard in the chest with the barrel of his M16. The Consulate is still on the line.

"Why are you poking me with your gun?"

"Go back or I'll shoot you."

"Why are you threatening to shoot me?"

"Because you came here when I told you not to."

"You didn't tell me anything."

"I did, I fired shots. Now go back or I'll shoot you."

"I want to go to Salim Village."

"You have to go through a checkpoint."

"This is a checkpoint!"

"No it's not."

"Yes it is, and it's the only way to Salim Village."

"You have to go through an official checkpoint."

"This is an official checkpoint, I've passed here many times after showing my passport."

"No it's not. Only humanitarian cases are allowed through here."

"That's not true! Many people cross here. You and I both know that."

I explain what's going on to the Consulate. The soldier who wears three stripes is Ariel Ze'ev. He's a crazy man. He leads a group of four soldiers who spend days wandering up and down this road, detaining people, obstructing their paths, punishing them, shooting at them. The group of four wander around, without a vehicle, suggesting that they believe they are quite safe.

Now he tells me this is his country, he's in charge here and I'm not going to Salim. I'm going back the way I came or he's going to shoot me. It's 9.30 a.m. and I ask the Consulate to speak to the IDF for me, and if they refuse permission, to ask them to fax a map and directions of how I can get to the village. I know it's impossible. The army has dug up all the roads and surrounded Salim and two neighbouring villages with a 10km ditch. The only possible route is through another two checkpoints, and then a half hour walk down the settler road, where Palestinians may not walk. Anyone on the road is likely to be hassled by soldiers or, even worse, armed settlers. No ambulances can get into the villages, and already two people have died at Azmout waiting for ambulances on the other side.

I tell Ze'ev that I intend to go to Salim, that I have spoken to someone at my Consulate (he listened in after all!) and that I'm not leaving till I get permission to go.

So begins the long wait. Shortly after, he stops a car, detains the driver at gunpoint, puts him against the wall, and parks the car in the middle of the road to Salim. He shoots at anyone who approaches the checkpoint. His three stooges sit against the wall of a house, looking bored and depressed. It is raining. I make more calls. Three Internationals will join me later I hear. The ISM media office prepares a press release to send out. A shepherd is next. He is detained at 10.30 and made to sit against the wall. His sheep are left to their own devices. Later two Internationals will try to retrieve them. They will not be good shepherd material and will be relieved when his brother appears and rounds the sheep up. They do manage to retrieve the donkey and tie it to a tree though. The shepherd is in for a lousy day. At about one Ze'ev will decide he is cheeky, cuff him and make him squat facing the wall. He will join another man who dared to question Ze'ev's responsibility.

A gynaecologist will join those who are not cuffed. He was given permission to cross earlier. When he returns to the checkpoint, Ze'ev will fire a shot in his direction and tell him to go back. An International will walk to him and walk back with him. Ze'ev will take his ID and make him sit against the wall. "Why?" the International will ask. "Because he didn't go back when I told him to" Ze'ev will say. I will phone the Israeli Human Rights Group HaMoked, in front of Ze'ev, explain the situation to them and pass the phone to the doctor. After the phone call Ze'ev will threaten the doctor and then give him back his ID and tell him to go.

Every now and then Ze'ev will ask me if I have my official answer. Not yet, I will tell him. More phone calls with the Consulate. "Where exactly are you?" "What's your passport number?" She will give it to the Israelis, even after she promises not to!

The three Internationals arrive. It gets chaotic at times and decisions seem arbitrary and strange. Some pass with impunity, some cross without any problem. Others are detained for wanting to go from one village to another. Others are allowed to go. Some are shot at long before they get near, and don't come any closer. Ze'ev will assault at least eight of the men during the course of the day, kicking, punching, banging heads against the wall. Sometimes Internationals will get between Ze'ev and the detained, sometimes it happens so quickly no one knows it is coming. Ze'ev's mood will fluctuate throughout the day, as it does every day. He would be in danger of a mental health section in the UK. Here he gets a gun, limitless ammunition and three soldiers and three villages to order around.

Several times he announces loudly that he is not human. Time passes. I remind the Consulate that all I want to do is visit a friend for a cup of tea. I remind Ze'ev that I am not at war with him, and neither is he at war with me. He's stopped threatening to shoot me now. At one point he wants to discuss where I bought my Doc Martens, and how similar they are to his.

Two-thirty and the Consulate rings. The Army spokesman has told her that I am allowed to pass, and that he will clear it with the soldiers. Several times the radio goes and Ze'ev speaks into it. But he says nothing to me. By now I am moving about freely. I go off to show an International where the sheep are.

"Where are you going?" asks one of the soldiers. "To look for sheep," I reply. "Why, am I under arrest?" "No," comes back the reply.

I go to get cigarettes from the shop in Azmout. I meet a man who has grazes and tells me was assaulted by soldiers trying to cross the valley. I ring HaMoked again, and they speak to him and take his details.

Four pm and I ring the Consulate again. She is surprised to hear from me. "They told me that they spoke to the soldiers and you have gone to the village," she says.

"Can I go to Salim?" I ask Ze'ev. He ignores me. I ask a soldier, he asks Ze'ev. "No" comes back the reply. I speak to the Consulate again. The man who gave permission left the office at three. "No problem," I tell her, "I'll just come back tomorrow and you can ring him then!" I tell her.

I turn to the soldier. "You guys must really enjoy my company," I say. "I'll be back again tomorrow and then I'll go to Salim." Ze'ev suddenly comes to life: "Go now," he says, pointing to the village.

Some of the men are detained until 10pm. It is cold and raining. I sleep the night in Salim. People are increasingly worried about the checkpoint, many avoid it, some can't. Arbitrary decisions are made. Arbitrary detentions and assaults take place every day. They don't believe the world will help. They don't know how it will stop. None of the three villages has produced a suicide bomber. The only possible explanation I can see for it is that the Israelis are trying to crush the villages. It may be working. Many villagers have given up and moved into Nablus. The settlers have been down and stolen sheep, wild pigs have appeared on the land inexplicably, wells have been contaminated.

I remember the discussion with the soldier at one point during the day.

"Don't you agree that Israel has the most moral army in the world?" he asks.

"No" I respond.

LOCALS AND INTERNATIONALS REMOVE CRIPPLING ROADBLOCK
by Lasse Schmidt, 2 March 2003

The road between Jenin and Berqin is essential not only to the 5000 people living in Berqin. It is the eastern gateway to the provincial capital of Jenin and is used by people living in a dozen villages in the eastern part of the Jenin District.

After closing the road for a week the Israeli army finally closed it completely on Thursday by building a roadblock from one mountainside to the other. The narrow valley was comprehensively closed off to all vehicles and persons not able to climb the five-metre-high pile of dirt and rocks.

By Saturday the roadblock had been removed by ISM volunteers working with the Berqin Municipality, thereby allowing traffic to use the important gateway to Jenin for the first time in a week.

The four ISM activists present in Jenin became aware of the roadblock early Friday and went to inspect the site the same day.

Saturday morning they left their homes in Jenin armed with just a shovel and three pickaxes. Several phone calls to the municipalities of Jenin, Qabatia and Berqin asking for a bulldozer to do the dirty work ended up without success. Instead the four international activists, two Palestinian men and a 13 year old boy started what seemed an impossible task—to remove the roadblock by hand.

Passing Palestinian townspeople offered their enthusiastic encouragement and the labouring crew sometimes numbered as many as twelve. After five hours of hard toil the result was a narrow bumpy road usable by four-wheeled cars.

At that point a bulldozer finally arrived and started work. The municipality of Berqin had expected Israeli soldiers to turn up and start shooting at the workers. But after five hours without any military interference they decided to lend their support to the action.

In half an hour the bulldozer cleared a narrow pass through the roadblock and the bumpy area surrounding it. The mayor of Berqin had emphasised to the driver of the bulldozer that he should only partially remove the roadblock. Years of experience have taught the Palestinians that the bigger the operation the greater the risk of the army showing up the next day to rebuild the roadblock again.

By the late afternoon traffic was flowing easily in the Berqin Valley thereby saving everyone an arduous climb up a mountain of dirt and a long walk afterwards.

PRISON AND THE BEAST
by Huwaida Arraf, 18 June 2003

Dear Friends,

Thank you for the calls and the emails. I am embarrassed to have taken up your time with my case when there are so many other Palestinians who need your help. The officer filling out my release papers commented that I "must have many friends all over the world."

I was put under arrest today for "obstructing the work of soldiers" and though I didn't go to prison, I'd like to ask a few minutes of your time to tell you about what happened today, and the larger prison that all Palestinians in the Occupied Palestinian Territories are in.

I arrived at the Huwara checkpoint at around 12:30pm with a newly arrived American volunteer, Rick; we were on our way to Nablus. The queue was long, at least 70 people, and it didn't look like the three Israeli soldiers who were manning the checkpoint were letting anybody through. A few of the Palestinian men, who had already been at the checkpoint for over an hour, seeing my companion was an International, advised us to walk around the checkpoint to avoid what would surely be another three-hour wait, at least; "If you have an American passport, you'll pass, no problem."

Though we were in a hurry to get Rick to the ISM training in Nablus, there was no question that we'd refuse to take advantage of the racist system that would allow an American into Nablus, but require a resident of Nablus or a surrounding village to wait for hours, to be checked by Israeli soldiers and then given a verdict of whether he/she could go home, to work, or to school.

So we waited. Soldiers make Palestinians stand in a female line and a male line and so our Palestinian friends, who were trying to save us time, urged us to at least get into the shorter female line. We did. Half an hour later a soldier came over and let a handful of women pass. I was one of the ones singled out to pass. Rick came with me.

When we approched the soldier who was to check our IDs, we noticed a family, a man, woman and two children, who were standing aside. Apparently the soldiers did not want to let the man through (he had a British passport) and his wife, a Palestinian from Nablus, was refusing to leave without him. They were also refusing to turn back. The soldiers kept asking of the Brit, his "hawiyya" (ID), insinuating that he had a Palestinian ID (in addition to the passport) and was just refusing to show it.

I then noticed two young Palestinian men, in their early twenties, crouching up against the cinder blocks that form the checkpoint, their hands tied behind their backs. An old woman was pleading with the Israeli soldiers, her son (one of the young men), was sick and had back problems and was on his way to Rafeedia Hospital in Nablus. She was trying to show the soldier her son's papers and x-rays, but he wasn't interested. "His back! His back!" she cried, but the soldier only yelled at her to go away. I interfered to ask the soldier why he was yelling at the old woman and holding the young men.

He said he wasn't interested. I learned from the two men, Rashed and Ramsy, that they had been held for three hours by that point (since about 9:30am) and the soldiers had confiscated their ID cards. They weren't told why. I got on the phone to HaMoked, an Israeli human rights organization in Jerusalem that often turns in complaints of abuses to the Military District Coordinating Office, and gave them the names of the young men. Rick and I decided that we would stay by Ramsy and Rashed until HaMoked was able to get back to us. Ramsy stood up to show us that his cuffs were on way too tight. It looked like he was losing circulation. I pleaded with one of the soldiers to loosen his cuffs, Rick pointing out that the boy could be seriously hurt. The soldier screamed at Ramsy to kneel "or else." Another soldier, calling himself a beast, said "I want to kill him today."

The soldiers told me to leave the area, as I was in a closed military zone.

A young man, named Nael, came through, asked the soldier if he could pass because he got word that his father passed away last night and he wanted to visit him before he was buried. The soldier told him to shut up and get back in line. When Nael persisted, the soldier called him a "son of a b★tch" and began pushing him. Nael stood his ground and the pushing got very rough. Another soldier ran over screaming and put his M16 to Nael's head. They grabbed Nael and pulled him away, one soldier still screaming and threatening to shoot. Rick and I followed and whipped out our cameras, "Hey, hey, calm down. Calm down!" Nael was also put in cuffs and told that he would be arrested and that he "would be seeing a jail cell and not [his] father." Another call to HaMoked.

The soldiers kept telling me to leave the area, as I was in a closed military zone and preventing them from doing their job—really annoying them. I refused, telling them that there was no way I was going to leave these guys when it was obvious the soldiers were being very abusive, and even if they considered serving the Occupation as their "job" there was no reason not to treat the people as human beings. This whole time they did not let anyone through the checkpoint, though every once in a while a soldier would get on the loud speaker and yell at the Palestinians to form straight lines and to stand behind the plastic barricades or else the checkpoint would be closed for the rest of the day.

By 3:30pm, more pushing, yelling, loosing and tightening of cuffs, Ramsy (the sick one) was released. One of the soldiers kept saying to us in English, "I want to kill him today." I asked why he couldn't realize that we're all human beings like he was. He replied, "I'm not a human being, I'm a beast. I'm a beast, OK, and I want to kill him." He came up behind Rashed, grabbed arms and tightened his plastic cuffs until they couldn't be tightened any more. When I protested, he yanked Rashed away and threw him behind an area of cinder blocks telling him to kneel so that he was out of sight. Rashed tried to stand up a few times, "my hands, my hands!" Another call to HaMoked. Nael, still cuffed, ordered from a young boy vendor, three colas, for me, Rick and himself.

He urged me to leave, assuring me that he would be OK.

It didn't seem like any of what we were saying was getting through to any of the soldiers who kept treating the people like they were less than human, denying entry to into Nablus to a new bride and her husband going to visit family, a husband and father, trying to enter with his family (the soldiers only let the wife and kids go) and a half dozen others, as people were ordered to approach one by one, one every 10 minutes or so. The self-described "beast" confiscated two bikes and one trolley—things that Palestinians trying to make a living in an economy with a 70% unemployment rate use to transport the bags and luggage of other travellers for a small charge. (As Palestinians often have to walk distances, owners of trolleys, bikes, and donkeys offer rides or transport of heavy bags for a nominal fee.)

A young boy came up to me to tell me that Rashed had been released. I guess I had had my back turned, and at first didn't believe it. But Rashed came up to the front of the line to wave and confirm that he was let go. I went up to him, "Are you going to try the other way around? Take care." He smiled, "Thanks." Only Nael was left until the "beast" ran after a Palestinian man who was given permission to pass, and for no reason, tied his hands up and pushed him down behind some cinder blocks, where Rashed was only minutes before. By now the soldiers were getting pretty annoyed with me (perhaps because the HaMoked calls were working) and a police jeep pulled up. By 4:30 I was taken away. Rick was given the option to leave and it seemed best, though I was worried about him travelling alone on his second day [in Palestine].

I was released at about 11pm from Ariel (settlement) police station. An anonymous friend (a veteran from the first Intifada who had spent 11 years in jail for actively organizing the popular resistance) made the 40km drive in the dark on the windy settler road to pick me up. Rick made it back OK. HaMoked rang to check up on me. Nael was not released.

If you can, please call or write to inquire about Nael Suwaydi from Abu Dis, arrested at Huwara checkpoint on June 18, 2003 for daring to come from Abu Dis to Nablus, without permission, to pay respects to his father. I never did give Nael my condolences.

Tel: + (972) 36 080 339
Fax: + (972) 36 080 343
Israeli Minister of Defence, Shaul Mofaz: sar@mod. gov. il
Israeli Foreign Minister, Silvan Shalom: sar@mofa. gov. il
Contact the Israeli Embassy in your country:
http://www. embassyworld. com/embassy/israel1. htm

In solidarity and struggle, Huwaida

I apologize if any of this is incoherent. I'm a little tired.

NABLUS TO TEL AVIV
by Neta Golan, 28 June 2003

My father passed away last week. I took Nawal, my two-month-old daughter, and attempted to go to Tel Aviv to attend the funeral and grieve with my family. Nablus, the city I live in, was besieged and completely sealed off. This has been the case for most of the last two years. Israeli soldiers threatened to shoot anyone approaching the checkpoint.

I had a letter from the hospital regarding a checkup that Nawal needed in Ramallah so we arrived at the Hawara checkpoint in an ambulance. The ambulance stopped at the designated place. The soldiers did not shoot, thank god, but they also did not approach us. After about half an hour the driver decided to try to speak to them. He stepped out of the ambulance. Guns were pointed in his direction. He stepped back in. All we could do was wait. All the while settler buses headed for the settlements that surround Nablus whisked past unchecked. Swallowing my outrage I thanked god that my baby was not suffering, that no one in the ambulance was in critical condition. The soldiers had no way of knowing that. But had they known it is likely it would have made no difference.

A year ago I was accompanying an ambulance through a checkpoint in Jenin. A young man with a bullet in his head was sprawled at the back of the ambulance, a doctor was pushing air into his lungs with a manual respirator. I sat next to the driver and said nothing while we waited and watched the patient's condition deteriorate. I know that being confrontational with soldiers can often aggravate a situation. I could not risk that happening. I calmed myself and waited for an opening. I offered the solider a cigarette. He accepted. I gave him another one for the other soldier, and then I ventured:

"Is it really necessary that we wait so long? This guy is dying." The soldier looked embarrassed, "We have to make sure he is not wanted."

"If you find out he's wanted you can come and pick him up from the hospital. He's not going to run away. He has a bullet in his head."

"I'll see what I can do."

That day we spent an hour and a half at the checkpoint, time that assured that the young man's brain damage was irreversible. The soldier, a young man himself, was just doing his job.

On the day of my father's funeral we were "only" delayed for an hour. It was the third time Nawal had made this journey since her birth. Despite the risk involved in getting in and out I came often because I knew my father was dying. I needed him to see his first grandchild, to tell him I loved him, to say goodbye.

After the funeral we spent a week with our Israeli family. My husband who is Palestinian is forbidden to enter Israel—Palestine that was occupied in 1948. It was hard that he could not be with me. But I knew that I was privileged to be able to grieve with my family.

I kept thinking of my friend Amal, one of the most beautiful women I have ever seen. With huge hazel eyes and dark black hair. Her family was forced to leave Palestine for Jordan before she was born. Her husband, Abed, is from the West Bank. They have two beautiful children. If she leaves the West Bank to see her family in Jordan, she will not be allowed back. Her parents have only seen their grandchildren in pictures. Her father was old and ill and she could not see him. He died and she could not be at his burial or comfort her mother. Today she refuses to accept that her father is dead. It is not death that she can't deal with. For people living under occupation must live with death every day. It is that fact that she was forced to choose her husband and children over her parents that she cannot live with. Her hair has suddenly begun going white.

The policy of denying spouses of Palestinians residency is one of the many forms that ethnic cleansing takes here. It is a policy as old as the state of Israel but Sharon takes special pride in it. In his election campaign he boasted that he had stopped Palestinians from entering Israel (greater) by stopping family reunification completely. Amal will never see her father again. Many thousands of Palestinians share her fate.

Back home in Nablus, Nawal and myself came back to our family and to the routine of waking up every night from the explosion of homes being destroyed or tanks thundering through the streets and shooting. In the meantime Nawal has learned to smile and when she smiles she shines like the sun.

8

AMBULANCE ACCOMPANIMENT

HOW I BECAME A TERROR TOURIST
by Shaista Aziz, July 2002

It's official. I am a terrorist. I am a twenty-six-year-old British Muslim woman. I have spent two weeks in Nablus, Palestine, as a volunteer with the International Solidarity Movement. The ISM is an organisation that calls for non-violent direct action to show solidarity with the Palestinian people. The Israeli army website refers to international volunteers such as myself as 'terror tourists'. We are viewed as being the enemy along with two million Palestinian civilians in the West Bank who are under Israeli curfew.

'Terror tourists' come in all shapes and sizes, nationalities and ages. It's a near impossible task to profile one unless they carry an Italian passport. Five hundred Italians were turned back by the Israelis recently; they were planning to volunteer with the ISM. I spent two weeks with Americans, Canadians, British, Norwegians, Danish and Japanese 'terrorists'. It was one of the most amazing experiences of my life.

[…]

I spent much of my time volunteering with the Palestinian Red Crescent Society (PRCS), taking patients to hospital. The ambulances are the only thing that move in

Photograph by Jennifer Midberry.

the city that is under curfew twenty-four hours a day. The ambulance drivers are continually stopped and harassed. The drivers and paramedics are often strip-searched. One young paramedic was taken inside a tank and made to strip in front of nine soldiers. They told him that they were looking for explosives. When they found nothing they told him that he could leave and reminded him that he would never be their (soldiers') friend.

Working with the paramedics was an amazing and eye-opening experience. The first time I faced a tank was less than two hours after being in Nablus. My legs turned to jelly when the barrel of the tank turned to face the windscreen of the ambulance. I began to question what the hell I was doing in Palestine and if I was up to volunteering with the ambulances. The ambulances that I travelled in were regularly stopped and searched. Patients were made to wait in the heat whilst their IDs were checked and the ambulances were searched for 'bombs'.

I began to adopt different strategies when it came to dealing with the soldiers. Sometimes I would engage with them, it was my way of showing them that I wasn't scared of them. I would ask them why they were doing what they were doing. If I was met with a stony face and silence I would keep my mouth shut and just stare at them.

Whilst working with the ambulances I saw how those guns and tanks are used against the civilian population of Nablus. We were called out to see a ten-year-old girl who had been shot in the side of her stomach because she had been looking out of her window. She had two bullet wounds, entrance and exit. The paramedics had been called out to re-dress her bandages. When the little girl saw her wounds she began to scream. Her father calmed her down and wiped her tears. Once the paramedics had finished with her she got up unaided and insisted that she would walk out of the ambulance alone.

One night we were called out to the old city to attend to an old man who must have been in his seventies. He had seven gunshot wounds to his body. I don't know why he was shot. When the ambulance arrived we were hurriedly ushered into the house and were told that soldiers had occupied the house opposite and that there were snipers on the roof. The paramedics patched him up as best they could and then we left to go on our next job.

Every day the ambulance drivers risk their lives to take care of the sick. They feel passionately about helping their people and when they can't get to a patient because of the checkpoints and harassment they get very frustrated and angry. I was told about one paramedic who was arrested by the army, they accused him of being a suicide bomber. He was taken to an army base and his ambulance, which was fitted with special equipment for premature babies, was seized by the army. That was three months ago, no one has seen the paramedic or the ambulance since. His wife and children don't know if he's alive or dead.

The Palestinian Red Crescent Society has one hundred ambulances that operate across the West Bank, taking care of two million people. Two years ago forty-five ambulances were donated to the PRCS, but they never reached the organisation. Instead the ambulances were seized by the Israelis and are stationed at the borders of Jordan, Egypt and the port of Haifa in Israel. The manager of the PRCS has been told that the ambulances are being checked for 'bombs' by the army.

[…]

OCCUPATION FORCES RAID PRCS
Occupation forces enter Red Crescent Society in early morning raid
International Solidarity Movement, 11 July 2002

FOR IMMEDIATE RELEASE

[NABLUS] Internationals received a distress call from the Palestinian Red Crescent Society (PRCS) office at approximately 2am. The Israeli army had surrounded the building with tanks and soldiers and forced the staff out into the parking lot.

Five Internationals walked from the Union of Palestinian Medical Relief Committees (UPMRC) office to the PRCS with hands raised, calling out to the soldiers. The peace activists demanded that they be allowed to observe the situation and two of their number went into the PRCS offices joining a third already there and one more is riding with an ambulance.

Marcus Armstrong (UK) is reporting that the army is holding the identity cards of two paramedics and preventing them from going out on ambulance calls.

The army is conducting a house-to-house search in the neighborhood surrounding the PCRS and has also entered a nearby mosque.

For more information contact: Marcus Armstrong (UK) [number withheld], Tommy Nielson (Denmark) [number withheld], Emma Bleach (UK) [number withheld], Mike Mcurdy (USA)[number withheld], Neta Golan (Israel) [number withheld]

ENDS

BIRTHS IN JENIN
by Tamara, 15 July 2002

LAST NIGHT I am sitting outside the Red Crescent sharing a chocolate roulade with Rebecca Murray, who has been riding in the ambulances in Jenin for a month now. There is a soft breeze blowing, offering some relief from the powerful Palestinian sun. Jenin has appeared peaceful for hours. Without any warning, the medics (all men) are lunging towards the ambulance.

"Injury!" they shout, and Rebecca pulls me over to get in the ambulance with her. "Just one," the driver tells us. Suddenly, I am handed a vest, and the door slams shut. Within moments we are speeding down a rocky dirt road, trying to find someone who I've been told has been shot. I try to brace myself. I've only seen gunshot wounds in photographs. We are flying over potholes, thrashing about in the back of the ambulance. It seems like we've been driving for ever. We are in the hills searching. We can't find the victim. We are driving in circles. I look down at myself, unbelieving. I am in an ambulance in Jenin.

Finally after more than thirty minutes we come across a car full of waving people. The victim has not been shot, she has fallen and seriously injured her back, is nine months pregnant, crying in panic, and in labor. They load her into the back of the ambulance, and I sit at her head, petting her forehead and squeezing her hand. She says she has to push. All of a sudden, I am thrown a pair of gloves. "You do it."

The mother's headscarf is still pinned under her chin. She is in a heavy black velvet dress and covered in a sheet. Only her undergarments have been removed. I am perplexed. How am I to do an exam under a sheet at sixty miles an hour on an unbelievably bumpy road with male medics staring on at woman who is horribly and terribly ashamed? I try patting her reassuringly, cooing to her in English. I have yet to learn the Arabic words for breathe and relax. She is very distressed, but still insisting that she has to push. I ask the driver to please tell her that I cannot help her if I cannot see. She consents, but only if I work under the sheet. The baby is not crowning yet, I am relieved … we still have time. We get the mother to the hospital, and both mom and baby are stable. As we pull out, I can see the red glow of gun fire from a tank. We ask the locals exactly where it is so we can get to the next call safely. More often than not the ambulances are stopped and searched, but tonight we escape the watchful eyes of the Israeli army.

Today I will go to an interview at the maternity hospital, and hopefully ask them questions that will help me bridge the gap between cultural sensitivity and being able to give adequate care. I am scheduled to work the ambulances from 6 to 11pm tonight and will also be teaching a summer camp for children from 8 to 11am. Last night several houses were destroyed again, but no one really cares. I hear explosions all morning; a baby cries at the sound of a fighter jet. I am told this is not news, this is just the way things are.

(I am looking forward to my shift tonight. I feel very comfortable in the ambulance, and am enjoying the privilege of working directly with the people.) I love you all. FREE PALESTINE!

JENIN FEVER
by Tamara, 17 July 2002

The heat permeates everything, turns muscle into melting modeling clay. Bodies droop over chairs, eyes hooded and heavy, lids fluttering at the gates of sleep. Fever creeps up through my limbs, my cheeks are flushed. I feel sickness in every cell, and I fight to stay awake. I don't want to be sick again. I came here to work, not sweat in silence in the stale blank apartment. "I'm not contagious," I tell myself. "It's just the water," and with that bit of self convincing I trudge to the Red Crescent, my poor Arabic morning greetings more slurred than usual.

A newborn has been left by the roadside. We ride to the hospital to claim him, and bring him to an orphanage in a surrounding town. This sort of abandonment is rare here. Mothers delight in their families, and towns are close knit, but Jenin is devastated. The economy is hard struck, the water lines cut, the sounds of gunfire and bombing have become background noise, the muzak of the Occupation. Even the most hopeful voices carry a ring of fatality in them.

The nurses have named him Abdullah. He has charcoal gray eyes, and a headful of dusty black hair. I cradle him in my arms, kissing his forehead with ridiculous desperation. A Jewish woman with a Palestinian baby in her arms, trying to transfer some sense of love and belonging to this little one.

I carry Abdullah into the ambulance, fussing with his blankets. The radio crackles, the driver answers. I have been ordered to go back to the dispatch center. They say the Israeli soldiers won't let Internationals go with ambulances outside of the city. I try to protest, but I am suddenly washed with a feeling of despair. All at once I feel useless. This stupid American woman condescending enough to come into this town, and think that I could help. The problems here are complex, and weighted with issues I have never had to organize around before. My naivety is heavy about me. I cannot work any more today. I am physically ill, and mentally pained. I know I cannot show my sorrow or my rage to my Palestinian friends. I haven't earned it. I have only touched the skin of their suffering, what lies beneath I cannot even imagine.

I am dizzy walking backing to the flat. Homesick, and heartsick and embarrassed. In bed I listen to my walkman. Ani sings me an activists' lullabye:

I'm no heroine. Least not last time I checked.
I'm too easy to roll over, and I'm too easy to wreck.
I just write about what I should have done, and sing what I wish I could say,
And I hope somewhere some woman hears my music and it helps her through her day.

We paid for this Occupation, sitting in our air-conditioned houses, never questioning where our tax dollars are sucked away to. My big woman's ego has been leveled, and I am just a little girl with a fever struggling to make sense in the rubble, in the heat of Jenin.

ISRAELI ARMY ATTACKS JENIN HOSPITAL
International Solidarity Movement, 31 July 2002

FOR IMMEDIATE RELEASE

[JENIN] The Israeli army, obviously not learning from the first time they did this, has once again rammed a utility pole. This time the military vehicle escaped unscathed, but has left the hospital without power. The wires, crackling with electricity, are hanging down at such an angle that ambulances have only a four inch clearance. Should the wires touch the vehicles they could kill the people inside.

Medics have to make the tough decision of driving under these wires or keeping patients from the hospital.

This continues the Israeli policy, especially in Jenin of attacking the civilian infra-structure.

Activists also report that at 4am one building containing eight apartments was destroyed for no apparent reason. This leaves dozens more people homeless and increases the desperate humanitarian situation in Jenin.

The International Solidarity Movement is opposed to the horrible and tragic civilian attacks happening in Israel and Palestine and call for an end to the Occupation as an end to the violence.

For more information in Jenin contact:
Rebecca [number withheld], Tobias [number withheld]

ENDS

NO FORESEEABLE END TO THIS TOUR OF DUTY
by Eric Levine, 9 July 2002

On walls in Nablus there's a shaheed poster—a poster commemorating a martyr killed by the Israeli army—showing a middle-aged man standing in front of an ambulance. We're told he was the head of the ambulance service in Jenin.

[…]

Palestinian ambulances, ambulance drivers and EMTs [Emergency Medical Technicians] are under constant attack by the Israeli army—in spite of international law which says that people have a human right to health care, and that health care workers must be allowed to provide it.

Because of their protected status, ambulances are the only vehicles technically allowed on the roads during curfew. Especially under curfew, ambulances have become essential to every aspect of health care. People can't leave their homes to buy medicine, and they can't travel to the hospital for urgent outpatient care like dialysis. People who care for elderly or ill family members can't get to them. People who are discharged from the hospital after an illness can't get home. So ambulances have become the conduit for all health care, and they are constantly out on the road trying to make sure Palestinians survive. This is in addition to the continued need for emergency service, which is exacerbated by semi-daily shootings of Palestinian civilians by the Israeli army. (See Nablus reports on the army's random shootings of Palestinians during lifting/re-imposition of curfew.)

But every minute that a Palestinian ambulance is on the road or attending to a patient is dangerous. Although the Israeli army is forced to allow ambulances on the roads, soldiers take every opportunity to impede them, and to ensure that health care workers know they are unsafe. Every roving tank that crosses an ambulance's path stops the ambulance. At every checkpoint (which is not just one blockade on a road, but two, with the army controlling the space between), ambulances are stopped and may be delayed for hours, and then may be stopped and delayed again 100ft later at the other side of the checkpoint.

When Internationals are present, stopping an ambulance means checking the ID of everyone on board, including patients; searching the ambulance; searching the EMTs and possibly the patients; and waiting. The ambulance can't move until the army says it can. Often, the soldiers just stand there, delaying it.

When Internationals are not present, stopping an ambulance may mean doing all of the above, possibly strip-searching the EMTs, possibly beating them, possibly damaging the ambulance, and randomly delaying for hours.

These criminal violations by the Israeli army of the right to health care are only part of the incredible stress endured by EMTs. Many EMTs are young volunteers, in their early 20s, who have been living full-time at the ambulance depots for months, sleeping on mattresses on the floor between long shifts. Especially under curfew, there's little else to do—no other work, no school, no place to decompress. So, in addition to spirit-crushing 24-hour curfew and the daily threat of violence directed at their bodies both as Palestinians and as EMTs, they face the stress of being medics in a war zone, having no place to go "home for a break", no time for vacation, no foreseeable end to their tour of duty, witnessing daily military violence visited on their own community and land, and daily having to fight to get basic treatment to members of their community who need it.

To me, as an American Jew trying to understand how Palestinians are surviving this intense psychological and physical battering, it looks like amazing spirit of resistance combined with zombified carrying-on-with-life. But the truth is, I have no idea how they're doing it. We have the same questions about how Jews, queers and others survived in WWII concentration camps. How much deliberate crushing can a people take and still be alive? People survived the concentration camps, but not everyone came out whole.

Although for some Jews that experience reinforced the need to fight oppression, others have clearly lost their sense of justice, turning to violence and conquest. Will Palestinians be like those survivors in 50 years, using past suffering to justify evil acts? I hope not—they aren't yet.

9

HOME PROTECTION

INTERNATIONAL SOLIDARITY MOVEMENT INVESTIGATES HOSTAGE SITUATION, BLOCKS TANK IN NABLUS
Tear-gas fired at unarmed Internationals; one American and two Palestinian members of the press taken into custody
by Marissa McLaughlin, 30 June 2002

Volunteers with the International Solidarity Movement received notice today that the Israeli Occupation Forces had been holding a Palestinian family hostage in their home in Nablus since 2:30 AM. Five Internationals, Anila Kahn (Great Britian), Neta Golan (Canada), Marissa McLaughlin (Seattle, USA), Lisa [unknown] (Great Britian), and Sarah Reeske (New York, USA), proceeded to the home to check on the safety and well-being of the family. This home was not marked with an Israeli flag, unlike other homes that the army occupies. After finding no one on the lower floors the Internationals knocked on a locked door on the upper floor. After several minutes with no answer the Internationals opened a window and saw army rucksacks inside. We continued knocking and a Palestinian man spoke to us from the other side of the door. He told us that there were no soldiers inside and that everything was OK. We asked

Photograph by Garrick Ruiz.

him to open the door and he said that he couldn't because he had lost the key. We decided to wait around and see what happened.

A few moments later a Palestinian man came out onto a balcony and told us that the soldiers said that they would shoot us if we didn't leave. We called for more Internationals and were joined by Rae and Eric Levine (San Francisco and New Haven, USA), Suzy (Seattle, USA), and five other Internationals. The Israeli Occupation Forces threw five percussion grenades from the home but none landed near the Internationals. We made signs in Arabic and English reading 'Danger, Soldiers Here' and taped them to the home to alert the locals that soldiers were hiding in the home.

We decided to place Internationals on the balcony to try to negotiate the release of the family being held hostage by the Occupation Forces. Several Internationals moved to the balcony and tried speaking with the soldiers about the release of the hostages.

After an hour or so a bulldozer and two tanks began approaching the home from a side street. Sarah, Eric, Neta, Anila, and Marissa sat in the street holding hands to block the tanks' entry to the area. We greeted the tank driver with news of the World Cup scores and he responded with a thumbs up. We were served tea and cookies by a Palestinian neighbor and as we sipped our tea we sang a song, 'Palestine will be free', and flashed peace signs at the tanks. The driver of the foremost tank asked to speak to one of us without a camera. Suzy went up to talk to them. The soldiers demanded that the press and the people behind us leave the area. We counter-offered by inviting the soldiers to come out and drink tea with us and discuss the situation. The soldiers refused, saying that the children would throw rocks at them. We offered to protect them from the rocks but they still refused. After a few minutes the soldiers fired two tear-gas canisters at us but we remained sitting. The tank in the back fired a shell but apparently it was just fired into the air and no one was hurt.

After about 45 minutes of facing off with the tanks and the bulldozer, the soldiers in the house fired on the ground to disperse the people between us and the house. More soldiers arrived in a jeep. Soldiers jumped from the jeep and apprehended two of the three members of the press who were filming the event. Two soldiers then came to where we were sitting and grabbed Eric by the collar, pushing him to the ground. They then dragged him face down for about 25 feet. They yelled at him, 'Now will you get up?' They pushed him into the jeep and then one soldier turned to the rest of us, all females, and told us that we had one minute to leave or be arrested.

We decided that we had accomplished our goal, which was to alert the people that soldiers were hiding in the home, so we left peacefully.

After we left the soldiers went onto the balcony and told the Internationals there that they would leave if the Internationals left. They agreed and left.

JUST ANOTHER DAY
by ISM volunteers in Jenin, 3 June 2002

This was a heavy day of targeted house searches, arrests and demolitions.

At about 5 pm, during imposed curfew, two Israeli military operations took place simultaneously in the town and in the camp.

In the city six jeeps and one intelligence vehicle entered the old city, followed closely by three tanks. The soldiers were doing a targeted house-to-house search—using civilian Palestinian human shields—looking for a "wanted" man whom they apparently did not find.

Two female Internationals from America and Ireland approached and observed the military operation, concerned about the safety of the civilians in the densely populated neighborhood of Jenin's Old City.

As the Israeli army prepared to blow up part of a house they claimed held a "bomb factory", the International women asked permision to search the surrounding house for residents. Their concern was heightened by the fact that about two weeks ago the Israeli army detonated a house in Jenin, killing three children when their neighboring house collapsed from the blast.

The army refused their request and the commanding officer shoved both women repeatedly, referring to one as a "nazi dog". The women remained and asked again if the soldiers were sure that they had fully evacuated the area. Again the soldiers said yes, but despite this affirmation, shouting was heard just moments before detonation. A family that had been hiding, frightened, in a neighboring home came running out. The room that was blown up was subsequently observed by the Internationals as being completely empty other than a chair. No explosives were found.

A tank guarding the street was manned by a soldier who had been observed by several Internationals the previous day firing live ammunition directly at children in the camp. While the other tank fired in the air, this particular soldier fired at least 30 rounds, narrowly missing several small children. When he pulled his tank away from yesterday's operation, he forced an Israeli-Palestinian truck-driver, who was detained while trying to pass the site with his potato truck, to walk in front of his tank as a human shield. An International accompanied him. As this tank pulled out, this same soldier let out a spray of bullets aimed directly at a crowd of neighborhood children. Simultaneously in Jenin camp, the army conducted searches and arrested five men, including a local sheikh.

That night, the Israeli military operations continued. At around 10 pm, the soldiers entered a neighborhood next to Jenin Government Hospital and bordering the camp, and set up their operations base at a private girls' school.

At around 11.30 pm, prior to entering Palestinian homes, the soldiers fired numerous rounds of live ammunition from tanks moving on the road. A seventeen year old girl was shot in the thigh while in her home. At 12.15 am, the Red Crescent ambulance service received a call from the Israeli army to come pick her up. However, when the ambulance arrived it was fired upon and turned back. Two more ambulances were subsequently dispatched and turned away.

Finally, an Irish International was allowed to pass on foot, and found the girl bandaged, wrapped in a blanket, lying between two jeeps. Although she had been stripped naked, the army demanded their blanket and stretcher remain with them. Finally this was negotiated, and the girl was taken to hospital with the blanket and stretcher.

In the course of last night's operations, despite a total absence of any resistance, between 50 and 100 young men were taken from their homes and forced to lay on their stomachs for the duration of the house-to-house searches, which continued until past 3 am. The army was looking for a local leader and his sixteen year old son. When they did not find them, they vandalized their house and arrested five men in the neighborhood of the leader's brothers. Previously, when unable to locate another local leader, the Israeli army arrested his brother, sister and father in an attempt to make him turn himself in.

CHILDREN'S SUMMER CAMP IN ASKAR REFUGEE CAMP, NABLUS
by Dina Ramaha, July 2002

We are now two weeks into the summer camp here in the Al-Askar refugee camp. We host about 300 children, and we have several different programs that the children participate in.

My co-worker and I are responsible for the counseling and therapy of the children. We meet with groups of about 65 different children ranging from 12 to 16 years old. The children are so happy when they are at the camp. There are many classes such as: music, dance, Islam, art, counseling, health and Palestinian history. I take debka classes with some of the older girls, which is a traditional Palestinian folk dance.

The summer camp has changed Al-Askar. The children all seem to have a connection with one another, and the volunteers have become great friends of the children. Everyone in the village is aware of the new center that was built for the camp, and it has created a feeling of hope that their children can look forward to the future. I go to the camp almost every day, and I always attract about 15 to 20 children who follow me around the village. It's kind of like being Mary Poppins, but without all of the singing.

The camp was put under a great deal of strain when the Israeli soldiers bombed the home of five families, leaving 21 people homeless. Their goal was to punish the family of a man named Ali. They have been unable to find him for the last four months, and no one has heard from him, not even his family. So they went to the village of his family at 2:00 am and gave them three minutes to grab their children and get out of the house. The homes here are very close to one another, and the Israelis bombed Ali's family home by air, so many houses were destroyed. The village has come together to help clean what is left of the homes.

There is no such thing as home insurance here. Not like the US. Everything that they had is now gone. All they have is each other and the clothes on their backs. I visit Rasheeda, Ali's mother, every two or three days. Her faith in God has given her great strength. Her 75 year old husband, two sons, and daughter were all taken by the soldiers that same night. She said that she does not care about the house or anything in it. She just wants her family back.

ISRAELI ARMY CARRYING OUT COLLECTIVE PUNISHMENT IN NABLUS
International activists trying to defend homes and families
International Solidarity Movement, 2 August 2002

FOR IMMEDIATE RELEASE

[NABLUS] International activists are currently stationed in homes due to be demolished as part of the Israeli Army's policy of collective punishment. The Shakhshir family home is under threat of demolition as the Israeli Army moves throughout the city of Nablus demolishing the homes of Palestinian martyrs (shaheeds).

Seven International activists (6 Americans and 1 Irish) are now stationed in the Shakhshir family home in the Al-Aryone neighborhood of Nablus. The home is that of Ammar Shakhshir, who died on March 17, 2002. Israeli forces wish to demolish this home as revenge, a flagrant violation of the Geneva Conventions and International law banning collective punishment. Ten members of two families reside in the home, including the head of the family who is disabled due to a stroke. Among the family members are 5 children.

As of 9 PM, 4 homes had already been destroyed, with families thrown out of their residences by Israeli soldiers rampaging through the city. International activists witnessed Israeli tanks deployed on every corner of the Old City, while troops conducted house-to-house searches and used Palestinian civilians as human shields. (Footage available).

Article 33 of the Fourth Geneva Convention states "No protected person may be punished for an offence he or she has not personally committed. Collective penalties and likewise all measures of intimidation or of terrorism are prohibited. Pillage is prohibited. Reprisals against protected persons and their property are prohibited."

Over two dozen international activists are currently stationed throughout Nablus, including in the Old City and Palestinian Medical Relief Centers bearing witness and trying to stop Israeli atrocities. We call on the United Nations and governments signatory to the Fourth Geneva Convention to take immediate action to stop Israel's violations of international law.

For more information contact:

Jonathan ISM [number withheld], Susan ISM [number withheld], Dr. Ghassan Hamdam UPMRC [number withheld]

ENDS

AT HOME IN AL-FARA'
by Matt Horton, 12 August 2002

[…]

Al-Fara' camp is located between Nablus and Jenin in the region of Tubas. The camp like other refugee camps is crowded and impoverished. Despite closure and upwards of 65% unemployment, the people in the camp were well organized and in good spirits.

It was difficult to stay in the house of the Al-Ghoul family because they were facing much pain. Their son had blown himself up in an operation on 18 June 2002, 10 days after the middle brother was married. The only steadily employed brother lost his job soon after and now their house is going to be destroyed.

They were living with relatives, but because the camp is already crowded enough, it was a difficult situation. In addition, their house was not yet destroyed so their problem had not yet reached a resolution and the pain of the demolition was being drawn out and the inevitable delayed. They kept a smile on their faces, but it would occasionally break and tears would come to their eyes suddenly. One morning the father, a man of over 60 years, broke down crying in front of us. He was a refugee from Haifa in 1948 and now he was a refugee again. His whole life of struggle for his family to live better than him was about to be destroyed.

Our request was to sleep in the house at night and do what we could to save it or at least the neighbors' houses when and if the military came. In the day we were basically on vacation. There was no army to be seen, the weather was nice and the land was beautiful. The camp is in the midst of a rural farming area and sits at the head of the Fara' valley. The Fara' valley has its source in a natural spring which flows into the valley, making it green like a small Nile River valley. One day we were invited to a house in the valley and walked through orchards of limes and fruit, tomato fields and even a few palm and banana trees.

INTERNATIONAL DAY OF ACTION AGAINST HOME DEMOLITIONS IN PALESTINE
by The People of Nablus, 23 August 2002

The people of Nablus, Palestine, joined by international civilians and local Palestinian organizations will hold a candlelight march on Friday August 23rd 2002 and ask all people of the world to join them in a protest against the illegal Israeli policy of home demolitions.

The Global Campaign to Rebuild Palestinian Homes, states that "the systematic demolition of Palestinian homes throughout the Occupied Territories, together with the destruction of the Palestinian infrastructure including health records, records of citizenship and ownership of land goes far beyond mere retaliation for terrorist attacks. It is an attack on an entire people, an attempt to make the Palestinians submit to a mini-state under Israeli control."

History
The facts and figures of this brutal Israeli policy are stunning. According to the Israeli Commitee Against Home Demolitions "in 1999 about 100 homes were demolished, down from 277 in 1998. Yet 2000 demolition orders remain outstanding in the West Bank, another 2000 for East Jerusalem, altogether threatening some 6000 families. The Bedouin population, harassed and being driven into tiny "reservations", is also targeted." THE SUSTAIN Campaign maintains that "since the beginning of the present Palestinian uprising, or Intifada, in September of 2000, the Israeli military has destroyed more than 2650 Palestinian homes, offices, buildings and other civilian structures ..."

International observation
Since the end of June the International Solidarity Movement has had activists in Nablus homes that are slated for demolition. The Internationals are living in the intensely

oppressive atmosphere that permeates the lives of people who do not know if they will have a home or even be alive to see the next day.

"They [Israeli soldiers] locked the family in a room on the second floor, put all of their furniture in a pile on the first floor, burned it, pocketed the family's life savings, and detonated a plastic explosive on the first floor to weaken the structure so the bulldozer would have an easier time knocking it down. Tiles fell off the kitchen and bathroom walls on all 3 floors, glass broke throughout the home, and huge cracks appeared in the walls. The IDF pulled their bulldozer back though, because someone had called the media and they decided it wasn't such a good idea to bulldoze the home down with the family inside on International TV." July 2002 Marissa McLaughlin.

"One of the problems is that the military doesn't always evacuate the other homes, or warn the neighbors of a demolition. Again this is in a refugee camp, the houses are all really close to one another. This can mean neighboring houses also go down—with people in them. The brother of the family some of the other New Yorkers are staying with had the first floor of his home destroyed by tank shelling. He and his son were inside. His son was okay but he broke both of his legs and was wheelchair-bound, now he has canes." August 04, 2002 by Amanda Devecka-Rinear.

Israeli policy

The Israeli government has consistently upheld every facet of this ridiculous and illegal policy. A recent supreme court ruling made it impossible for the families to even have a 2 hour warning prior to demolition. An earlier court ruling highlights the injustice of the situation:

"The state's attorney said that while there was no evidence that the family had been involved in the son's deeds, the house demolition was justified because it would deter other potential terrorists …" Ha'Aretz Daily.

A child witnessing the destruction of his or her home is not going to limit the anger and hatred that will develop for the oppressive regime of the Israeli government.

International law

"Under the 1949 Geneva Conventions, collective punishments are a war crime. Article 33 of the Fourth Convention states: "No protected person may be punished for an offense he or she has not personally committed," and "collective penalties and likewise all measures of intimidation or of terrorism are prohibited."

In World War II, Nazis carried out a form of collective punishment to suppress resistance. Entire villages or towns or districts were held responsible for any resistance activity that took place there. The conventions, to counter this, reiterated the principle of individual responsibility. The International Committee of the Red Cross (ICRC) Commentary to the conventions states that parties to a conflict often would resort to "intimidatory measures to terrorize the population" in hopes of preventing hostile acts, but such practices "strike at guilty and innocent alike. They are opposed to all principles based on humanity and justice."

The law of armed conflict applies similar protections to an internal conflict. Common Article 3 of the four Geneva Conventions of 1949 requires fair trials for all individuals before punishments; and Additional Protocol II of 1977 explicitly forbids collective punishment."

We need your help ...

The people of Nablus ask you to join in solidarity against the brutal policy of home demolition.

Actions can include vigils at major Israeli, US and British embassies, street demonstrations and protests.

We also ask you to support the SUSTAIN campaign against the Caterpillar Corporation.

"Caterpillar D-9 bulldozers have become such an active part of the IDF's activities that the term "D-9" is as common to school kids here as "Apache" or "Cobra" helicopters, or the much more terrifying "F-16" fighter jets. The official IDF website documents their main purpose—home demolition .... The dozers (or, in some cases, pneumatic breakers) then demolish the homes, proceeding from the second floor to the first. The whole operation takes from 30 minutes to three days, depending on its scope and intensity." from The Electronic Intifada.

SLEEPING IN THE BED OF A SUICIDE BOMBER
by Paul Larudee, September 2002

The young wife of Amer Nabulsi (not his real name) had a special way of coping with his death. She decorated their room with pictures of children and young couples, valentine hearts, teddy bears, and other irrepressibly cute images. Some were happy, a few sad, and others in love. Some were cut from magazines; others were posters, cards or stickers. To these images she added her own words and symbols.

I sleep in their room, so her artwork surrounds me every morning and evening. Much of it is in Arabic, which I don't read very well, but the tears and broken hearts drawn with marking pens speak clearly enough, as do the few English words, "I love you and miss you."

The reason I sleep here is that she has fled the house, along with most of the family. Out of a total of ten family members, only Amer's parents are here, along with me and other members of the International Solidarity Movement from the US, Ireland, Italy, the UK and other countries. Israeli authorities have threatened to demolish the house, despite the fact that it is a war crime to do so. The Fourth Geneva Convention, to which Israel is a signatory, outlaws collective punishment of entire families or communities. We want to try to prevent this from happening, or at least put up non-violent resistance.

No one knows for sure why Amer chose to become an istishhad (one who martyrs him/herself). By Palestinian standards, he had every reason not to. He had a job, a home, a car, a loving wife and daughter. While not wealthy, he did not have to worry about becoming needy.

Furthermore, his mother and father consider suicide bombings to be immoral. They are deeply devout Muslims, but are among the vast majority who believe that any form of suicide is against Islam. They spend much of their time reading the Koran and praying. In spite of this, or perhaps because of it, they are quite liberal by local standards, and highly tolerant. Their youngest daughter wears jeans and wouldn't be seen in the hijab, or traditional head covering, and her relationship with her fiancé is anything but traditional, with her parents' blessing. Amer's father cannot talk for long about him without tears welling up in his eyes and his face being transformed by grief.

What led Amer to put on a vest of Semtex and cause his flesh to be scattered by its explosive force? Part of the reason might be the anger that he must have felt when his father suffered brain damage from a beating administered by Israeli forces. Mr. Nabulsi's left side was left partly paralyzed and he now speaks with difficulty, as if he had had a stroke. Still, that was seven years ago.

More recently, a friend was killed in a car that was destroyed by Israeli gunfire. His family also reports that he was strongly moved by both the news and personal reports of the Israeli invasion of Ramallah in early March, 2002, and especially the siege of the presidential compound. However, such experiences are common to most Palestinians, and do not necessarily make them suicide bombers.

What was the difference in Amer's case?

I can only speculate, but it may have been the strong sense of moral right and wrong, of justice and injustice, that his parents instilled in him. It permeates the family, and can be seen as they drop by for meals and conversation with their parents, in which I am invited to share. The small children get plenty of love and patience, but no indulgence. Even the slightest disciplinary action comes with a moral dictum, however brief.

It may be that Amer simply grew impatient with the injustice he saw around him. Perhaps it was the daily humiliation at the ubiquitous checkpoints, where Palestinians pass only with the permission of the soldiers on duty.

Perhaps it was the increasing sight of Israeli settlements, built on confiscated Palestinian land, on the hilltops surrounding the city.

Perhaps it was the arbitrary arrest and/or assassination of thousands of "suspects" by Israeli security forces, the use of torture, now considered legal in Israel, and the unlimited detention without charges.

Perhaps it was the refusal to allow him and 3.3 million others in Gaza and the West Bank to worship in Jerusalem, the holiest city in the country to all religions. Perhaps it was the diversion of water resources, the deaths of ambulance patients at checkpoints, the bulldozing of olive and fruit orchards, or the construction of settler roads, which Palestinians are permitted neither to use nor cross.

I have been with the family for two weeks now, and it is time to go, although our group will continue to maintain a presence at this and other homes, as the situation warrants. When the Israeli Occupation forces choose to commit war crimes, they prefer to do so away from the eyes of international observers.

I would have stayed even if the family had been a misanthropic group of wild-eyed fanatics, because a war crime is a war crime. However, they are kind, generous, and courageous, and we have bonded during my stay. We kiss each other on the cheeks and exchange contact information. They invite me to come to their daughter's wedding. I promise to call.

Suicide attacks against innocent noncombatants are also a war crime, and Amer's family is right to condemn them. However, I do not see wild-eyed religious fanaticism as the reason for the attacks. I see instead a resilient people without other means of resistance, pushed to desperation by the increasing pressures of ethnic cleansing, while their cries for help are ignored.

Is there a proud people anywhere that might not be driven to such measures to defend themselves?

NABLUS DECISION: RESISTANCE
by Hussein Khalili, February 2003

During the last four days of continuous Israeli Occupation Forces operations in the Old City of Nablus eight people have been killed and more than 50 injured. The IOF demolished one building and damaged hundreds of houses all around the Old City. Rat holes were opened by explosives in the walls of the houses in order to make it easy and safe for the soldiers to pass from house to house. The destruction is huge but without any results for the Israelis. Until now the IOF didn't even arrest one wanted person they didn't break the resistance. On the contrary the people's resistance has become stronger. All inhabitants of Nablus engaged in mass shouting and whistling in the evening of the fourth day of this operation. Hundreds of thousands of people were shouting and whistling for more than one hour in a very beautiful way to resist the Occupation. Thousands of people went out of their houses into the streets in a mass demonstration.

We were very tired that evening after four days of working in the rain. We were moving from one occupied house to another, delivering medicine, food and baby milk for the people under the siege. I went with Maria to have a break in our flat and to change our wet clothes. Half an hour later we started to hear noise from outside. Maria asked me what was going on. I opened the window and I found that all the people in the area around the neighbourhood where I live were shouting "Allah akbar" and many people were in the street already marching toward the Old City. We went down the stairs to the street. It was very beautiful to see all those people in the street and to hear the shouting from the hills in the north and the south sides of the city.

Hundreds of people moved toward the Old City and most people were outdoors shouting and whistling. I stopped and asked a guy about what was going on and he said:

"There was an announcement in the local TV asking the people to protest against the destruction and the killing which is taking place in the Old City."

One announcement on the TV mobilized all those people to go out and protest in the cold weather. I received phone calls from friends in different places in the city and they said that people were shouting and protesting in the camps as well. I heard a woman saying to her daughter while walking in the street:

"In April they succeeded to make us afraid but not any more. They are stupid if they think that this terror can scare us."

I have never seen anything as beautiful as this, Maria said. To me it was a very emotional experience and it took me back in time to the first Intifada. I am always surprised by the strength of my people even though I know how they can create ways of struggle. The first Intifada showed the people the power that they have and now when the people get the chance to use their power they use it. Now I really have a strong feeling that all this destruction and military presence in the streets of Nablus make the people stronger than ever and increase the resistance. The people create new ways of resisting. Every day there are clashes around the occupied houses and in the streets, hundreds of shabab [youths] attack the military vehicles with stones and Molotov cocktails, many demonstrations are organized from different places toward the Old City.

After six days the IOF changed their strategy and now they hide in very few houses trying to confuse the people but the people pass information among themselves about where the soldiers are. In this operation it was clear that the people knew how expensive freedom is and they know that to end this Occupation they need to pay the price and they did and they are ready to pay more.

During the operation volunteers from the UPMRC (Union of Palestinian Medical Relief Committee), the Red Crescent and the Union of Health Care Committees were working 24 hours a day rescuing injured people, delivering food and medicine to the people in the occupied houses. Many of them were forced to strip in the rain and many had been detained for hours but they still kept moving from one place to another in the rain risking their lives to help others. Those volunteers were heroes during this operation. I do not have words to describe how great they were.

The decision of Nablus is to resist.

10

THE OLIVE HARVEST

WHOSE RIGHTS, WHOSE OLIVES?
by Claire and Angie, 5 October 2002

The Israeli voice on the phone identified himself as Didi from Peace Now. 'You left a message asking about the level of fanaticism in the settlements in your region,' he prompted calmly.

Yes, I said, we were about to enter into the harvest season and were putting together a campaign for international volunteers to accompany Palestinian villagers—we were interested in trying to determine what was the likelihood of serious attack from settlements nearby.

The surreal conversation continued with Didi giving us a rundown on the scene in our area. 'Where are you based exactly?' I told him Hares, near Ariel. 'Ah, so Ariel isn't probably going to be too much problem, you know it's a big settlement, one of the biggest, but most of them are students and so on, you know, what we call "quality of life" settlers ... but Ravava is near you, isn't it, yes, they are quite serious, and then you've got Immanual, they're Orthodox religious, and because of the shooting there last year, and Ma'ale Shomron and Karnei Shomron, they could be dangerous, and

Photograph by Neal Cassidy.

Yakir and Nofim, they are bad, and Altei Menasche a bit further north, and Sharei Tikva and Els Efrayim to the west a bit [he was describing an area with a diameter of less than 20 km], but I wouldn't say they were going to cause as many problems as the settlers around Nablus, they are really crazy … your biggest problem is going to be Tapu'akh, definitely. Those guys, I mean they're as bad as the settlers in Hebron!'

Three days later in the village of Yasouf, Mohammed Obeid picked up the phone to call the Israeli police. 'They're at it again', he told the bored sounding voice on the other end, 'the settlers from Tapu'akh, they're down there on my land, picking my olives and threatening my family with their guns.'

The policeman told Mohammed to give him his 'position'. Mohammed told him that Yasouf was the Palestinian village on the hill opposite the recently expanded settlement of Tapu'akh. The policeman said he didn't know where that was and would call back when he had located it on a map.

Mohammed replaced the phone on the cradle and sighed. The policeman, who was sitting at a desk in Ariel less than 5 km away, had to be either stupid or lying. Tapu'akh could almost be said to be an outlying suburb of Ariel, and even Yasouf is marked on the 2000 edition of the Israel Road Atlas (the crude Israeli 'roadblock', however, which effectively seals off Yasouf to vehicular access, is not marked).

This was the fifth time in three days that Mohammed had called the police about the settlers on his land. If they didn't act soon it would be too late, and all the olives would be gone. Today was slightly different, however: an international activist, Angie from IWPS [International Women's Peace Service], had arrived at the village, and was also calling the same police, announcing her intention to accompany a peaceful delegation of Yasouf farmers down onto the land to approach the settlers and ask them to stop stealing the olives.

Perhaps it is because of Angie's call that, unusually, half an hour later, Mohammed's phone rings again and it's a policeman calling from a patrol car. 'We can't find your position', he says. Mohammed begins again to try to explain but the policeman interrupts him, uninterested. 'You have to come and meet us so that you can show us where you are', he explains, 'meet us in Jama'iin.'

'No. Please.' Mohammed is desperate, Jama'iin is too far away and impossible to reach by car from Yasouf, thanks to the roadblock. Were Mohammed to drive to the roadblock and walk to Jama'iin it would take him all day. 'Better that you come to Tapu'akh gate,' he tells them. Tapu'akh's entrance is a concrete, wire and tarmac confection, cosmetically augmented by heavily irrigated flowers beds and shrubs. It feeds onto the Yasouf road just to the unblocked side, making it five minutes by car alone from the main settler highway and Ariel.

'Can we meet there in ten minutes?' Mohammed asks. 'Alright,' says the policeman gruffly, and promptly hangs up.

Angie and the little band of elderly farmers (Rukaya, Rashid, Ahmad, Hasan, Mohamed, Yusad, Marouf and Issa) are approaching the area where the settlers were stripping the trees (they have stopped since they noticed the villagers on their way). Suddenly one of the settlers fires at them, a 'warning' shot that hits the ground on the path about ten yards ahead of their feet. The Palestinian villagers sit down, and Angie stands in front them calling out that she is a foreigner and that they have come peacefully and are not armed. Through the trees, although they are still a way off, Angie can see them and they seem to be discussing what to do.

Mohammed has reached the entrance to Tapu'akh, he is waiting a little way down from the entrance on the opposite side of the road—it's a deserted area but Mohammed is scared to get too close to the entrance in case the security guard in the watch tower fires at him. After a minute he sees the police car, he steps out into the road to wave, the driver looks at him for a split second and drives right past into the settlement. Mohammed—who is a sixty-something father of six—tries to run behind the car a little way to stop it, but to no avail.

He is standing there wondering what to do when an ear-splitting siren starts up and looking down through the entrance to the settlement, Mohammed can see the police car parked in the main square, and armed settlers amassing in response the siren, clambering into cars and racing off out of the settlement through the far gate which leads directly down the hill to the area where Angie and the farmers are stranded.

Mohammed is watching, but the police car does not follow the settlers. He waits for fifteen minutes but the police car doesn't move, not to pursue the armed and angry mob, nor to come and meet Mohammed as arranged. Angie and the villagers' calls for help from the police are not getting through, or they're getting the same message as Mohammed: 'We don't know where you are.' Now there are armed settlers, one with a dog, pouring down the hill towards their brethren on the hillside. There is a standoff but the settlers are beginning to get closer.

Angie speaks again to the police, and, although this is Yasouf-owned land and the settlers are the ones who are trespassing, stealing, shooting and threatening violence, this time the police's advice is simply for the villagers to 'leave the area'. The villagers do decide to leave, and it's as if this was the cue that the settlers were waiting for, and they rush at the group, throwing stones and shouting.

Angie stands her ground while the old men begin to walk back and she is soon surrounded by the angry mob, one man tears the camera from around her neck, another wrestles her bag from her hands. She tries to resist, but there are too many of them. She is about to speak when a settler cuts her off, barking, 'Leave, or there will be bloodshed and you will be responsible.' She tries again, 'I'm not leaving. Give me back my bag and my camera.' Her camera disappears while her bag is searched and papers torn up, ending up on one of the settler's backs, but her passport and money are thrown at her.

After a few minutes, most of them leave, heading down to watch the old villagers being chased further down the hill. At least one stone thrown met its target, when seventy-five year old Rashid Saleh is struck on his shoulder. Two settlers and a dog are left to guard Angie, who is insisting that she will wait there until the police come so that she can have the settlers arrested and get back her things. After almost an hour the two settlers leave her and as there are still no policemen on the scene, she heads back to Yasouf village.

Later that same day, Angie gets to Ariel police station and makes a statement. She is shown photographs of settlers from Tapu'akh who already have records on file at the station, but none of them look like the men who took her stuff. The policeman showing her the photos tells her that they have a lot of problems with Tapu'akh and that they do prosecute them, but they need evidence. However, they refuse to accompany her to the settlement so that she can identify the settlers or to help her search for her things. They allow her to write her statement and file it away.

Although it is 10 pm and dark by the time she is through, they drive her only to the entrance to the settlement and she is left to walk the three miles home alone. She leaves with the police promising that they will help to 'protect' the Palestinian villagers while they try to harvest their olives. The next day Mohammed calls IWPS because the settlers are back again. The villagers watch all day helplessly from their houses, but the police never respond and the settlers cart away sackloads more of the precious fruit.

The story of what's been happening in Yasouf begins to get out, and Arik Asherman from Rabbis for Human Rights has called around and managed to get a group of about twenty-five Israeli peace activists who are prepared to come to Yasouf to help the Palestinians to salvage what's left of the olives from the most vulnerable areas closest to the settlement. What begins as a scene of hope and unity ends in a terrible day. The settlers come down from their caravans on the hillside to abuse the harvesters, shouting obscenities and religious slogans, gesticulating rudely and jeering at the cameramen and journalists.

They are particularly harsh to the visiting Israelis, even confronting them physically in some cases. More worryingly, some policemen seem to agree with them: when a settler with an American accent tells an Israeli to get lost and 'go home', and the Israeli tells him to do the same, the policeman sharply rebukes him emphasizing, 'Actually, this is their land, their home.' A Canadian cameraman wants to interview the settlers, but the police and soldiers won't let him near them. Suddenly, Angie recognizes a settler, the one who was part of the gang who took her camera and bag, but for some reason, even though at the station she was asked to try to identify him, now police refuse to get involved, and seem much more interested in ending this increasingly uncomfortable scene.

And so, while the Palestinians are trying to ignore the crazy situation between two groups of Israelis, and just get on with harvesting, the Army suddenly declares the area a 'closed military zone' and first to have to leave the area are … the Palestinians and their 'sympathizers'. No one wants to go, so the police have to start physically pushing them away down the hill. When someone asks the commander why the settlers are still being allowed to stand there and gloat upon the scene, he tells them, 'Because you and the Palestinians are easier to get rid of.'

They try to set up their harvesting tools, their ladders and sheets further down the hill, but the Army keep advancing and forcing them all the way down. Some Palestinians are angry, and try to sit down in protest, but a hostile Army with guns at their finger-tips can be very persuasive. Some of the Israeli activists offer to take their places on the ground, but it accomplishes nothing, and after a few minutes, it's the Palestinians who persuade them gently to come away and wash their hands for the meal that the village had prepared in welcome and thanks—and in the vain hope of for once having something to celebrate …

[…]

YANOUN
by Hussein Khalili, 22 October 2003

For more than 300 years many generations of Palestinian farmers living in Yanoun, a small village of 150 people, east of Nablus, depended on raising animals and on olives, the Palestinian gold.

Yanoun is located 3km to the north of Aqraba and it is as ancient as the olive trees that cover the surrounding hills. There is an Israeli settlement located 200 meters from the houses of Yanoun called Itamar. The settlers used to attack the farmers in Yanoun, especially during the olive harvest when the farmers are picking their olives. During the last two years the settlers attacked the village every week.

This season from the very beginning of the olive harvest the settlers have been attacking the olive fields and the village daily, and have forced many families to leave the village. This is a unique and very dangerous situation, as it is truly the only village that has been vacated due to settler aggression and violence. A typical settler attack includes descending upon the village during the middle of the night, kicking doors and windows, climbing on the roofs, firing arms, and generally terrorizing the entire village. These ruthless attacks and the great fear that the settlers have induced have left the village completely abandoned and houses empty.

We went today to the village and talked with the people this afternoon. Currently there is no electricity and no water in the village because settlers have destroyed both the electric motor and the water tanks that supply the village with drinking water. We talked to many families who want to return to Yanoun tomorrow, but are currently obliged to sleep in Aqraba far from their land and their homes. These families are terrified of the settlers and the children especially are suffering immensely psychologically—some of the children would not stop crying because they thought that the Internationals were settlers.

Internationals and Israeli peace activists are sleeping in Yanoun with the two families who are in the village and tomorrow morning many families will courageously attempt to return to Yanoun.

MASSIVE ISRAELI SETTLER ATTACK ON FOREIGN VOLUNTEERS IN PALESTINE
Number of Internationals injured and hospitalized
International Solidarity Movement, 27 October 2003

FOR IMMEDIATE RELEASE

[YANOUN, NABLUS] Militant Israeli settlers attacked a group of international volunteers working with Palestinians to harvest olives in the olive groves near the West Bank village of Yanoun.

Immediately after a Palestinian operation in the illegal Israeli settlement of Ariel that killed two Israeli settlers and soldiers, a group of about a dozen armed Israeli settlers spotted the Palestinian farmers from their settlement (which is illegal under the Fourth Geneva Conventions), and descended upon the international volunteers, kicking, punching and beating them with stones and rifles butts. The Internationals were in front of the Palestinian workers, trying to protect them from the settlers. The injuries are as follows:

James Deleplain—US citizen, 74 years of age—repeatedly hit in the face, wound under his left eye and massive swelling, kicked in the back and both the right and left rib cage, with a broken rib and punctured lung. James had pneumonia two weeks ago and has been coughing since, therefore the beating, especially in the rib cage has left him in a very weak state.

Mary Hughes-Thompson—US and British citizen, 68 years of age—repeatedly hit in both arms. Possible broken arms. Speaking to Mary while she was on her way to the hospital, she stated "I am convinced they were trying to kill me."

Robbie Kelly—Irish citizen, 33 years of age—beaten in the face and body with rifle butts. Swollen mouth, bruised ribs and 7 stitches in his left ear.

Omer Allon—Israeli citizen, 24—cuts and gashes in both legs and bruises all over his body.

The Internationals' money and passports were stolen by the attackers, all of whom were teenagers. Palestinians in the area may have also been attacked but we don't have concrete information yet.

Internationals and Israelis have been providing a continual presence in the village of Yanoun, due to constant Israeli settler attacks on Palestinian villagers and their property. Last week the villagers of Yanoun left the village, not able to withstand the repeated attacks and denied protection by the Israeli police and military. They only returned a few days ago accompanied by Israelis and Internationals, hoping to monitor, witness and protect.

ENDS

PERMISSION TO PICK
by Kate Raphael, 1 November 2002

Dan, Lysander and I picked with a family whose orchards face an Ariel military outpost. The family was very afraid. When we sat on their porch having tea, one of the women, whose English is pretty good, told us that twice last week they had been told by soldiers to go home. Yesterday, gas was thrown into their field.

She asked Dan to talk to the soldiers and tell them they want to pick there for three days. I said I would go with Dan, since he would be leaving at noon and I was staying all day. As we walked into the grove, we heard shooting. I looked up to see soldiers at the checkpoint. I wanted to head up right away, but the family wanted us to go to their fields first. As soon as we got there, we smelled the gas and saw the spent canister on the ground. I called Angie at our house, told her about the gas and asked her to call the DCO, or District Coordinating Office, about it. Dan, Lysander and I got our things ready and headed up toward the checkpoint.

After about 100 meters, halfway between the fields and the checkpoint, the soldiers started yelling. One came out with his gun pointed at us. I yelled in Hebrew, "We want to speak with you. Is there anyone who speaks English?" They answered in English, "Who are you? What are you doing here?" I gave my standard rap, we're Internationals, we're here with the family who owns this land, we only want to pick the olives for four days. "You can't pick here, this is a closed military area. Go back." I produced my standard lie, that I had talked to the DCO, and they said we had the right to pick there.

They yelled, "You have permission from the DCO?" "Yes." "Let me see it." "I don't have it here, it was a phone call." "What's the license number?" I felt surprisingly calm, considering that I was being caught lying to men with guns pointed at me. Dan jumped in. "We don't have to give you a number. If this is a closed military area, let us see the order." The conversation turned ugly in a hurry.

"You have two minutes to get the fuck out of here, or you will have tear-gas on your heads." I hesitated. "I don't want to draw gas into the field," I said to Dan. "We can't back down," he answered. I felt that was true. The family was counting on us. They needed to see us take a stand, not just be told no and go away. I continued to argue with the soldiers, one of whom soon said to me, "One minute, or I shoot you." I called Angie back to see if she'd made any progress with the DCO. She said she'd left a message. In fact, the soldiers mentioned last Sunday's bombing but nothing about a shooting. While I was on the phone Dan continued to argue with the soldiers. I didn't hear all of what they said, but at one point, just as Angie was saying, "The Army has the last word," one of them said, "I'm just like the police in New York. I can do whatever I want." This was interspersed with one of them saying, "We don't want to make any problems," and Dan and me chorusing, "Neither do we."

I noticed their pretense at not speaking much English had vanished, though the one who kept threatening to shoot us ended one of his threats with, "Sorry I don't speak English so well. Speak Hebrew perfectly." "Your English is fine," I couldn't help saying. I realized we had overstayed this confrontation. Dan quickly agreed, we were not accomplishing anything: we had made our point, we would go back and talk to the family.

They were already picking, and we started picking too as we told them what had happened. They said if there was any more gas, they were going to leave. I fervently prayed that wouldn't happen. A few minutes later, we saw a cloud of gas. The family said they were going to finish the tree we were on and move, but the gas didn't come into their field, so they changed their minds.

Claire called and said the DCO was apparently out of town, but she had talked to his secretary who said we did have permission to pick. I couldn't believe it. I asked if there were a number or anything I could give to the soldiers. She said she didn't get that, and gave me the phone number so I could call. I called the number three times before it was answered. When I told the secretary what I wanted, she said, "Where are you exactly?" I tried to explain. She kept saying, "I need to know your exact position, or I can't help you." I tried getting one of the family members to tell her, but she didn't understand, or pretended she didn't. "I can't help you," she said and hung up.

I felt I was starting to know what Palestinians feel like, but then I reminded myself that the Palestinians can't even make those calls.

[...]

TWO PROTESTORS INJURED TRYING TO PROTECT PALESTINIAN OLIVE TREES!
Partial success in delaying massive destruction
International Solidarity Movement (ISM) and Grassroots International Protection For Palestinians (GIPP), 4 November 2002

FOR IMMEDIATE RELEASE

[Falami, Qalqilia District] This morning at 8:00 am Palestinian Falami farmers along with a group of approximately 20 International civilians were attacked by hired Israeli Security Personnel as they tried to peacefully protest the destruction of the Palestinian agricultural land.

Israeli government contractors along with Israeli private security overlooked by the Israeli military continued to chop down trees and even managed to destroy 10–15 trees. As the group of Internationals peacefully came between the contractors and trees ready to be chopped down the hired security personnel (hired security personnel are usually Israeli soldiers or Israeli police) began to aggressively push volunteers away from the trees. Volunteers who wouldn't step away from the trees began "hugging" the trees as their bodies were being pulled away by the security personnel. Many volunteers had been attacked by the Israeli security and three had sustained minor injuries.

Adam Keller, late 40's Israeli citizen, a volunteer from the Gush Shalom Organization was attacked and kicked by the security personnel and was almost cut in half by a chainsaw as he hugged the tree while the contractor was chopping the tree.

Tom Dale, 18 year old British citizen was also attacked by the security personnel as he stood chatting with a group of volunteers. Tom was also beaten and kicked as the Israeli military stood by and watched and sustained bruises on his body.

Emily Winkelstein, 27 years old and a U. S citizen sustained scratches on her body as she was being dragged away.

Heidi Niggeman, 29 years old a German citizen was beaten and punched in the stomach as she tried to stop a contractor/worker from Chopping down a tree with a chainsaw.

Dan O' Reilly-Rowe, 25 years old Australian/ American was kicked in the stomach and attacked repeatedly by the security personnel as he held on to save the tree from being destroyed. Dan was nailed to the ground 5–6 times by the security men and is suffering from a twisted ankle.

Yesterday and today Palestinian farmers and Internationals have been partially successful in delaying any more destruction of their land.

Tomorrow morning November 5, 2002 at 8:00 AM Palestinian farmers and International volunteers will again sit on the land. The French Ambassador along with members of the Israeli Parliament will accompany the Palestinian farmers in a joint attempt to stop the Israeli destruction of Palestinian land.

Photos and video footage of todays attacks available by calling below.

For more information contact:

Heidi Niggeman [number withheld], Huwaidaa Shapiro [number withheld], Osama Qashoo' [number withheld]
ISM OFFICE [number withheld]

ENDS

ALL BECAUSE OF A SMALL OLIVE
by Uri Avnery, 2 November 2002, The Other Israel

Why has the Sharon–Ben-Eliezer–Peres government collapsed? Because of a small olive.

It started like a children's tale: Once upon a time there was a small olive in a Palestinian village. It grew and ripened on a branch of an old tree in a grove on the top of a hill. "Pick me! I want to give my oil!" the little olive pleaded. But it went on ripening, and the pickers did not come. They could not reach it, because the settlers had set up two mobile homes on the hill, and the whole area became a "security region" of this outpost. When the owners of the grove approached, the settlers cursed them, beat them up and started shooting. This happened at dozens of locations all over the West Bank.

The villagers called the IDF, which now controls all the Palestinian territories. But the army did not come to protect them. Many of the army officers are themselves settlers. The army considers that its job is to defend the settlers, and does not like the idea of confronting them. When the army did interfere, it was to drive the villagers out of their groves near the outposts.

In their plight, the villagers called on the Israeli peace organizations. They found them willing.

The Israeli "peace camp" consists of two parts. One, centered around "Peace Now", is connected with the Labor party, which was a pillar of the government. The party chief served as Minister of Defense and was, therefore, responsible for all the iniquities committed in the Palestinian territories.

The other part of the peace camp consists of many radical groups, each active in its chosen sector. "Gush Shalom" is a political and ideological center. "Ta'ayush", an Arab-Jewish Israeli group, is aiding the besieged Palestinian population. "B'Tselem" collects and publishes data, as does the "Alternative Information Center". "Physicians for Human Rights" does a wonderful job in the medical field, while the Women's Coalition for Peace and Bat-Shalom combine human rights activities with a feminist agenda. "The Committee against House Demolition" initiates the rebuilding of homes destroyed by the army, and "Rabbis for Human Rights" is acting on behalf of the (unfortunately, tiny) religious community that does not follow the fanatical nationalist banner. "Machsom

Watch" reports and tries to prevent abuses at the checkpoints. "Yesh Gvul" helps soldiers who refuse to serve in the occupied territories. "New Profile" is active in the same area. The list is long. Activists of different groups frequently cooperate, and many belong to more than one.

The activists of these organizations volunteered to help the villagers. They went out to pick olives and to defend the villagers as a "human shield". They were joined by European peace activists, who come in shifts to help the occupied Palestinian population. On some days there were dozens of Israeli and international activists in the groves, on Saturdays there were hundreds. They were dispersed in different villages, went up the hills and were attacked by the settlers. In dozens of incidents, the settlers started shooting into the air and at the ground around the olive pickers.

During long weeks, the public did not hear anything about these events. There is a conspiracy of silence in the media concerning the very existence of a radical peace camp. "Peace Now" is considered somehow as belonging to the national consensus, and therefore its actions are (scantily) reported. The actions of the more principled and energetic forces ("The Deep Left" in the words of former Prime Minister Ehud Barak, who abhors them) were not reported at all, unless there was bloodshed. But slowly, reports about the War of the Olives began to infiltrate the media: about the settlers driving the Palestinians away and robbing them of the olives they had picked; about settlers who picked the olives in the groves themselves after driving the owners away; about settlers setting fire to groves; about the former Chief Rabbi, who announced that Jews are justified in taking away the fruits for which the Arab villagers had toiled, because God has given the fruit of the Land to the Jews.

The conspiracy of silence was finally broken when a group of famous writers organized a token olive picking. The media, which had ignored the devoted work of the hundreds of anonymous activists, were happy to join celebrities like Amos Oz, A. B. Yehoshua, David Grossman and Me'ir Shalev. The olive picking became part of the consensus.

[...]

This is an example of the working of the "small wheel" doctrine formulated by us decades ago: a small wheel with a strong independent drive turns a bigger wheel, which turns an even bigger wheel, and so on, until the whole big machine starts operating.

That's how a small political group, with an independent and determined agenda, can drive decisive political processes when the timing is right.

We still have a long way to go. The danger of fascism is still hovering over this country. However, it has now been proven that things can be moved in the opposite direction.

Perhaps the small olive on the hill is mightier than a one-ton bomb.

AN IMPORTANT STEP IN THE RIGHT DIRECTION
by Ghassan Andoni, 27 October 2002

Despite brutality, intimidation, physical attacks, and continued provocations, Palestinian villagers and ISM international and local activists are proceeding with harvesting olives.

Many of the olive groves that were out of reach for villagers for years are being harvested. This year no one could expropriate the olive harvesting season. For the first time in years the Occupation army and Israeli settlers were forced to accommodate the determination and strong will of Palestinian villagers and international activists. For the first time those peaceful, empty-handed, decent people proved that power, aggressiveness, and intimidation have limits. That the occupier cannot always dictate the rules of the game.

This is the time in which people discovered the strength of being peaceful and determined at the same time; that people could step out of their fears and practice their natural rights against the will of the occupier; it is the time in which the empty hands and proud souls won against guns and Occupation violence. It is the time in which peace and justice stepped forward and greed and aggression retreated.

The first days of the campaign were hard. Settlers and soldiers used all the oppressive tools available to crack down the will of the people. Settlers burned olive groves (Mazraa Alsharqia); they moved into Palestinian olive groves along with foreign workers and harvested and stole olives (Jayyous); they physically attacked olive harvesters by shooting at them and throwing stones (in almost all places); the army prevented harvesters from arriving at their fields; they forced harvesters out of the fields; tear-gas, sound bombs, and machine guns were fired at the peaceful harvesters; many were arrested; and some were injured.

All of this did not stop the harvesters from coming back again and again. As an army officer in Yasouf said "Today we failed and you won."

Today we won because we were full of determination, because we were peaceful, because we were active and they were reactive, because we controlled our feelings of anger and did not respond to their intimidation, because they went out of control.

We won because we struggled for life and they stood against it, because we waged peace with more determination than their desire for war. Today we won because no one, regardless of how cunning and smart he is, could disguise the Occupation or could turn the issue into an existential war or a war against terrorism. We won because we fought for life to continue.

We won because hundreds of Palestinian villagers became proactive in defending their rights. We won because of the great local community leaders who showed a great level of leadership and demonstrated an outstanding ability in leading the campaign. We won because what was a dream is on its way to becoming reality. Civil disobedience is spreading widely and is becoming an important and integral part of the Palestinian efforts to end the Israeli Occupation.

We won because we fought out of hope and not out of desperation. This is the glory of Palestine; seeds of hope can still be planted in the midst of the overwhelming despair.

We are winning a campaign but we know that it is only a step in the road to end the Occupation. A huge amount of work still lies ahead of us all. We need to stand against the concrete monster, we need to dismantle the inhuman network of road blocks and checkpoints; we need to protect the land from settler greed. We need to deprive the Occupation of its tools of oppression and control. We need to cut the Occupation's claws. We need to force the occupiers to adjust to the needs of an active civil-based resistance.

With this campaign we started the first steps down a long road. With more determination, and with more massive and regular work, we will be able to move steadily towards peace and justice.

11

THE APARTHEID WALL

STOP THE WALL "SNAKING THROUGH THE WEST BANK"
by Jamal Jumma', 15 August 2003, Miami Herald

Palestinians have been watching with great despair Prime Minister Mahmoud Abbas' visit to Washington. Amidst the rhetoric of negotiations, over 100 bulldozers are working non-stop every day to continue construction of the Wall. This construction highlights the actual path that the Road Map is paving. While President Bush was correct in calling the Wall "a problem" and referring to it as "snaking through the West Bank," on the ground there is no sign of an end to what has been called the largest "project" ever in Israel.

In this context, the negotiation process seems void of any meaning, or a smoke-screen for what is being implemented on the ground.

Expected to be the largest land grab since 1967, the year Israel occupied the West Bank and the Gaza Strip, current projections suggest the Wall (misleadingly referred to as the "security fence"), with an expected length of 400 miles, will secure Israeli control of almost one-half of the West Bank. The Wall is snaking its way up to 4 miles inside the West Bank, and in some areas may cut 10 miles into the West Bank. It

Photograph by Radhika Sainath.

consistently follows a path that ensures maximum settlement annexation and large-scale control of Palestinian lands.

The Wall takes on a number of horrific constructs. In some areas, it consists of an 8 meter (25 feet) high concrete edifice with armed watchtowers hovering over residential areas. In others, the Wall is layers of electric fences and buffer zones of trenches, patrol paths, sensors and cameras. Whatever the structural differences, the effects are the same.

Life in these open-air prisons is intolerable. Palestinians will be imprisoned in walled ghettos, deprived of the most basic human rights. Such oppression and misery are already taking hold in the areas where the Wall is currently being built. Some 10% of the West Bank is already affected by the destruction created by the Wall's first phase. Building the Wall has involved razing agricultural land, damaging irrigation networks, isolating water resources and demolishing homes, stores and community infrastructure. With the daily subjugation of closures, sieges and curfews, people have become particularly dependent upon their lands for mere survival, but they are unable to access them. The fertile lands of 51 villages have been either confiscated or are isolated and unreachable because of the Wall.

The latest opening of three "crossing points"—in addition to dividing Palestinian lands—only further highlights the institutionalization of the land theft caused by the Wall. In less than a month since the gates were opened, people have been shot, beaten, humiliated and prevented from accessing their lands. Such scenes are a part of the daily Palestinian landscape under Israeli Occupation and around the Wall. This Wall and its so-called crossing points are inhumane and illegal.

For us, and for all who have witnessed what is taking place, the Wall is nothing less than a collective noose around the Palestinian areas and the Palestinian people. In Qalqilia, where Wall construction is nearing completion, close to 15% of its 41,600 inhabitants have been forced to leave, unable to survive in what many in the community call the Apartheid Cage. In Palestine, and among various solidarity groups, the Wall is referred to as the Apartheid Wall—as part of a colonial project that includes the long-term policy of occupation, discrimination and expulsion.

The Wall will guarantee the impossibility of creating a free and sovereign Palestinian state. Consequently, the recent usage by Israeli Prime Minister Sharon and US President

Bush of the terms "viable" and "state" take on particularly cynical and empty meanings. Their increased calls for a "state" run in direct parallel with the impossibility of such a state existing, as the sealing of the fate of the Palestinian people into ghettos of the dispossessed takes hold.

In Palestine, the demand to stop the Wall is in the forefront of calls being made by the public. We ask that you join us in this urgent call.

NONVIOLENT PROTESTERS ATTACKED IN MARCH AGAINST THE CONSTRUCTION OF THE WALL
Jaggi Singh, 29 December 2002

Up to 500 Palestinians, supported by more than 100 Internationals, converged on the village of Jayyous today after two separate marches passed through several villages in the Qalqilia district in the West Bank. The rally was to demonstrate clear opposition to the building of Israel's so-called "security fence", better known as the "Apartheid Wall". A large section of the wall is being constructed in Qalqilia district. During the marches through district villages, demonstrators were confronted by soldiers who used tear-gas against marchers. Still, the marches continued to Jayyous, where speeches were given denouncing the wall at a local school. From there, Palestinian farmers and Internationals tried to march to the local fields, near where the wall is being built. Private contract security were in place, armed with loaded and pointed M-16 rifles.

A BAD DAY IN JAYYOUS
by Moosa Qureshi, 29 December 2002

We made our way down the hill towards the Israeli bulldozers which were working on the Apartheid Wall. I know that Radhika and I were in front and behind us a line of French Internationals, arms linked, in white T shirts. Radhika and I were not alone in heading the peaceful procession, but the situation was so tense and noradrenergic that my memory is unsure. I remember Radhika, myself, some blurred faces, a line of white Francophone T shirts, and then a chequered crowd of Internationals and Palestinian women. And I remember the soldiers.

"Stop."

We stopped.

A few of us went round the back of the soldiers with cameras and snapped shots of Israeli guns pointing at the procession. The French volunteers looked rather worried but ISM workers were relaxed. We were trained to expect this.

And yet, as events unfolded, I found myself again today.

We remained in a relatively calm stand-off with the soldiers and private security guards for some minutes. This was broken by the sudden arrival of the Israeli Border Police. The crowd broke apart like the sea before Moses as the police jeep bludgeoned its way through and rolled down the hill. Israeli soldiers took out what looked like baseball bats and dispersed the Internationals with threatening gestures. I found myself smiling at a soldier as he raised his bat towards my face. I always smile when I'm nervous.

Life in the Palestinian territories is strangely predictable. The Border Police always means trouble.

Sound bombs are easy, they really don't bother me. Tear-gas is a different story. It chokes you and makes your eyes water, and can permanently damage the epithelium of your airways. The tear-gas used by the Israeli army is far more pernicious than the variety used by western governments. Onions help some.

Young Palestinian men responded by throwing stones and the spiral of violence was set in motion. Rubber bullets were flying everywhere. A young Palestinian cameraman was caught in the double crossfire, his shoulder dislocated by a stone and his thigh struck by a rubber bullet. In some way, I suppose he symbolised the bizarre tragedy of this conflict.

Let me draw a brief sketch of our situation. A hundred metres down the road, two jeeps. About ten Israeli soldiers and Border Police standing round these jeeps, and others hidden in the fields on either side of the road. Most of the Internationals dispersed behind us. I can honestly say that I only saw ISM volunteers holding their positions, but perhaps this is because they were my friends. Two houses bordering the fields on the edge of Jayyous were occupied by men, women and children, trapped by the crossfire. Daud, a native English Muslim, and myself had decided to stay on the road near these houses, to protect as well we could the two families.

As the guns fired and the stones rained, eventually one of the families decided to vacate their home. I asked Malin and Roba to go into their house to escort the women and children out. The other family decided to remain in their home. Daud, myself, Lovisa and a Palestinian journalist by the name of Mustafa stood at their door.

Again, a lull in the conflict and again, it was deceptive. At this point, the Israeli soldiers took decisive and immoral control.

Radhika was walking downhill towards us with some food and beverages wrapped in a clear plastic bag. She handed me the bag. As we looked on, some soldiers marched up the road. They seemed to be heading past us, up towards the town. And then suddenly they snatched Mustafa.

I guess this was a personal failure on my part. Mustafa was behind Lovisa and me. Radhika tried to grab him back but an Israeli soldier knocked her to the ground. She's only a slender girl so she went flying. The soldiers retreated rapidly, dragging Mustafa with them, waving their guns in our direction, as we watched helplessly. My only excuse is that I had never been in such a situation before and it happened so unexpectedly. Anyway, it happened.

Lovisa and I started walking towards the soldiers. We held our hands up in the air and advanced slowly down the hill. I had my passport in my left hand. We were about eighty metres away the first time they yelled at us to stop.

"Let him go," Lovisa shouted back at them, but we stopped. "We only want to talk."

One of the Israeli soldiers sitting on the front bumper of the jeep yelled, "We don't want to talk."

We advanced a few more steps until a soldier pointed his rifle at us.

"One more step, and I shoot you."

The soldiers were young and nervous, and we stopped again. Patrick and Lisa had now joined us. Lisa spoke loudly to the soldiers in Hebrew. "Why point guns at us? Let's just talk."

The soldier dropped his gun just a fraction and we advanced a few steps. Again the rifle cocked up towards us and we stopped. I quietly whispered a prayer that we would secure Mustafa's release. This innocent Palestinian journalist would surely suffer at the hands of the Border Police. They are infamous for their brutality, even towards Internationals. And then we advanced a few steps further. It was a strange process. Lisa in Hebrew and I in English, speaking loudly but calmly, and advancing a few steps until the gun pointed towards us. Then repeating the process again and again, until finally we all four stood just twenty metres away from the two jeeps. All the time, the Israeli soldiers and police were jeering and dancing and making faces. They knew and we knew that they held all the cards.

The jeep started up and now Israeli soldiers were marching up towards us en masse. Lisa recognised the face of the soldier leading them and murmured, "We don't stand a chance."

He also recognised her. "So we meet again. This time you are with new friends," looking at Lovisa and me. He told us that they were arresting Mustafa for throwing stones and that we would all be arrested if we did not make way for the jeep. In reality, he did not want to arrest us. Fifteen soldiers and Border Police just pushed the four of us out the way and the jeep rolled through with Mustafa locked inside. If we had resisted, then Israeli justice would have convicted us of assaulting a police officer. Mustafa had not thrown a single stone.

Both jeeps were now heading uphill into Jayyous. We followed in their wake. As they drove through the streets, they dropped canisters of tear-gas. Patrick handed me an onion. I couldn't breathe, my nostrils and my throat burned. I walked with my right eye half open, my left eye closed tight in pain. But we had to follow because the Israeli army had not yet finished their business in Jayyous. We caught up with them outside a Palestinian house. One jeep had parked outside and an Israeli soldier was kicking the door violently. It opened from inside. Three Israelis marched in holding their guns in front of them. We heard the sound of furniture crashing inside and then they brought two bearded Palestinian men out. Hands up, against the wall, bodies searched. Neil tried to photograph the scene but was told that his camera would be smashed. I just held my camera down by my side and nonchalantly snapped two photos. They didn't know where the flashes came from and I won't know what the photos will tell until I return to England.

Radhika and Malin and I were asking awkward questions and doing our best to peacefully intervene, while not responding to provocation by the soldiers. They found nothing on the two men and eventually released them. And so on to another Palestinian home. It was some time before they left Jayyous.

Lisa and I now wandered the streets of the town together. As we walked, Palestinian children would shout out to us from the balcony windows where they were caged. "Peace be with you" or "Hello". There was a curfew in Jayyous and nobody was allowed to leave their home. Now and again, a Palestinian man or woman would ask us to escort them to their home. It was while we were escorting one young man that we heard more bad news which we had to investigate.

As we walked through the door of her house, Lisa and I saw a red-faced tearful Palestinian woman sitting on the floor, surrounded by family and women from neighbouring homes. Her right arm was in a sling. The two Israeli jeeps had split up and we had not been able to monitor all their activities. We saw now the broken hinge of the door where the soldiers had forced their way in. And we saw the young boy who had been thrown viciously against a wall. And we saw the mother whose arm had been fractured or broken while she was trying to protect her young boy.

One grizzly-haired old man in the family spoke good English. "Who is the terrorist?" he asked. "Palestinians or Israel?"

They gave us tea to drink and the woman with the broken arm kissed Lisa on both cheeks as we left. Lisa is Jewish, American and anti-Zionist. They know this.

Tonight as we patrol the houses of Jayyous through till dawn, the old man's words will reverberate in my mind. "Who is the terrorist?"

There is pain and anger and truth in this question.

A COMMUNITY RISES UP TO STOP CONSTRUCTION OF THE APARTHEID WALL
by Drew Penland, 8 January 2003

The Apartheid Wall, now being built at lightning pace in Occupied Palestine, is officially being constructed for Israeli security. But cutting through the flimsy rhetoric its true illicit nature is clear: an illegal attempt to steal Palestinian land by force.

For the village of Rasatiye in the Occupied West Bank the stakes are high. If the wall is built the community will be on the Israel side of the wall. Locals have been told, much to their despair, that after the wall is constructed their land will join a number of illegal Israeli settlements and become part of Israel.

Today I was among an ISM team that assisted a non-violent attempt to stop the construction of the Apartheid Wall in the small village of Rasatiye in Occupied Palestine. The mood of the community this early morning was buoyant. About 150 local Palestinians and a dozen ISM activists were called to gather at the community mosque over the mosque loudspeaker, a device almost exclusively used for the Muslim call to prayer five times a day. Otherwise the mosque loudspeaker is only used in times of emergency, like when a wall is being built by a foreign occupier that may in effect kill your community.

There was a sense as the last of the locals gathered that local people were happy to take non-violent action to try to stop the destruction of their community. Community opposition to the wall is strong. They know that their land is part of Sharon's plans for a greater Israel; they, however, as Palestinians are not.

We moved to the site of where the wall is being constructed. It was a place familiar to me because several days earlier I had visited the site and was shocked to see ancient olive trees being ripped out of the ground in the area around where the wall is to be built and being placed in a pile near a road.

Olive trees are the very essence of Palestinian society and intertwined with the fate of the Palestinians. Since the beginning of this intifada they have met a devastating fate. Reportedly over one million have been destroyed or removed from Occupied Palestine in the last two years. Some of the stolen olive trees are trucked to Israel and resold by Israelis in nurseries to other Israelis.

On that day a group of local Palestinians were also feverishly taking what they could from what had been one man's poultry business. The building and the neighboring house were reportedly slated for destruction. The wall not only destroys the land but also any adjacent buildings. Across the street a shiny new elementary school built with Swiss Aid money has also been threatened with demolition.

At that time I recall a local farmer sitting powerless as his land was being destroyed. He wept openly with his hands on his head. The weeping farmer and his land being stolen is not a first for me, it is a heartbreaking sight I have witnessed all over this part of Occupied Palestine.

Today two behemoth machines of destruction, the largest bulldozer I ever recall seeing and huge backhoe, were jackhammering the land and noisily making a huge mess of a previously pristine agricultural area.

Four Israeli boys guarded the worksite. Two were heavily armed Israeli soldiers, pimply geeks of about 18 years in real life who appeared to be mild-mannered. The other two were armed private security guards, one sporting Rayban wrap-around sunglasses, a bleached blond swath of hair and an unjustifiable swagger, the other darker with good English and a small trace of sincerity amidst his need "just to do his job". These were the boys who were imposing this arrangement on the village of Rasatiye.

As we marched today towards the site the "boys" seemed caught completely by surprise. They appeared not to know how to react as we stopped the huge backhoe in its tracks with little real struggle by surrounding it with people. One of the security guards soon brokered a deal with locals that the crane and bulldozer would be let go if it left the community. We marched it right out of the community. It felt like a real victory for the community, but the soldiers were not about to let the people win.

Our procession stopped and was at a standstill merely watching as the machinery moved into the distance. The soldiers were about 200 meters away and retreating steadily. Then, one soldier shouldered his rifle and shot a canister of tear-gas from his M-16. One canister and then a second sizzled over head and landed in an area where there were women and children. The crowd parted to avoid the noxious gas as it rose around us and I got a fair dab in my lungs.

Then he took aim for real. He visibly aimed his gun straight into the crowd and a shot rang out that was followed by screaming. A local man had been shot. As I approached I thought maybe he had been shot with a real bullet. I saw a very coura-geous boy, the man's son, pick up a hot tear-gas canister and lob it away from the area of his fallen father. Someone yelled out that he had been hit with the tear-gas canister. He appeared to be in great pain and his son, brave soul, was crying.

Attacking peaceful demonstrators when they were at a standstill as a non-violent action came to a conclusion was the most cruel and cowardly action I can recall: a savage act to terrorize a peaceful demonstration of farmers and activists. The man was brought to the village and an ambulance called.

The soldiers continued to leave and my attention turned immediately to two more military jeeps that were moving through the village towards us.

VIOLENCE AT THE GATE
by John Petrovato, 19 July 2003

On Tuesday, July 15th, four foreign journalists conducted an interview with Sharif Omar, a prominent member of the Jayyous village and leader of the local Land Defense Committee. Sharif has participated in many nonviolent actions against the building of the "Security fence"/ Apartheid Wall and has been instrumental in keeping the issue on the table during the current peace negotiations between the Palestinian Authority and Israel.

What was puzzling to the journalists however was why there had been so much protest against the fence if the gate to their fields had been open and Israel has given permission for them to travel to them. They would ask "How many times have you been prevented from going?" or "How many times have the gate been locked?". The answer by Sharif would be "None, but…". Seeing that Sharif was having some difficulty translating his thoughts on this matter into English, I politely interrupted and asked if I could try to clarify. I suggested that while the gate was indeed "open", it does not mean that travel is safe, easy or even advisable. Because of random beatings, the detaining and the intimidation that farmers must suffer, passing through the gate is a very frightening experience for the people.

Many men have reportedly been detained at gun point, forced to sit in the hot sun for many hours, beaten by fists and rifles and kicked. Other forms of harassment I had personally witnessed include the forcing of the villagers to provide their identification cards (passports), give explanations of their destinations, reasons for traveling, etc. Further, one must attempt to imagine the very experience of having to travel daily through a gate in which one would not know the outcome; having to interact with guards who had beaten them or someone they personally know in the past; never knowing when that individual will again decide to beat them; further, knowing that these individuals may beat and detain you at gun point without any fear that they will be punished for their actions and that one has no legal recourse to contest such violence.

Another problem that farmers have to deal with is the presence of the Israeli military roaming on their farmlands. Even on this particular day, an Israeli military APC drove aggressively toward the tractor that I was traveling with and forced it to stop. The soldiers jumped out with their machine guns ready in their hands and demanded the Palestinians' identification cards. They, like the civilian security guards, asked them questions such as where they were going, what business did they have here, how long did they plan to be there, etc. The farmer would humbly reply "I am merely going out to irrigate my fields and the land which you are driving on has been in my family for dozens of generations." After some 15 minutes of questioning and searching of the tractor's cargo, they "permitted" the farmer to continue.

The journalists did find it "interesting" that Israeli civilian security guards engaged in violent activities which they had no authority to do (security guards are not the police or the military, but civilians hired to protect construction equipment, etc.). However, they dismissed it as insignificant in and of itself. As opposed to the journalists, I would make the argument that the use and actions of civilians in terrorizing a population is extremely significant. For it illuminates the power dynamics between Israeli civilians and Palestinian residents in the West Bank.

Such forms of daily violence and terror are condoned by the Israeli state. It is not essential that violence is conducted by civilian security guards or the violent ideological settlers. It appears that by allowing such forms of violence against Palestinians to continue without punishment, the state of Israel seems to use these various forms of violence to reach their objectives: the confining of the growth (and ultimate destruction) of Palestine. It must be asked whether the episodic and unruly nature of sporadic violence conducted by civilians and individual soldiers is as powerful as the formal and controlled Occupation. Is it even more powerful? Is violence understood and accepted as exercised only through guns and tanks, or does it also occur through daily interactions with a power such as the individual soldier and the individual settler or civilian?

IF IT BLEEDS, IT LEADS
by Greta Berlin, 28 July 2003

Thirty to forty Internationals marched up the road to the gate in the Apartheid Fence separating the farmers of Aneen from their land. The Israeli government had grabbed acres of land for this horror, this fence that is making Palestinians into another Polish ghetto. They say it's for security, but it's a land grab that is as egregious as the land grab of the South African government.

We were joined by another thirty Israeli peace activists who marched the long winding road to the road, the road that the Israeli army had filled with roadblocks and broken boulders the size of small cars. Up we marched to the razor wire, the huge gate in front of us, the Palestinians behind us. The Israeli settlers and the army stood there with armored personnel carriers and guns.

Within a minute, the Internationals were shaking the gate, cutting the lock with the bolt cutters, shaking and shaking the sides to pull them down. "Boom", the first noise bomb went off in front of us. Then tear-gas, then noise bombs, then more tear-gas, this time aimed directly into the crowd of Internationals and Israeli peace activists. As we crouched and covered our ears, the first International was hit, Andrew shot in the stomach with a rubber bullet, then, seconds later, Thomas, shot in the back as he clung to the side of the gate, its outward swing turning him toward the Israeli soldiers, making himself a target.

I walked quickly toward Thomas with another ISM International to see if he was OK, and the army shot directly in front of me, a rubber bullet grazing my right calf as I stepped in to help Thomas. The Israeli army says it doesn't shoot at women. It is not true.

Within five minutes, the gate was open and five of us were wounded with rubber bullets, Kelly wounded in the back as he tried to carry Sam away. He had been shot twice in the leg as he tried to pull the onerous gate down.

Five wounded, tear-gas now being shot directly into the seventy of us, so we pulled back. Razor wire covered the other side of the gate, and the Israeli army stood directly in front of our banners, our bodies, our passion to help the Palestinians. It was certainly no match.

We stood there for several minutes, the Israeli peace group and us, and we shouted, all of us, over and over again … Free, Free Palestine … one, two, three, four … we don't want your stupid war … five, six, seven, eight, stop the fighting, stop the hate. The media shot footage as fast as they could. After all, if it bleeds, it leads … and we peacekeepers, the people holding the line against Israeli aggression … the people who are there because Israel refuses to allow UN peacekeepers in, we all bled.

CAMP AGAINST THE THIEVERY OF LAND
Another tent goes up to block the Wall
International Solidarity Movement, 8 July 2003

FOR IMMEDIATE RELEASE

Monday July 7, 2003, another solidarity camp went up in the West Bank in protest over the thievery of land and in an attempt to stop the apartheid wall being built by the government of Israel. Citizens from the USA, Sweden, France, the UK joined Palestinian villagers as they set up a peace camp in the village Arrabony in the north of the West Bank.

Arrabony is a village by the northern border of the occupied West Bank, 8 km northeast of Jenin, with around 900 inhabitants. This small village is another one of dozens of Palestinian villages, towns and cities that will be affected with lands stolen and the livelihood of inhabitants devastated, by Israel's Apartheid Wall. With the wall complete 800 dunums of land will be confiscated from the people of Arrabony, leaving approximately 2000 dunums in the hands of the villagers.

International volunteers from the USA, the UK, France, and Sweden together with the village's inhabitants set up a peace camp in Arrabony, in the path of the wall's construction, in protest, and will follow with non-violent direct actions targeting the construction-work in the whole northern Jenin-area.

Similar protest tents have been set up and are maintained in Deir Ghosoon (Tulkarem region), Mas'ha (Salfit region) and Jayyous (Qalqilya region), where farmers are camping out on their land, which has already been isolated from them.

We invite all people to join us in one of these areas against the confiscation of land and the creation of Palestinian ghettos, and we invite journalists not to ignore the voices of the people and the devastating facts that Israel continues to create on the ground, despite talks about peace and a "roadmap".

For more information contact:
Huwaida [number withheld]
Jenin: Tobias [number withheld] or [number withheld]
Tulkarem: Flo [number withheld]
Jayyous: Sharif Omar [number withheld] or John – [number withheld]
Mas'ha: Yousef [number withheld] or [number withheld]

ENDS

GATHERING FIREWOOD TOGETHER
by Oren Mendicks, 11 August 2003

Perhaps only an Israeli can fully appreciate the surrealism of the following situation: Israeli, Palestinian and International peace activists, living together in an olive grove deep inside Palestinian territory, deep inside "Intifada Land". Palestinians and Israelis gathering firewood together, discussing politics and strategies for action. At night, frightened, not of each other, but of the Israeli army. No wall or fence separating us. This is the daily routine in the West Bank Palestinian village of Mas'ha. The Mas'ha protest camp against the wall was initiated last April by Nazeeh Shalabi, a farmer from Mas'ha who will lose all of his land behind the wall.

Marketed to the Israeli public and the world as a reasonable security measure to separate Palestinians from Israelis, the wall, in reality, only separates Palestinians from their land. Mas'ha, almost four miles from the border with Israel, will lose 98% of its land, and almost all of its commercial life because of the wall.

Why are Israelis joining Nazeeh in protesting the wall? Increasingly, Israelis realize that the wall represents yet another means of deepening the Occupation, under the pretext of security.

In fact, the wall is a means of silent ethnic cleansing, because life in these prisons will be unbearable, driving Palestinians out. The wall surrounds the nearby Palestinian city Qalqilia. About 7,000 of Qalqilia's 40,000 residents were already forced to leave their homes.

On a deeper level, the wall is a new version of the hated Jewish Ghetto. Only this time it is we, the Jews, who are building the ghettos, and locking another people in them. By doing so, we are creating an internal ghetto for ourselves. After 2,000 years of exclusion, Israel has returned to the old ghetto mentality.

For many Israelis, creating fences and walls is unacceptable. It will close the door on possibly the last chance for decades to start a process of true reconciliation with the Palestinians. Being together in the camp has proven to us that real security lies in the acceptance of one another as equals, in respecting each other's right to live a full, free life.

In contrast, many Israelis favor the wall for the exact same reason, but reversed. They cannot afford to really see the Palestinians, because by doing so, they are forced to see the humiliation and pain they inflicted during 100 years of colonization.

In short, they prefer a wall to a mirror. Preventing human contact "helps" not only in dealing with the past, but also in preparing for a dreadful future, because only if the Palestinians are "those behind the wall" can they be demonized, stripped of humanity, and eventually disappear without our conscience shrieking in pain.

Jewish history knows this only too well. This is why we joined the people of Mas'ha in the protest camp.

Last week another Mas'ha farmer, Hani A'amer, requested our help. The wall will pass one meter from Hani's doorstep, cutting him completely from the village. Hani's home will be trapped between the separation fence and the Elkana settlement fence. According to the army, Hani and his family will only be permitted to leave three times a day through a special gate.

We moved the camp to Hani's yard so people could witness this monstrous plan. Shortly after, 150 soldiers stormed the camp and brutally dragged off, jailed, and interrogated all 45 of us peace activists. The next day, another group of 24 Israeli activists were arrested in the same manner.

Regardless, our struggle against the wall continues. We, Israelis, Palestinians and Internationals, will not allow the wall to separate us. We will keep the Mas'ha camp alive till the world helps us end this shame, which turns an entire people, in fact two peoples, into prisoners.

As Israelis, we realize that Palestinians are not only losing their freedom—we are losing ours as well, because as prisoner and jailer, we are shackled together.

12

THE LARGEST CONCENTRATION
CAMP IN THE WORLD

"WELCOME TO THE EREZ CROSSING"
by Jennifer Loewenstein, 28 July 2002

The sign on the way out of Gaza really says this. Yes. Greetings. Welcome to a half a mile of concrete barriers and barbed wire. Welcome to electrical wires and fortified soldiers' bunkers. Take no notice of the machine guns pointed at your head. Follow the arrows and obey the signs. Put your hands up, leave your bags behind you, walk slowly, show us your passport, tell us what the hell you think you're doing in this human garbage dump. No, you can't be trusted. You're living in Gaza.

Welcome to the Erez Crossing. Make yourself at home.

A young, blue-eyed soldier with a crew cut and a machine gun watches me enter the main office at Erez. I say a meek "shalom"; I don't want to get into a conversation. But he wants to know where I'm from and what's my name. His eyes pierce mine and he grins in an unpleasant manner. He looks like the stereotype of a Nazi soldier, I catch myself thinking. Don't. Don't have that thought. It's not allowed.

Outside, another 100 meters away, is the last guard post. I pass by it easily, handing over my gate pass, and feel relieved to see that my taxi is waiting for me. But in between me and my last few steps at this God-forsaken transit point is a family of four, a mother, father, and two young children—sitting on the pavement in the sun, the 100-degree-Fahrenheit, humid Gaza sun—waiting for the master boys in uniform to deign to let them back into prison. How many hours have they been kept there in the withering heat?

The soldier at the gate shouts for the father to approach in the tone of voice used for disobedient dogs. I feel sick. "I'm so sorry. I know my country is paying for this." They're the only words I can find and I utter them in broken Arabic. The father looks at me surprised. "Never mind. It's not your fault."

Worthless lives can sit for hours at the gates of an inferno. No one will ever know. And the man who waited at Ben Gurion airport for ten hours to get permission to return to his Gaza hovel was finally allowed in—without his wife and daughter, who were threatened with deportation for no apparent reason. You never heard about him either or the hundreds with similar stories. Or about the woman sitting in the back seat of a taxi with her child one early morning this past June: soldiers in a nearby outpost fired bullets through the window of their car killing them both. They have no names, no faces, no relevance.

More than 150 people have been murdered by the Israeli Occupation Forces in the Gaza Strip just since the middle of March. Three made news in the US. The *New York Times* labeled them "suicide bombers" though they had no explosives on their bodies. They were 14 and 15 year old boys stupidly driven to trespass into the Netzarim settlement, illegally situated on their land. They were shot in the head and chest, ridden over by an armored vehicle that disemboweled and utterly disfigured them, and left to the mercy of dogs until the next afternoon. Do you remember them?

Are we really surprised that an F16 warplane would drop a 2000-pound bomb on a family home at midnight killing 15 people, nine of them children and two of them mothers? Where has the outcry been up to now that over a million human beings—treated like refuse, spoken of like vermin, drained of the trappings of basic dignity—live in a ghetto walled off from humanity surrounded and strangulated by an occupying army that kills them at will and with complete impunity? Why should 15 more deaths matter when the hundreds of others never did?

Because this time the killers were so purposefully indiscreet.

When I step into my taxi for the weekend trip to Ramallah my Arab Israeli driver greets me tentatively at first. I thank him for being at Erez so promptly; for not making me have to wait in that miserable place. Anguish fills me when I turn back to look at the entrance to Gaza. Let me try to forget for a while. "Where are you from," I ask the driver in Arabic, in an attempt to focus my thoughts elsewhere. "I am Palestinian," he answers me in a voice of controlled calm.

Erez, it seems all your greetings have failed.

ISRAELI ARMY DESTROYS ROAD THAT INTERNATIONALS AND PALESTINIANS HAVE BEEN FIXING FOR DAYS
International Solidarity Movement, 15 July 2002

FOR IMMEDIATE RELEASE

[Breij, GAZA] International peace activists have been accompanying Palestinian mechanics to a water well close to the edge of the illegal Israeli settlement of Netzarim, so the mechanics would be able to fix a well that had been damaged 15 months ago. The well is the source of water for Palestinians in the mid-Gaza region. The work began on Thursday and continued on Sunday July 14. Part of the work included creating a road, in place of the existing rough dirt road, that leads to the well to facilitate access, as the locals will have to oil the well daily to maintain its functioning.

Palestinian workers and Internationals returned to the well today to find that the road to the well had been destroyed. The Israeli military has dug deep trenches in the dirt road as well they constructed roadblocks. The Israeli Army also bulldozed the grape and fig crops of Palestinian farmers located in the vicinity of the well. The structure around the well had been entered into, though it is not clear whether the soldiers had damaged the well itself. Soldiers from a nearby army tower shouted obsenities and threats at the group trying to examine the damage, while two Merkava tanks were brought into the area to threaten the Internationals and local civilians.

The International Solidarity Movement is considering the next steps and actions. There is no rationale for denying a people access to water, or purposefully causing such large-scale destruction of Palestinian land and infrastructure.

For more information on the well, please call:
Mr. Kamal Al-Bughdadi, Mayor of Breij [number withheld], David Skjor-Duving
(Denmark) [number withheld]
For information on the ISM in Gaza: Garrick Ruiz (USA) [number withheld]

ENDS

A LONG NIGHT IN GAZA
by Garrick Ruiz, 23 July 2002

[…]
   Yesterday five of us from ISM arrived in Rafah at the southernmost end of the Gaza
Strip. This is my third visit to this hardhit city. Two of us from ISM as well as two jour-
nalists, one from the US and the other Dutch, ended up staying with a family near
Salahadeen gate. This is an area in the Yibna refugee camp here in Rafah along the
Egyptian border and an area that sees intense attack from the Israeli military every
night. Some members of ISM had stayed with this family a few days ago so we knew
it would be a long night but I don't think anything could have really prepared me for
just how long it would be.
   I want to give names to the people in this story because they all have names but I'm
going to use fake names so as not to have any possibility of my words being used to
target anyone. The father of the family is Mohammed. Mohammed has eight children
and his wife to think of. His home was severely damaged almost one year ago by Israeli
tanks and bulldozers. They can no longer stay in their own home so they have moved
down the street a few meters further away from the Egyptian border to a neighbor's
home. Just a few quotes from Mohammed (I'm amazed at the sense of community
under such horrific circumstances):

> I am original here, my family has lived in the Gaza Strip for hundreds of years. Simply I
> want my house, I want to continue my life as I am. I take care of my neighbor's
> children. They take care of mine, there is no question. Where else can I find that? When

I left my house I hoped to return in one or two or three hours. I think now I will never return. Why not?

[...]

Mohammed used to work as a construction worker inside Israel untill the beginning of this Intifada. Now with the closure he has no source of income.

Mohammed stays up every night now until at least 4:30 or 5:00 am. He sits outside with some other men from the community, keeping track of where the tanks are, what's happening, if he and his older boys need to run, if the whole family needs to move, etc. At best he gets 2–3 hours of sleep per night. This has been going on for more than a year. And he loves to talk about his life and the situation that they live in and so I learned a lot last night.

Something like a timeline of last night:

11:30 p.m. We go outside. The shooting usually starts around midnight or 12:30. Almost immediately tonight we hear a series of gunshots from a tank. Mohammed tells us that there is already a tank at the end of the street. I can see the flashes of tracer bullets shooting by at the end of the street.

12:00 Tanks begin to move. We hear them roll behind us around the building we are sitting in front of. More shooting but still only sporadic rifle and machine gun fire at this point.

At this time Mohammed shows me some of the damage in his neighborhood. He points out where homes had been demolished, where a medical clinic once stood and he shows me many streams of bullet holes from machine guns. He points out how many of them stitch through houses in places where people could not even possibly stand, much less attack a tank from.

"Why?" he asks. "Why do they shoot at these houses at places where no one could possibly fire back?" "Why do they shoot here? There is nothing military here, only regular people." I have no answers for him, though it seems clear to me that the answer is that the Israelis don't view them as regular people. They view them as dogs or vermin or all the other racist terms so common once amongst the Nazis referring to Jews that now are so common in Israeli culture.

12:50 Tanks shoot down the street we are on. We all have to stand against the wall so as not to draw gunfire.

1:00 The news starts to spread of the assassination of a Hamas leader in Gaza City. It happened around 12:30 or 12:45. We go inside and turn on Al-Jazeera (the CNN of the Middle East—Mohammed translates for us). We got the following information in bits and pieces over the course of the night but I'm including it all here for sake of ease: at least 11 killed, eight children dead, about 100 injured from an F-16 attack. Five homes were destroyed. The assassination was targeting Salah Shihadah, leader of the military wing of Hamas. He, his wife, his three children, five other children and one other man are known dead.

We watch as people from the area pull bodies and pieces of bodies from the rubble. Others are being rushed to ambulances, bleeding heavily. Children are screaming everywhere. Children's faces and bodies sliced open by shrapnel. One child bleeding from his head sitting drooling, unable to control his body.

Have you seen these images in the US or has once again the voluntary censorship of the US media won out? That was the face of state terror last night. That is what the world should see, but I know that it won't. All this comes after Hamas has announced only a few hours before that it will stop suicide bombings to allow the peace process a chance to move forward. They were apparently very close to signing a deal. This morning we learned that the attack was ordered by Sharon and the minister of defense. The rest of the Israeli cabinet did not even know. The message is clear to Palestinian organizations. Talk about peace and we will hit you harder.

I just heard that Sharon declared the action a great success but expressed regret about civilian deaths, how nice of him. The death toll is now 15. The assassination weighs heavily on us the rest of the night.

[...]

PROTEST LABELS ISRAELI ARMY "MURDERERS"
Blood stains military vehicles in Ramallah
International Solidarity Movement, 23 July 2002

FOR IMMEDIATE RELEASE

[OCCUPIED RAMALLAH] Over 40 foreign civilians confronted the Israeli army outpost in Ramallah today in protest of the brutal Israeli attack on Palestinian civilians in Gaza City yesterday and calling for an end to the Israeli occupation of Palestine. The demonstrators, representing the United States, England, France, Puerto Rico and Japan, carried black flags with the words "Gaza 23. 07. 02" painted on them. Four of the black flags were planted into the ground around the Israeli tanks, as the protestors chanted and waved Palestinian flags.

A group of the protestors also scaled the walls around the army post carrying buckets and cans of paint. One armored personnel carrier and one Israeli army truck were doused with red paint, while the words "Murderers" and "US $" were painted on another armored personnel carrier.

Pictures and video footage available.

For more information, please call: Huwaida at [number withheld] or [number withheld]

ENDS

RAFAH UNDER SIEGE
by Kristen Ess, 19 December 2002

Block O is almost empty now. Most of the people have gone. The sewage flood is knee deep in places. One old man is walking around the muddy edges. His house is flooded. The 8 meter high, 10 meter deep prison wall the Israeli military government is building as it devastates Rafah is growing. Reddish brown steel riddles the landscape that the Israeli military has destroyed. The standing houses are now made of bullet holes.

Across from them, lining the wall, are sniper towers, green and draped in dark mesh. Israeli driven Caterpillar bulldozers have created another wall with home rubble—bed springs, a plastic rocking horse, some torn sheets, and the concrete that the homes were built with. This rabid destruction has further complicated the sewage drainage system in the area. A friend and engineer in the Water Municipality of Rafah says the way to drain the flood is to break this wall apart to allow a simple flow.

The houses cannot be rebuilt. The area is under siege. "When the tanks and bulldozers came, the people were panicking in the dark. They were grabbing for their children fast. The noise is of crushing concrete and people screaming. They ran out of their home into sewage water." The man telling me this paces with his hands in his pockets. He offers a cigarette and says, "You are welcome here."

There is nearly nothing left, nothing to come back to as the Israeli military moves through crushing homes, infrastructure, life. This is ethnic cleansing. But some people here are saying, "If we just had one person standing beside us, just one set of eyes from outside, we would take a stand in our homes. We would stand up here."

A deaf man in the north did not hear the Israeli soldiers megaphone demand that he run from his home and he was crushed, as was an elderly man who told his neighbors he could not be humiliated by Israel anymore. The Israeli military government is targeting agricultural land and factories in order to crush the Palestinian economy, whatever might provide for survival here. This is part of the ethnic cleansing process. It's psychological, economic, physical.

A doctor here told me, "They're destroying our schools and hospitals. The factories they say make bombs are just factories. If we make cheese they say we're building bombs. They are destroying our fields, everything. They're doing this so we have to buy their vegetables, all of their products, so we have no economy."

A farmer, now living in a tent after the Israeli military bulldozed his house and most of his area in the north of Rafah, told me, "They are not letting us grow things. They just bulldozed my fields. This is my land. I won't leave. We won't leave. They can kill me here. They will kill me here."

Due to this specific targeting of infrastructure, and to the constant closure of the Gaza Strip, unemployment has reached 80% at times. Five people looking for jobs left their home in the Khan Younis refugee camp this week. They tried to leave the Gaza

Strip through an Israeli military checkpoint that only allows products to pass through. Israeli soldiers shot and killed every one of them. For a few days the Israeli government and the corporate media put them on Israel's so-called "wanted" list.

A guy from Mawasi has not been home in two years. He told me this in Rafah, about 15 minutes from home. He says, "The Israeli government does not want any young people to be in Mawasi, they want to drive everyone away."

There are no schools in Mawasi, save for a movable school caravan described as being "only for emergency cases." By this they mean for the young children, to give them something to do that might possibly help normalize their lives. They are so stressed by the constant Israeli attack that 50% of the kids are wetting their beds. Sixty-one percent of Palestinian children suffer from anemia in this area, not from a lack of food to be eaten, but from a lack of appetite. A UNRWA doctor told me, "They're too nervous to eat. They're scared all the time."

The Israeli Defense Minister is in Washington getting approval for an increase in the already 12 million dollars per day that Israel receives from the US.

CAMP RAFAH
by Polly Wilkens, 13 January 2003

[…]

The demolition of now almost 600 homes clears the way for a security barrier that allows the IOF [Israeli Occupation Forces] to construct the 40ft tall wall that will divide Egypt from Rafah and in the future separate all of the Gaza Strip from the rest of Palestine. Internationals stayed with one family whose mother has not been allowed to see her family in Egypt for seven years. She was unable to be present at her mother's funeral two months ago.

The ISM presence in Rafah has been short-lived thus far and has continuously worked to establish a proactive relationship of trust in an economically devastated community made fearful and desperate by years of Israeli oppression.

[…]

Two Internationals were staying with a family whose house was under severe threat of demolition. During their evening meal they witness the initial warning of inevitable destruction by tank shells that came through the ceiling and walls followed by rapid gunfire into the house at body level. They escaped with only minutes to spare before the house was razed to the ground by bulldozers that worked throughout the night.

During the days that followed while people retrieved their salvageable belongings and repaired damaged water lines, the tanks fired rounds to scare them away. The Internationals were present and approached the tanks with banners and a loud speaker. They withstood tear-gas bombings and gunfire to protest the tanks' presence and their terrorism to the people. The tanks ceased their firing.

On January 3rd the Internationals, following the lead of the local community, set up the first tent on the site of this demolished house to prevent tanks firing at the existing houses and the busy street behind them. During that night one family moved back into their home, sensing greater security from the International presence.

The next day the Internationals went to the site of a home being destroyed by two bulldozers which were protected by three tanks. The ISM members ran to get in front of the massive D-9 American-made bulldozers while being filmed by media and fired at by the tanks. The bulldozers did not cease their destruction and pushed the Internationals without reserve into the rubble, causing serious risk and endangering their lives.

Inevitably the Internationals left the scene when the risk of being crushed with the rubble became too high but succeeded to draw the attention of the world through a televised report on the BBC. On top of this site, the Internationals established their second presence along "no man's land", erecting the tent under the fire from the on-looking tanks. After the first night of this tent's presence, the local police chief told the Internationals that he believed the tent was responsible for the de-escalation of gunfire.

The Internationals maintain a 24-hour presence at the tent sites in order to ensure the tent's survival and the safety of the communities. During the past week of non-violent protest and action no lives fell victim to the tanks' violence and the community's fear seems to have decreased dramatically. The Internationals want to establish a permanent presence through a worldwide campaign to "Camp in Rafah." Join them to protest the destruction of homes that makes way for a pointless wall of oppression.

THEY SHOT A REPORTER
by Chris, 14 January 2003

Two hundred meters away and they grazed the back of his head. One centimeter lower and we're attending his funeral instead of visiting his hospital room. He's going to be fine. He was in very good spirits in the hospital, but I'm still really pissed. Let me take it from the top.

We went to the meeting spot about one kilometer away from the checkpoint [to Tel Sultan] where we met up with the villagers. We had apparently been misinformed: 100–200 people want to come with us, but almost all wanted to see us in action before joining us. So, we had five women with flags there. No matter, though, these five women along with big bags of medical supplies would accompany us. We also had local reporters as well as the Reuters news agency there with us. We began walking towards the checkpoint.

We made it about half of the way there when we got our first notification that we weren't welcome: a rifle shot off to our right. We ignored the warning shot and continued. The Israeli Occupation Forces fired several more shots, each progressively closer. One of them was so close that the bullet kicked up a small stone that bounced along the ground and hit me lightly on my right ankle. With each shot, we stopped for a few seconds and then proceeded slowly. Finally the IOF had had enough and fired the nearly fatal shot.

We were scared and angry at that point, and further reflection has made me even angrier. As we approached the checkpoint, we seemed to have more power than the IOF. Obviously they're the ones with the guns, jeeps, tanks, helicopters, F-16s and training, but on our side we had world opinion.

We were escorting older women while carrying medical supplies and world opinion simply wouldn't stand for a bloodbath. The IOF wanted to get rid of the media in order to tip the scales their way. Of course, they couldn't shoot an international media member, because that would be a huge story, so they went after a local Palestinian reporter. Their sharpshooter grazed his head (intentionally or unintentionally, meaning they may have meant to kill him), and all of the media immediately took off (not that I blame them). Now we were just a bunch of activists with a few video cameras, which clearly gave the IOF the advantage. They used this man as a pawn in their game.

They were so determined to keep residents and medical supplies out of Tel Sultan that they shot and nearly killed a reporter.

After this we tried talking to them with our bullhorn. After several minutes of this while we continued slowly approaching, they responded over their loudspeaker. Naturally, they told us that we couldn't come through and that we should turn around and go back. We refused and the situation came to a standstill.

After a while they sent a jeep out to negotiate with us. Angela (from New York) went out and came back several times.

After a standstill in negotiations and a few more warning shots the Palestinians and we decided to back off and go home. The whole thing took about two hours.

I got about an hour and a half of it on tape.

American cops in riot gear will never frighten me again.

WAITING FOR THE DECLARATION OF WAR
by Kristen Ess, 26 January 2003

The Israeli occupying army attacked Gaza City again last night. They murdered 12 Palestinians and targeted infrastructure. They destroyed homes, shops, roads, and electricity. Over 40 people are injured.

Friends called throughout the night, terrified. "What can we do? We sit here and wait." Another who left his home in the Zaytun neighborhood which was surrounded by tanks told me from his safe place, "They are close to here now too. Listen." He held the phone out to the air. Tank shells and missile fire were heard throughout the Gaza Strip. This morning a friend from a Gaza City NGO was at what was once the print shop we use. It is the place that prints human rights pamphlets and posters. Now it is completely destroyed.

The occupying Israeli military went into Beit Hanoun again. They closed the main street with sand and barbed wire. There is no way out.

Israeli soldiers just shot a man in Rafah's B'razil refugee camp. One man in the area told me, "It's just getting worse here."

Israeli "Defense" Minister Mofaz is talking about a full occupation of all of the Gaza Strip.

These assaults constitute war crimes under humanitarian law. The targeting of civilians and civilian property during the above incursions are grave breaches of Articles 33, 53 and 147 of the 4th Geneva Convention, which also prohibits collective punishment.

This is occurring while the Israeli military government dissembles that it has a democracy and is holding elections. Its funding is coming from the United States which continues its ten year assault on the Iraqi people via bombardment and sanctions. We wait for its official declaration of war.

ISM ACTIVISTS PROTECT GAZA HOSPITAL AT REQUEST OF UNAIS AND HOSPITAL DIRECTOR
by ISM volunteers in Gaza, 6 February 2003

The United Nations Association International Service (UNAIS) and the Medical Director of Al-Wasa Hospital have requested that the ISM send a team of activists to protect Al-Wasa Rehabilitation Hospital after it was attacked last night by the Israeli Army.

At 11.45 last night a house 70 metres from the hospital was destroyed by a missile fired from an Israeli attack helicopter.

At 12.15 two of the hospital's nurses were killed by Israeli soldiers who had occupied a residential building across the street. Abdul Al-Karim Lobbad (21) and Omar Hassan (21) were both killed by a single bullet fired through a hospital window.

The hospital accommodates 50 patients with serious disabilities and cares for around 100 other patients on a day care basis. It is clearly marked as a hospital with signs that can be seen from 400 metres away.

The ISM is sending three volunteers from the UK and the US to provide an international presence in the hospital so that it can keep functioning.

For further information contact: Olivia on [number withheld] or Joe on [number withheld].

WATER WARS AND ASSASSINATION
by ISM, Rafah, 17 February 2003

Today in Rafah water workers were able to continue their repairs on the Tel Sultan wells, which were demolished by the Israeli Army on January 30. They had the help of nine ISM activists (three UK, four US, one Italian and one French) who stood between the workers and Israeli military towers from which soldiers regularly fire upon Rafah Municipality water workers. Tomorrow, the activists intend to sleep at the wells to protect the water workers' equipment.

Also today a Palestinian ISM activist traveling from Rafah to Gaza City witnessed the assassination of Nahed Abu Ziad, whom the Israelis suspect of being a leader of the Hamas organization in Gaza. The activist watched as regular soldiers cut the road she was traveling on. Plainclothed assassins then fired into the car in front of hers, killing Abu Ziad and wounding the driver. Both Ziad's body and the wounded man were taken away by the Israelis.

The activist's account of the assassination differs from the official version of events, which claims that the Israelis were trying to capture Mr. Ziad but that he died of his wounds in hospital.

For further information on the Tel Sultan action contact Olivia on [number withheld].

For further information on the Nahed Abu Ziad assassination Jehan on [number withheld].

US EMBASSY SUPPORTS OWN CITIZENS SHOCK!
by David Watson, 5 March 2003

Two American nationals staying at a protected house in Rafah in the Gaza Strip expressed pleasant surprise when a midnight call to the US embassy resulted in a halt to the military attack on the house they were staying at late last night.

Machine gun fire had been clearly audible over the phone line when the initial call was made to the International Solidarity Movement media centre and the two ISM peace volunteers reported being uncomfortably close to rockets and tank shells that were being fired.

The couple had used a loud speaker to inform the IDF forces that they were US citizens but it had no effect.

When in the first place the media centre had called and explained the situation on the embassy's emergency line a rather bizarre question was asked.

"Huh can't this wait till the morning?"

The answer was that by that time the two people in the house might be dead if the assault continued so your intrepid media co-ordinator gave an emphatic no.

But when the case was passed on to the US Military Attache the two Americans were delighted to report that good support was given and the official promised to ask the military to cease their attack which they did within minutes.

"He was a cool guy," said one of the volunteers.

ISM ACTIVISTS OPEN ABU HOLI CHECKPOINT
by Raphael Cohen, 19 April 2003

Three ISM members based in Rafah—Alison from Scotland, Francesco from Italy and Raph from London—arrived at Abu Holi checkpoint, the main ingress to Khan Yunis and Rafah from the north, at 3:30 this afternoon.

We were greeted by a queue of 25 vehicles and a crowd of people. Those at the head of the queue told us they had been waiting since 7:00 in the morning. The atmosphere was one of patient frustration, nobody knowing whether there might be a brief opening to allow them through. The Gaza strip is currently enduring its fourth day of closure as ordered by the Israeli Occupation to mark the Jewish holiday of freedom, Passover. The effects of closure are to even further isolate the Gaza strip from the outside and to divide it into three sectors between which movement is not permitted.

Israel has justified its action as a response to a resistance attack on the edge of the Gaza strip at the main crossing point for goods between Israel and Gaza. The draconian, disproportionate and arbitrary nature of this response clearly makes it an act of collective punishment in contravention of the Geneva Convention.

Palestinians present became aware of us and moved forward with us to the head of the line of vehicles. This small crowd at the front clearly made the hidden soldiers nervous and a voice came over the loudspeaker of the tower warning us all to move backwards or we would be shot. We took this threat seriously and stepped back a few yards to call the British Embassy and consider what to do. The embassy advised us to leave.

As we could not be sure that our shouting into the wind was audible, we decided that Alison and Raph would slowly and deliberately approach the tower and attempt to communicate the desire of the Palestinians to pass through the checkpoint. Francesco was to wait behind and observe. We intended to make a case for those with particular needs, be they medical or social.

Alison and Raph linked arms and walked in as unthreatening a manner as possible about 10m up the road. We then stopped to shout that we were Internationals from the UK who wished to talk to them. As we got no response we walked forward another 10m and shouted again. The loudspeaker told us to go back (in Arabic). We were then asked to show our papers and we waved our passports in the air. We continued to shout that we were peaceful Internationals who wished to talk and then were told in English to wait.

We sat down in the road for about 10 minutes. A jeep then pulled out from the tower area and parked behind the drums. The tower told us to approach. Alison and I got up, linked arms again and went towards the jeep. Once we were next to it, four soldiers got out and we were called over.

Two soldiers took up a firing stance behind blocks on either side of the road and we talked with the other two. The soldiers asked in English where we were from and we showed our passports. We made our request that the checkpoint be opened for a short period for all to pass, or if they were not willing to allow this, that the sick, old and young be allowed through. The officer said that the checkpoint was closed and no one could go through, these were his orders. One of the two snipers, probably a Russian, said (in Hebrew to his colleague) that he wanted to go home and wanted peace. This was relayed to us in English by his co-sniper who said he wanted peace but the Palestinians did not. We said the Palestinians too wanted peace.

The second sniper warned us that we were in danger from the Palestinians. In the interests of our objective I did not comment. The officer then suggested the checkpoint would open at 3am. In response to our concern for the humanitarian cases present he indicated that the Israeli military liaison officer would come to the scene. They instructed us to go back. The Palestinians were eager to hear our report on what was said and we decided to wait for the DCO.

The white jeep finally appeared after about 20 minutes and Alison and I again linked arms, walked to the checkpoint itself and engaged the two soldiers. The main speaker was eager to see our passports. He asked if we were just tourists as per our visas (we said yes) and explained that all humanitarian cases required coordination with the Palestinian liaison. We explained our concerns and the soldier indicated the possibility of a 30 minute opening after a man and sick child had been brought through from the Gaza side of the checkpoint. He made no promises but said he would check with his senior officer. We returned and the news seemed well received by the Palestinians. The white jeep drove off.

After some 20 minutes, the original four soldiers came out and removed the barbed wire across the opposite lane and moved the barrels from our lane. This caused much cheering and hooting of horns from the Palestinians with us. People rushed to their cars, only to see the soldiers return the barrels. Finally, the other side did open. Everybody rushed to their vehicles in great excitement. Once the traffic had gone through, the white jeep came back and our convoy was ordered forward. The first vehicle edged towards the checkpoint, a young man jumped out of the back to move the barrels and we watched as everybody sped past, smiling, clapping and waving.

Our sense of exhilaration lasted only until the taxi ride home when we heard the news from Nablus of the killing of a journalist.

ON THIS SIDE OF THE MIRROR
by Lora Gordon, October 2003

On Yom Kippur (to specify, October 6), the most holy day on the Jewish calendar, the day of atonement in which we are supposed to cease every form of work in order to pray and request forgiveness from God, the army began construction on a new permanent checkpoint in the Gaza Strip. Another slice.

Tanks cut off the main road between Rafah and Khan Younis (the city just north of Rafah) by driving ten tanks right in front of the European Gaza Hospital, the only decent hospital south of Gaza City, and the road has been closed for days. Nothing can get to Rafah, many things in Rafah are simply not available right now, things like medicine, the ability to cash checks, basic supplies. People who study or work in Gaza City and Khan Younis haven't been to work or university for days. It makes me think of high school, when snow and ice could shut a city down.

Upstairs from our apartment, Rasha can't hide the small relief she feels from this reprieve of study. I wonder how much the relief Rasha feels has to do with getting let off the hook from dealing with checkpoints. The week before this closure, she spent five hours one day waiting for Abu Holi to open so she could go home and the next day it closed all night, leaving her to sleep at her friend's sister's house in Gaza City after waiting for four hours in a hot taxi in line with hundreds of cars waiting for the checkpoint to open. I compare our worlds, like parallel universes, squinting at each other from both sides of a mirror.

When tanks cut off the main road people trying to get home used the sandy road and tanks cut that road too, shooting all the time, and bulldozers followed, demolishing anything anywhere near Moraj settlement, mostly olive trees. They are still demolishing. They've also started construction of something, people are saying it's a permanent checkpoint, another Abu Holi.

Nobody knows much, not even the human rights organizations are going, nobody is risking going near the place because the tanks are shooting anyone who approaches. Nobody has dared approach since the first day of the incursion, when the army invaded without announcement, taking people by surprise as they drove to and from work.

They injured four people, including a doctor who was shot in the head and is in critical condition in the European Gaza Hospital where he used to work. In addition Rafah has accumulated another shaheed [martyr], Said Abu Azzum, 26 years old, who was driving with his wife and their two sons on a routine trip to Khan Younis, without any idea what was happening some meters down the road; shot in the heart as he turned a corner. He had no job, no money, and no house, and now he leaves behind a 21-year-old widow with nowhere to go, a 4-year-old and a 6-year-old with nowhere to go. They couldn't even have the wake in his sister's house where he used to stay because it's near the border and because it's too small to accommodate visitors, so they sat for three days in a cousin's house in Shabura so that people wouldn't be afraid to come and pay their respects.

When I went on the third day, his mother was angry. She said, where is your camera, where are the journalists. Not one person from the media had come to photograph her. I was embarrassed. I hadn't brought my camera, thinking it disrespectful to bring journalism to a wake. She said, if you're going to write, at least take notes that I can see, write in your book that Sharon and Bush murdered my son, from the comfort of their offices.

On the same day Said Abu Azzum was killed, Mohammed's older sister Wisam was coming home from the European Gaza Hospital where she works as a nurse when she heard the army had cut the road, and her taxi went with the other taxis towards the sandy road to bypass the tanks, but not fast enough. Tanks drove into the road as they were crossing into Rafah and began shooting indiscriminately, and it was at this point that people were injured and killed upon running from their cars to try to reach safety. Wisam was part of a group of women that walked together after the men had left, holding a white mendeel to signify surrender and peace.

The tanks shot at them anyway—is this the way to tell this story?—as they were walking (the words are so vile), and they lay down on the ground in the sand for a half an hour while a tank rode back and forth right next to them, a meter away, vile bastards, before retreating.

Wisam did not walk to Rafah, she ran, in bare feet (having left her sandals somewhere on the ground), and arrived in her family's home, her abaya torn, with the black glove of a woman she didn't know that somehow found its way to her shoe, found her family and cried for hours, she says she's never going back to work. The road is closed in any case so for now it's not a question.

She is taking her respite with her family, in Tel Zorab, farther from the border than the main street in town but not so far that their third floor flat can't be seen by the Zorab sniper tower, which effectively keeps them from using the kitchen and one bedroom. The tower shoots all day and night. It shot at us while we were eating kabbab in the living room, and as Wisam impressed me from room to room with the delicate furnishings in her home. She said, "Yesterday, I couldn't stop thinking about your friend Rachel. I thought I was going to meet the same fate."

So it goes. There is nobody in Rafah who doesn't feel the effect of this new blockage. Feryal is wondering where she will go if the road is closed when she gives birth to her fifth child, who is turning in her belly for the ninth month. When I visit them, her daughter Rula tells me they've closed the road. What can we do? We want to see the world, we want some fresh air, we can't go anywhere, we're Palestinians.

Rula is 7 years old. Her older brother Mohammed, 11 years old, has been given an assignment by school to draw something related to human rights. He draws a world, an armed man shaking hands with an unarmed figure. The armed figure is America, he tells me, and the unarmed is Israel. Palestine is a cloud raining down lightning bolts of anger onto them, separate, alone, excluded from the conversation, unable to hold anything but its own fire and tears.

THE BATTLE OF TEL ZORAB
by Michael Shaik, 7 April 2003

At 5 p.m. activists were having a meeting at the ISM Rafah headquarters when they received word that armoured bulldozers were demolishing Palestinian homes in the Tel Zorab area. Immediately, they broke up the meeting before scrambling to gather their equipment (fluorescent clothing, megaphones and banners) before piling into a large taxi.

When they arrived at Tel Zorab they found a large group of Palestinians who were peering around the corners of buildings to watch the bulldozers at work and carefully avoiding exposing themselves to fire from the tank that accompanied the bulldozers or the military towers from which snipers dominate Rafah's border areas. Unfurling their banners the group approached the area where the bulldozers were operating, to the cheers of the Palestinians.

Leaving their Palestinian supporters behind, the activists found two bulldozers working together to tear down a Palestinian home. The bulldozers were accompanied by a tank, which, upon seeing the activists, immediately began firing its machine gun into the air and at the rubble of a building that had already been destroyed.

Leaving a couple of activists behind to film and monitor the situation, the remainder advanced cautiously as the tank continued to fire into the air and at nearby buildings so that on a few occasions the activists were showered with shrapnel. Undaunted, the activists continued their advance upon the war machines until they came close enough for the tank's crew to hurl sound grenades at them.

[…]

When the activists began to block one of the bulldozers in its demolition work, the driver got out the vehicle and told them to leave the area since this was his land, not theirs and they had no business being there. They replied that this was not his land and that they were civilians in a civilian area and it was he, as a soldier, who had no business being there. The driver then got back in his vehicle and attempted to resume his work but was blocked by four activists who stood in his path.

A battle of nerves then took place as the bulldozer drove very close to the activists who stood their ground until he withdrew. This happened several times until the driver gave up and pulled back so that the tank could fire its machine gun over their heads before one of its crew opened a hatch and threw a tear-gas canister. Unfortunately (for the tank crew) he had misjudged the wind direction so that the gas blew back into their tank.

Meanwhile, the bulldozer had approached the house it was trying to destroy from another direction but was blocked by four other activists who stood in its path, with their backs towards the partially destroyed house.

The British Consulate then informed the activists that they had received word from the Israelis that they intended to arrest the activists. Shortly thereafter an Armoured Personnel Carrier arrived on the scene and the activists positioned themselves so that they could easily withdraw towards the Palestinian areas.

(Israeli soldiers operating in the Gaza Strip are generally terrified of the Palestinian resistance fighters and almost never venture out of their armoured vehicles. There are many Palestinians in the Gaza Strip who have lived all their lives under occupation and with tanks roaming their streets but have never seen an Israeli soldier.)

After the tank had created a smokescreen several soldiers in full combat gear rushed out of the APC and towards the activists who quickly withdrew so that the soldiers ran back into the APC without capturing any of them.

At this point an enormous explosion occurred as a rocket was fired from the Zorab tower into an abandoned Palestinian home.

The APC then began firing its machine gun at the feet of the activists as another bulldozer tried to resume its work before being blocked by a group of activists. Once again the bulldozer driver approached within inches of the activists before stopping. The bulldozer driver then began blowing his horn in a musical manner and then wrote down his phone number and held it to the windscreen while pointing at one of the female activists.

Shortly thereafter, the soldiers in the APC rushed out to arrest the activists but failed again as the activists withdrew towards the Palestinians. When the soldiers withdrew to the APC the activists resumed their positions.

At one point one of the tank's crew climbed out of the top of the tank and tried to tackle one of the Italian activists but only succeeded in partially pulling off his trousers before he escaped. As the soldier fled back into the tank, its machine gun fired into the windows of some Palestinian houses to cover him. (At no point were there any members of the Palestinian resistance in the area.)

At about 7 p.m. it began to get dark and the armoured vehicles began to withdraw. They were "covered" in their retreat by another rocket fired from Zorab tower which hit a nearby house and showered the activists with rocks.

The activists then left the area to by welcomed by the Palestinian spectators who cheered them and shook their hands.

This was the first action the Rafah ISM team has undertaken to prevent home demolitions since the murder of their comrade Rachel Corrie in a similar incident three weeks before.

PART THREE: ISM UNDER ATTACK

13

RACHEL CORRIE, BRIAN AVERY AND TOM HURNDALL

IN CONVERSATION WITH THE US CONSULATE
by Michael Shaik, 14 February 2002

Diplomat: I'm sorry but it's Shabbat and we can't contact anyone in the Army because they're all on holiday.

ISM: On holiday? Then what are they doing demolishing houses in Rafah and shooting at international volunteers for?

Diplomat: I'm sorry but we don't have anyone we can contact in the Army.

ISM: Then phone the Department of Foreign Affairs and tell them to contact the Army. [The standard protocol under such circumstances.]

Diplomat: What are they doing in the area?

ISM: They're trying to stop house … Can I speak to the Consul please?

Diplomat: Please hold a minute …

Photograph by Khalil Hamra. © Associated Photo Press, 2004. Reprinted with permission.
[The scarf reads "Palestinian Children's Parliament".]

Ingrid Barzel: How can I help you?

ISM: This is an emergency call about a group of international peace activists in Rafah Town that are being fired upon by Israeli troops. I'm phoning you because I want you to get in contact with the Army and advise them that there are American nationals in the area and ask them to please exercise restraint.

Ingrid Barzel: Please advise your people there to leave the area.

ISM: Look they're in the area and they don't intend to go anywhere. They're trying to stop houses being demolished by military bulldozers.

Ingrid Barzel: We have a travel advisory against traveling to the Gaza Strip and if these people are there they are there illegally. [This is untrue: to enter the Gaza Strip one has to have a special authorisation stamp in one's passport and all the Rafah activists have one.]

ISM: What if one of them gets killed? Will you hide behind your excuses then?

Ingrid Barzel: They're not excuses. It's State Department procedure endorsed by the Secretary of State.

ISM: So what you're saying is you take no responsibility for the welfare of your nationals doing peace work in the Gaza Strip even if this means one of them gets killed because of your inaction?

Ingrid Barzel: We do not accept any responsibility for anyone who ignores our travel advisories and illegally enters the Gaza Strip.

ISM: What is your name?

[Pause]

Ingrid Barzel: I'd be happy to give you my name. It's Ingrid Barzel.

I also got in touch with the British consulate who said they'd phone me back but seem to have got in touch with the Gaza military headquarters and the Dutch consulate which was on holiday and had an answering machine operating.

RACHEL CORRIE'S LAST E-MAIL TO HER MOTHER
by Rachel Corrie, 28 February 2003

Thanks, Mom, for your response to my email. It really helps me to get word from you, and from other people who care about me.

After I wrote to you I went incommunicado from the affinity group for about 10 hours which I spent with a family on the front line in Hi Salam—who fixed me dinner—and have cable TV. The two front rooms of their house are unusable because gunshots have been fired through the walls, so the whole family—three kids and two parents—sleep in the parents' bedroom. I sleep on the floor next to the youngest daughter, Iman, and we all shared blankets.

I helped the son with his English homework a little, and we all watched *Pet Semetery*, which is a horrifying movie. I think they all thought it was pretty funny how much trouble I had watching it.

Friday is the holiday, and when I woke up they were watching *Gummy Bears* dubbed into Arabic. So I ate breakfast with them and sat there for a while and just enjoyed being in this big puddle of blankets with this family watching what for me seemed like Saturday morning cartoons. Then I walked some way to B'razil, which is where Nidal and Mansur and Grandmother and Rafat and all the rest of the big family that has really wholeheartedly adopted me live. (The other day, by the way, Grandmother gave me a pantomimed lecture in Arabic that involved a lot of blowing and pointing to her black shawl. I got Nidal to tell her that my mother would appreciate knowing that someone here was giving me a lecture about smoking turning my lungs black.) I met their sister-in-law, who is visiting from Nusserat camp, and played with her small baby.

Nidal's English gets better every day. He's the one who calls me "My sister". He started teaching Grandmother how to say, "Hello. How are you?" in English. You can always hear the tanks and bulldozers passing by, but all of these people are genuinely cheerful with each other, and with me.

When I am with Palestinian friends I tend to be somewhat less horrified than when I am trying to act in a role of human rights observer, documenter, or direct-action resister. They are a good example of how to be in it for the long haul. I know that the situation gets to them—and may ultimately get them—on all kinds of levels, but I am nevertheless amazed at their strength in being able to defend such a large degree of their humanity—laughter, generosity, family-time—against the incredible horror occurring in their lives and against the constant presence of death.

I felt much better after this morning. I spent a lot of time writing about the disappointment of discovering, somewhat first-hand, the degree of evil of which we are still capable. I should at least mention that I am also discovering a degree of strength and of basic ability for humans to remain human in the direst of circumstances—which I also haven't seen before. I think the word is dignity.

I wish you could meet these people. Maybe, hopefully, someday you will.

THE KILLING OF RACHEL CORRIE
by Tom Dale, 18 March 2003

Many of you will of heard varying accounts of the death of Rachel Corrie, maybe others will have heard nothing of it. Regardless, I was 10 metres away when it happened two days ago, and this is the way it went.

We'd been monitoring and occasionally obstructing the two bulldozers for about two hours when one of them turned toward a house we knew to be threatened with demolition. Rachel knelt down in its way. She was 10–20 metres in front of the bulldozer, clearly visible, the only object for many metres, directly in its view. They were in radio contact with a tank that had a profile view of the situation. There is no way she could not have been seen by them in their elevated cabin. They knew where she was, there is no doubt.

The bulldozer drove toward Rachel slowly, gathering earth in its scoop as it went. She knelt there, she did not move. The bulldozer reached her and she began to stand up, climbing onto the mound of earth. She appeared to be looking into the cockpit. The bulldozer continued to push Rachel, so that she slipped down the mound of earth, turning as she went. Her faced showed she was panicking and it was clear she was in danger of being overwhelmed.

All the activists were screaming at the bulldozer to stop and gesturing to the crew about Rachel's presence. We were in clear view as Rachel had been. They continued.

They pushed Rachel, first beneath the scoop, then beneath the blade, then continued till her body was beneath the cockpit. They waited over her for a few seconds, before reversing. They reversed with the blade pressed down, so it scraped over her body a second time. Every second I believed they would stop but they never did.

I ran for an ambulance; she was gasping and her face was covered in blood from a gash cutting her face from lip to cheek. She was showing signs of brain haemorrhaging. She died in the ambulance a few minutes later of massive internal injuries. She was a brilliant, bright and amazing person, immensely brave and committed. She is gone and I cannot believe it.

The group here in Rafah has decided that we will stay here and continue to oppose human rights abuses as best we can.

I want to add that more than 10 Palestinians have died in the Gaza Strip since Rachel.

AT THE MEMORIAL FOR RACHEL IN RAFAH
by Tobias Karlsson, 18 March 2003

Today we held a memorial ceremony for Rachel Corrie in Rafah. ISMers from Nablus and Jenin and activists from the Christian Peacemaker Team in Hebron arrived to pay respects to our murdered friend.

We marched in silence through the city, 15 Internationals with more and more Palestinians joining en route. By the time when we arrived to the spot where the bull-dozer took Rachel's life, we numbered about 200.

We held a ceremony, planting flowers next to a small memorial. I planted three flowers—from ISM Jenin, ISM Sweden and the third from a close friend of Rachel's.

The army was notified in advance that we would hold this ceremony to honor our friend whom they murdered two days ago. Still they couldn't respect us enough to stay away.

Less than 15 minutes after we arrived, they sent out an APC that drove up and started to cover the area with thick white smoke. We continued our ceremony by walking out in the 3–400 meters-wide desert landscape that is the so-called security zone on the Egyptian border. The APC followed us as we walked up to the barbed-wire fence and hung an ISM-banner and laid more flowers on the ground.

Activists and Palestinians (who have not been able to enter this area for many years) started to confront the vehicle, putting flowers and posters of Rachel on it. The soldiers acted somewhat restrained in the beginning. One activist was even able to climb the APC and hand over a Rachel poster through the lid on top of the APC.

After half an hour, several more vehicles approached—three bulldozers and two more APCs. When we saw that one of the bulldozers—Number 949-623—was the same one that killed Rachel, things got very emotional. We were all outraged and many activists were crying.

The soldiers now took a more aggressive approach, driving around the crowd at high speed, putting lives of activists and Palestinians in great danger. Some activists tried to stand in front of them but had to jump out of their path not to get run over. The soldiers threw some percussion-grenades and some tear-gas (that dispersed in seconds in the dusty Rafah wind).

The peace activists responded by covering the military vehicles in flowers and pictures of Rachel. Eventually they all left, except for the first APC and we decided to end our session with a sit-in. We all sat in a minute of silence before we marched together out of the no-man's-land that is normally entered only by the Occupation army's killer-machines.

We must never forget Rachel Corrie, the sacrifice she made, or the other international aid and press workers that the Israelis have killed.

THE SHOOTING OF BRIAN AVERY

by Michael, 5 April 2003

Today the Israeli army of occupation operating in the Jenin area imposed its second day of curfew on the people of the city. Groups of young men and boys continued their resistance to the curfew by venturing out onto the streets to throw stones at tanks and other military vehicles.

At about 6.30 pm Brian and another ISM activist were at the ISM's Jenin head-quarters when they heard the sound of gunfire coming from the centre of the city, about two blocks away. They left the apartment to investigate and had travelled about 100 metres when they saw two armoured personnel carriers advancing towards them at low speed. There were no Palestinians on the streets in the area, armed or otherwise.

At the sight of the armoured vehicles both activists stood still and raised their hands above their heads.

When the first armoured personnel carrier was 50 metres from them it fired a burst of machine gun fire (an estimated 15 rounds) at the ground in front of them so that they were sprayed by a shower of broken bullets and stones. Tobias, Brian's companion, leapt aside. He had fled about three steps when he looked back to see Brian lying face down on the road in a pool of blood.

Tobias and Brian were then joined by four other ISM activists who had arrived at the scene of the shooting by a different route. All six of them rushed to help him as the two armoured vehicles rolled past without stopping. He was conscious but when he raised himself from the ground they saw that his left cheek has been almost totally shot off.

The activists then performed first aid on him and phoned for an ambulance which took him to the Martyr Doctor Khalil Suleiman Hospital in Jenin where he was treated for shrapnel wounds to his face including bone fractures below the eyes, lacerations of the tongue and lacerations of his left cheek. A specialist was called in to examine his injuries and recommended that he be transferred immediately to a hospital in Afula in Israel but his departure was delayed because the Israeli military refused to grant his ambulance safe passage for more than an hour.

From Afula Brian was transported to a hospital in Haifa by helicopter.

Under the Israeli Army's own rules of engagement soldiers are not permitted to fire warning shots with mounted weapons. They may fire warning shots with light handheld weapons and must aim away from the people they are warning.

When he was shot Brian was wearing a fluorescent red vest with a reflective white cross on its back and front.

VIOLENCE IN ISRAEL ALTERS LOCAL MAN'S LIFE
by Susan Broili, 27 June 2003, Herald-Sun

CHAPEL HILL—As he lay badly wounded for two months in an Israeli hospital, Brian Avery dreamed of coming back home to Chapel Hill.

"The biggest thing I was looking forward to was having some privacy and some peace and quiet," Avery recalled.

The 25-year-old Avery, a 1996 graduate of Chapel Hill High School, was shot in the face April 5 in the Israeli-occupied West Bank city of Jenin.

Members of Avery's Palestinian-backed International Solidarity Movement to Protect Palestinian People said an Israeli armored personnel carrier fired the shot that hit him. The Israeli government, in a statement issued to the *Chapel Hill Herald*, said the soldiers in question did not shoot the self-described peace activist.

Since he returned home June 7, Avery has found some of the peace and quiet he longed for. He spends time reading, taking walks and allowing the lush beauty of his hometown to help him heal.

"There's so many trees and flowers," he said.

Avery already has undergone three surgeries to rebuild his face. It will take at least four more to restore his features.

He almost made it home physically unscathed from his time in the dangerous West Bank region, where he also acted as a human shield.

After almost four months of volunteering for the ISM, Avery had planned to leave the day before he was shot. But his taxi to the airport could not pick him up because of an around-the-clock curfew imposed April 3 by Israel Defense Forces, said his father, Robert Avery.

His speech muffled by his closed and injured jaw, Brian Avery spoke recently of the events that left him with pulverized facial bones and teeth, an injured eye and a road map of scars.

[…]

Last week, his mother Julie showed the vest she said Brian wore that day. Stained with blood, the red vest had a white fluorescent band on the front and back with the word "doctor" in English and Arabic.

As he and Karlsson walked, Avery said, they heard military vehicles approaching. At an intersection, two Israeli armored personnel carriers came into view, he recalled.

"We stopped with our hands held out so it was clear we weren't holding any weapons. After a few moments, they just opened fire (from about 50 feet away)," Avery said.

He said he remembers the sound of shots, but that everything immediately afterward was mostly a blur. He does recall the ambulance ride to a Jenin hospital and to another hospital in Afula and finally the helicopter trip to a hospital in Haifa.

"The last thing I heard was the helicopter, and then I woke up in the hospital in the intensive care unit," Avery said.

His father Robert—who went to Israel April 9 to be with his son—said Karlsson told him he started running away, then looked back to see Brian, lying on the ground in a pool of blood.

Robert Avery said he also spoke with four other ISM members who said they witnessed the shooting. The four had heard gunfire close to the ISM apartment—apparently the same gunfire that prompted Brian Avery and Karlsson to investigate.

The four other ISM members arrived at the intersection in time to see Brian Avery and Karlsson standing still on the other side of the street, Robert Avery said.

Robert Avery said he went April 13 to see the US ambassador to Israel, Daniel Kurtzer, in Tel Aviv about what had happened. After that visit, the US State Department requested that Israel Defense Forces conduct an investigation into the shooting, Robert Avery said.

The Israeli government commented on that investigation as part of a statement sent to the *Chapel Hill Herald*.

"The results of this investigation found that the soldiers in question were not involved in the shooting of Brian Avery. What did occur to Brian Avery is truly a tragedy, and Israel does regret all incidents which alter innocent people's lives," a spokesperson from the Israeli government said in the statement.

"It's still an ongoing case," Robert Avery said.

He said he continues to be in contact with the US State Department and Congressman David Price's office, which he said has been very helpful.

"We are still involved," said Stuart Patt, spokesman for the consular affairs bureau of the US State Department.

Patt said the State Department is looking into the findings of the Israel Defense Forces' investigation of Avery's injury.

"We're also seeing if [Israel] will continue to help with his medical expenses," he said. "We're still very much engaged with his situation and trying to come up with a satisfactory solution for him."

Robert Avery said he does not know if the issue of blame will ever be resolved.

"I would just like for (Israel) to accept financial responsibility for his recovery," he said.

Brian Avery is not covered by health insurance and faces "enormous medical expenses," his father added. He said Israel did cover the expenses for Brian's two-month stay at the hospital in Haifa.

The recovery

In the hospital, Brian Avery received 2,000 e-mails from around the world, said his mother, who spent a month in Israel when her son was hospitalized.

His spirits remain good in large part because of his prognosis for recovery. Doctors have said they can restore his face, not 100 percent but "darn near," Robert Avery said.

Brian's tongue, split by the bullet, has healed fully. He said he is not in pain anymore, but that he is uncomfortable at times. Liquids remain his only nourishment.

"He wants steak and lobster," said Julie Avery.

Emotions run deep about the shooting. Anger flashes when she speaks about it. Still, she and Robert Avery say they have a lot to be grateful for. Brian could have died that night had it not been for a lucky combination of efforts to save him, Robert Avery said.

Brian's fellow ISM workers administered immediate first aid and used a cell phone to call for an ambulance. In a Jenin hospital, a doctor performed a tracheotomy that allowed Brian to breathe. The US Embassy in Israel arranged for a helicopter to take Brian to the hospital in Haifa.

THE SHOOTING OF TOM HURNDALL

by Tom's Rafah Group, 12 April 2003

On 11 April 2003, 10 members of the International Solidarity Movement in Rafah, Gaza Strip, Palestine, were planning to set up a tent in an area that an Israeli tank often uses to shoot into the houses and streets of a refugee camp called Yibna. Several Palestinian community members had initiated the project, gathered the supplies, and accompanied us to the area at around 4:30PM. When we arrived at the area, the tank was already there and had been shooting into the street. A nearby Israeli security tower had also joined in and was firing repeated, single, sniper shots.

An American International was accompanied by two Palestinians to go closer and get a better look at the area, and was wearing our trademark fluorescent orange jacket with reflective stripes. The tank and tower fired live rounds at the ground and buildings on both sides of her, making her movement difficult. She quickly returned to the rest of the group that was positioned behind a large roadblock but in view of the security tower. We made a consensus decision to call off the action, and return the next day as the Palestinians were uncomfortable with the gunfire.

At about 4:45PM, shots began to hit the buildings and street around us, and we became concerned for some children who were playing on the roadblock near us. Many had scattered, but a few were left. Thomas Hurndall, a 21 year old activist from London, UK, noticed that one small boy was still on the mound and under fire. He quickly lifted the boy and moved him behind the roadblock. Tom was about to leave when he noticed two small girls still in front of the roadblock and in the line of fire.

He was moving to help them when an Israeli soldier in the tower, about 300 meters in front of him shot a high caliber sniper bullet directly into his head. He was wearing an orange fluorescent jacket with reflective stripes, and was in full body view of the tower. The British Embassy had been informed of his presence, and had in turn informed the Israeli military.

Palestinians lifted his body and moved him to the pavement about 5 meters behind the roadblock. Two trained medics administered first-responder medical treatment, and used safety pads to try and stop the bleeding.

Palestinians then lifted him into a nearby taxi and rushed him to Al-Najar Hospital. On the way, they took care to try and stop the bleeding.

At around 5:15PM, he was transferred in an ambulance to Europa Hospital in Khan Younis. It takes about 30 minutes for an ambulance to get there as there is an Israeli roadblock on the main road. Without this obstruction it would only take seven minutes.

After much negotiation with the British Embassy and the Israeli military, Tom was taken to a nearby Israeli settlement from which he was taken by helicopter to Saroka Hospital in Be'er Sheva, Israel. He is currently on full life support and in a head cast. Several of his friends have joined his bedside, and his parents are on the way.

GETTING TOM TO HOSPITAL
by Alice Coy, 12 April 2003

Yesterday I was with Tom Hurndall and a number of other Internationals and Palestinians when he was shot in the head by an Israeli sniper from a tower. At the time he was trying to help move two young girls from the line of fire. They had been shooting into this residential street for several seconds and most of us had retreated.

There was absolutely no provocation for the shooting. There had been perhaps eight high-velocity single sniper rounds into the street before Tom was shot. The shrapnel from one of the shots grazed another International's arm. Tom was wearing a high-visibility orange reflective jacket. There was absolutely no resistance activity at this point. It was an unprovoked, offensive shooting into a civilian, residential street.

I attempted to administer first aid. He had both entry and exit wounds in his skull. He was taken to Al-Najar Martyr Hospital in Rafah, and then by ambulance to the Europa Hospital near Khan Younis. I was with him all this time with two other Internationals. The situation was incredibly critical. Despite the massive amounts of brain damage he was still alive. However the Europa Hospital, despite having very talented doctors, does not possess the medical equipment Tom needed. It was urgent that he be transferred to a better-equipped hospital.

We were advised that the best chance he had was to be taken to a nearby settlement and then flown by helicopter to an Israeli hospital. We were in contact with the British consulate in Jerusalem. It took two hours of watching blood leak from his head, of being told we must wait yet another five minutes, of twice the duty officer at the British Embassy in Tel Aviv hanging up on me, before the details were finalised.

We went with Tom in an ambulance the five minutes to the "checkpoint" where after a very tense few minutes of being ordered via megaphone by unseen soldiers in an area where Palestinians would normally be shot almost on sight he was finally turned over into the care of soldiers, one of whom said he was a doctor. They refused to allow any of us to travel with him.

Tom was 22 years old, an intelligent, kind, young man. He was shot like thousands of Palestinians by an unseen, unaccountable Israeli soldier. I am still in shock at losing my second friend in under four weeks.

I feel like a Palestinian.

HELP US TO MAKE A DIFFERENCE

by Sophie Hurndall, 17 May 2003, speech at Freedom for Palestine Rally, Trafalgar Square, London

I have been asked to speak at this rally as the sister of Tom Hurndall. As many of you may know, Tom was shot while trying to save children from Israeli army fire. While I would emphasize that my family have no political affiliation, what Tom and we discovered during our separate visits to Israel and Gaza has caused us deep concern.

I am here today to describe our experiences.

My brother Tom was a keen and talented photographer—he was also a caring human being. He travelled to Gaza because he had heard about human rights abuses taking place in the occupied territories and wanted see for himself the way in which Palestinians were living, and to photograph and document what he saw. Tom is now lying in hospital in Israel in a deep coma. His brain has suffered severe damage and the doctors have said he is unlikely to regain consciousness.

In the days before Tom was wounded he sent e-mails home detailing several incidents he had observed in which civilians had been shot by Israeli soldiers and also a helicopter attack in which 46 civilians were wounded, some of whom later died.

Tom had already sent us photographs including one of a boy of about 7 or 8, who posed no threat, being shot from an Israeli tank.

Tom was himself shot as he was trying to help a group of children. Waiting at the end of a street in Rafah, he saw machine gun fire being directed at a mound of earth on which about twenty children were playing. Most of the children fled but three young children were too scared to move, two girls and a boy aged between 5 and 8. Tom walked forward and picked up the little boy, named Salem Baroum. Having brought Salem back to safety he returned for the second child. Tom was shot in the head by a single sniper bullet as he leant forward to pick up the little girl.

The IDF released reports that Tom was armed, clothed in army camouflage and firing at the soldiers when he was shot. These reports have been reflected in media around the world, especially in Israel. These reports are not true. Many of you will have seen photographs of Tom in his fluorescent orange activist's vest. We have photographs of Tom immediately before and after the shooting—from several independent sources.

There were over ten eyewitness reports of Tom's shooting from Internationals, including the accounts of journalists—all of which support the fact that Tom was fired at with no justification and that there was no cross-fire. But what is extraordinary is that to this day, not a single one of these witnesses has been questioned by the IDF or the Israeli authorities. How can any credible inquiry be conducted without questioning them? Indeed some of these witnesses have since been arrested and detained or unlawfully deported.

It was clear to all that Tom did not pose a threat to the Israeli army or to anyone else. He was with a humanitarian organization which was involved in peaceful protest and which was known by the army to be present in the immediate area at the time. He acted in a way which every decent human being should have seen as natural and necessary in going to the aid of a young, helpless and desperately vulnerable group of children.

Many of us would not have had the courage to do what Tom did. In return for his courage and selfless commitment, he is likely to have paid the ultimate price. Tom is the victim of a direct and deliberate shot to the head.

Our request for an explanation about the shooting is not unreasonable. My parents, my two other brothers and myself have spent much of the last five weeks at Tom's bedside in Israel, and also in Gaza trying to find answers. In spite of numerous repeated requests during that time, through the British Embassy in Tel Aviv and the media, we have been bluntly refused an explanation from, or any communication with, the Israeli forces. My parents have even been shot at while travelling with British Embassy officials in Gaza. They have now been refused entry unless they sign a waiver absolving the Israeli army of any responsibility if the army shoots at them as well.

Is this what freedom and democracy are in Israel?

My family is campaigning for an independent, public inquiry into Tom's shooting. Not only for Tom, but because every day Palestinian civilians are maimed and killed by the Israeli army. Tom showed us this through the e-mails he sent home. Any act of violence—whether by Israeli or by Palestinian—should be subject to the same prosecution and a fair trial. Yet clearly this is not happening. Palestinians suspected of committing violence against Israelis are assassinated without trial as in the helicopter attack mentioned earlier. Yet an Israeli soldier is very unlikely even to be reprimanded for outrageously heavy-handed tactics.

We cannot stand by silently and allow people like Tom, Rachel Corrie, Brian Avery, Iain Hook and James Miller to become such tragic victims. If we don't make a stand to make the Israeli government accountable for its actions, then there will be no end to this terrible loss of life in Palestine.

Help us to exert pressure for proper accountability and an end to this indiscriminate loss of life. Please contact the foreign secretary, Jack Straw, to reinforce our demand for an independent and public inquiry. And please look at our website— www.tomhurndall.co. uk.

Help us to make a difference.

FAMILIES SEEK TRUTH OVER ISRAELI DEATHS
by Chris McGreal, 20 October 2003, Guardian

The family of a British peace activist shot in the head by an Israeli soldier is considering applying to the courts for permission to turn off his life support machine.

Doctors in Britain have told Tom Hurndall's family that he does not feel a thing. But his family find that hard to believe as they watch the twisting body and contorted face of the 22-year-old who is in a "vegetative state" after being shot in April.

"Tom can move, he flails, he turns his head from side to side from his shoulders upwards and grimaces," said his sister, Sophie, 24. "He looks like he is in agony. He looks like he is in hell. It is the most heart-rending and torturous thing to watch." Ms Hurndall said the family may seek a court order aiming to end Tom's life. It could take up to six months to obtain, and then a further 14 days for him to die.

"For me, Tom has already died but there's still no closure," said Sophie. "At the same time, it causes so much suffering and pain going in to see him. It's just an innate instinct to help him, to stop him suffering."

The Hurndalls, from Tufnell Park, north London, are one of three British and American families struggling to extract from the Israeli government and military the truth about how loved ones were killed or horrendously wounded by soldiers.

All three families have accused the authorities of fabricating evidence, suppressing investigations and covering up deliberate killings.

Tom Hurndall's mother, Jocelyn, wrote to Tony Blair last week demanding he exert more pressure on Israel to hold a transparent inquiry. Writing in today's *Guardian*, she calls the Israeli government a "deeply immoral regime which is cruel beyond human understanding".

The three victims were all shot in Rafah, a refugee camp in southern Gaza which the Israelis call a "war zone":

- Tom Hurndall, a student photographer volunteering with the International Solidarity Movement, was shot as he tried to protect children under fire from Israeli soldiers;
- James Miller, a 34-year-old British television cameraman, was killed a month later. His relatives are travelling to Israel next week to put pressure on the military to make its inquiry public and to admit it lied about the circumstances of his death;
- Rachel Corrie, a young American peace activist, was crushed to death by an army bulldozer in March. Her parents are still trying to obtain a copy of the military investigation which cleared the driver.

The Corries had been told the report was secret until they found that the Israeli government was covertly distributing it among members of the US Congress to prevent an independent investigation.

In only one case has there been a proper investigation: the death of Iain Hook from Felixstowe. He was head of the UN rebuilding programme in Jenin when he was shot by an Israeli sniper in November.

The army falsely claimed he was shot while standing among Palestinian gunmen in the UN compound. Israel paid compensation to Hook's family but attached confidentiality clauses which suppressed a public admission of culpability for what some of the UN worker's colleagues have called "cold-blooded murder".

All four families have carried out their own investigations after swiftly losing faith in the Israeli authorities.

"Sincerity isn't a word I would use in conjunction with the Israeli military," said James Miller's brother, John. "I have absolutely no confidence in what they tell me. I think the Israelis operate a war of attrition that just grinds you down in the hope you'll give up."

The Hurndalls have concluded that Israel has no intention of seriously investigating the shooting of their son, who was wearing a bright orange jacket, and had already carried a small boy to safety and was stooping to pick up a girl when the bullet struck.

The army investigation said that a sniper in a watchtower fired at a man wearing camouflage clothes and carrying a gun. The military came up with five theories for how the student came to be hit, all built around the claim that there was an unidentified gunman on the scene.

His father, Anthony, a lawyer, visited Rafah and compiled his own 50-page report in July. The report, seen by the *Guardian*, concludes that the army invented the gunman to justify the shooting. Mr Hurndall's report accuses the army of lying, withholding evidence and major factual errors.

"The events described are two different events: one real and the other a fabrication," Mr Hurndall wrote in his report. "The distance from the tower is about 150 metres [500ft]. For an experienced soldier, it is not possible to believe that he was under any misapprehension that Tom was a Palestinian gunman."

Mr Hurndall wrote that the chiefs of staff had given "the clear signal to their soldiers and to the international community that in Israel soldiers can and do deliberately kill and maim innocent civilians, Palestinian and international, without cause and with impunity".

In May, the Israelis promised the foreign secretary, Jack Straw, that there would be a "full and transparent inquiry" into Tom's shooting, but this has yet to materialise. In July, the then foreign office minister responsible for the Middle East, Baroness Symons, wrote to the Israeli foreign minister, Silvan Shalom, pressing for a military police criminal investigation after seeing a copy of the Hurndall investigation.

Evidence

"Their report contains very powerful and disturbing photographic evidence to support the written account that they, and a considerable number of witnesses, have given of Tom's shooting," she wrote.

The Israelis took two months to reply, and then only to say that a decision on a criminal inquiry was still being considered.

The Israeli government said it had shown "goodwill" by offering to pay Tom Hurndall's medical and repatriation costs. But, four months after he was flown home, the family says they have not seen a penny.

Nearly six months after James Miller's death, his family is still battling to see the army's investigation. Miller was shot as he left Rafah filming bulldozers destroying homes. The fatal bullet came from an armoured vehicle he had approached waving a white flag and shouting to the soldiers. The next day, Colonel Avi Levy, Israel's deputy commander in Gaza, said that Miller had walked into a battle.

"Troops in an armoured vehicle were searching for weapons-smuggling tunnels along the Egyptian border when the soldiers came under fire from rocket-propelled grenades. The troops returned fire," he said. A day later, Col Levy went further and said Miller had been shot "from behind", possibly by a Palestinian.

Neither claim was true. Video footage suggests there was no gun battle and the only shots came from an Israeli soldier. The postmortem said that the bullet struck him from the front and ballistics tests showed it came from an Israeli gun.

The family's lawyer in Israel, Avigdor Feldman, has called the killing "criminal", saying the soldier had targeted Miller.

Army investigators belatedly ordered the guns of 15 soldiers impounded for ballistics tests, but only nine were secured and they had consecutive serial numbers. They are only likely to be the real weapons used on the night if they were carried by soldiers who joined the army on the same day, were issued guns at the same time and were all assigned to the same unit. The ballistics tests have yet to be carried out.

Miller's brother, John, said the family was given an assurance by the Israeli deputy defence minister, Ze'ev Boim, that the results of the investigation would be released."We were told we would be able to see it in its entirety. Ze'ev Boim said it at a press conference in Paris and in an interview on television," he said. "Now they say they won't show it to us because the military police investigation is under way."

Cindy and Craig Corrie have been similarly frustrated. Rachel Corrie, 23, was crushed under the blade of one of the army's monster bulldozers as it prepared to destroy Palestinian homes in Rafah.

The army said the driver had not seen the young woman. The government refuses to let the Corries see the evidence that led the military to clear itself, but Rachel's parents were able to read a copy of a report circulated to the US Congress after meeting a sympathetic congressman who left it on his desk and walked out of the room.

"Having read the report we still have questions," said Cindy Corrie, noting that the Israelis changed their account several times and misrepresented evidence.

Mr Corrie said: "They say that the doctor that did the autopsy said that her death was probably caused by tripping on the debris or perhaps by being covered by the debris. Well, that statement is not in the autopsy."

The Corries were disturbed by an incident as they visited the site of their daughter's death in Rafah. For their own safety, the Israeli army had asked them where they would be and when. The Corries complied. But in the middle of dinner with a Palestinian family, the Corries looked out of the house to see a bulldozer heading toward the building.

"It was surprisingly aggressive and provocative considering they absolutely knew who we were and why we were there," Mr Corrie said.

The British and American families emphasise that their cases are no worse than the suffering of hundreds of Palestinians whose children have been killed by the army during the three-year intifada.

Even the most blatant cases of extrajudicial killing by soldiers are rarely investigated by the military police, and usually only after adverse publicity. Only nine soldiers have been charged with illegal killings; so far, there has not been one conviction in three years.

But the families of the foreign victims find it telling that even under diplomatic pressure, and with greater media attention, Israel has shown little interest in getting to the truth that the Hurndalls, Millers and Corries are seeking.

"Our primary objective is to see a criminal prosecution for the chap that pulled a trigger and the person that gave the order, if there was such a person. Secondly, there is an acceptable level of acceptance and apology, and thirdly financial restitution," said John Miller.

"With Iain Hook, the Israelis settled with a gagging order. That shows they have some acceptance but they just don't want negative PR. There's no possibility we'll sign confidentiality clauses that allow them to hide. That's the point of this, that everyone should know what goes on."

Sophie Hurndall agrees. "If we were to accept hush money, it would be totally wrong. What's going on in Palestine is horrific. Tom is a symbol of that horror. If we were to compromise what we could do with that symbol for money, I don't think it's even an option. It would go against everything Tom was and what he believed."

Israeli officials said they were unable to comment while investigations continue.

© The Guardian, 2003. Reprinted with permission.

TOM HURNDALL DIES AS FAMILY RECEIVE NEWS OF THE INDICTMENT OF HIS KILLER

by Carl Arrindell for The Tom Hurndall Foundation, 14 January 2004

Tom Hurndall, the British photographer shot in Gaza while shepherding young children out of the line of fire, died last night at 7.45pm. His death came nine months after an incident in which he was shot in the head by an IDF soldier which left him in a vegetative state.

The traumatic nature of his injuries has meant that at any time Tom has been vulnerable to serious infection and his death came after his body was unsuccessful in overcoming an episode of pneumonia.

At a hearing on Monday, a soldier arrested last week in connection with the shooting of Tom Hurndall has finally been indicted on six charges: Aggravated Assault; two counts of Obstruction of Justice; Incitement to False Testimony; False Testimony; Improper Conduct.

The decision of the court to prosecute the soldier on a charge of Aggravated Assault rather than attempted murder is based on the assumption that the soldier did not intend to murder Tom.

The family believes that based on its own extensive investigation and the soldier's testimony that he shot Tom using an advanced telescopic lens, it is improbable that the shot which entered Tom's forehead was intended to do anything other than kill.

The family will be pressing its lawyers to ensure that the appropriate charge—murder—is applied in this case. The family lawyers were advised by the prosecuting judge yesterday afternoon that in the event of Tom's death, the charges are likely to be changed.

The new charges shall be either manslaughter or murder. The maximum penalty for Manslaughter is 20 years imprisonment and for Murder there is only one penalty—life imprisonment.

Tom's family have made it clear that they will be satisfied with nothing less than the full prosecution of the person responsible for murdering Tom and they expect the imposition of the maximum penalty in this respect. They additionally expect that the harshest penalties should be imposed on all those involved in the obstruction of justice.

A second soldier has been detained and is expected to be indicted on charges of Obstructing Justice and False Testimony.

The indictment of this soldier and his testimony have totally destroyed the credibility of the initial IDF investigation and Field Report. It was this Field Report—presented to the British Embassy in Tel Aviv and later to the family of Tom Hurndall last May—that totally exonerated the soldier(s) responsible in the shooting of Tom Hurndall.

It is very much the case that if it were not for the ceaseless campaigning and lobbying on the part of Tom Hurndall's family and friends and in particular the family's own investigation (which amassed 14 independent eyewitness statements along with photographic and ballistic evidence) a military police investigation is not likely to have been instigated and the truth would have remained concealed.

The family now assert that the existing initial inquiry procedure is by its nature flawed and prone to abuse and they ask that the IDF immediately review its initial inquiry procedure with a view to replacing it with an independent inquiry.

They further call on the Israeli Army to radically examine the current rules of engagement and to take steps to eradicate the existing culture of impunity which exists in the Occupied Territories.

The family hope that the prosecution of those responsible for the shooting of Tom Hurndall and the prosecution of those responsible for the deliberate fabrication of evidence will send the strongest message to all soldiers on the ground in the Occupied Territories "that the shooting or killing of innocent civilians and breaches in basic human rights will not be tolerated."

THE DAUGHTER I CAN'T HEAR FROM
by Cindy Corrie, 11 May 2003, speech at Sylvester Park, Olympia, Washington

To all moms here, happy Mothers' Day. This is a day some of us wait for in order to have a little reward for all the time we have spent in our lives reminding and making sure that all of the family birthdays, Fathers' Day, and important days in our families' lives are properly acknowledged. We deserve this day! We have earned it!

I have had lovely Mothers' Days in my life. When my children were younger, I had to remain in bed until they could serve me breakfast there—French toast (sometimes a little crispier than usual) and orange juice—always lovingly, sometimes messily, most often safely prepared. There were gifts—handmade cards, poems, drawings, and coupon books. The latter promised hours of house cleanings, meals to be prepared on one of my busier days, and sometimes an unlimited number of hugs.

I think I always collected on the hugs. I probably didn't redeem all of the other coupons offered, but I knew on those Mothers' Days that my children's hearts and minds were filled with finding creative, tangible (and inexpensive) ways to say "I love you, Mom." I am not sure that even now they completely, consciously understand that their greatest gift to me has always been simply in their being.

This Mothers' Day, of course, is a unique one for me. As my kids grew into adulthood and as we spread out across the country, on Mothers' Day I could count on a phone call from each of them—three kid calls in one day. (For AT&T and Sprint, Mothers' Day is winning the lottery.) This year, I hear from Chris and Sarah by phone and in person. Not from Rachel, who on March 16 was killed by a bulldozer in the Gaza Strip, while trying to protect a Palestinian home from demolition. Rachel is, though, powerfully with me—in the same way, I am sure, that other mothers have their lost children powerfully with them on this day.

The possibility of Mothers' Day 2003 having more than the usual significance was sparked for me before Rachel died—a week before, when I was in Washington DC with other women gathered to challenge the pending war with Iraq. I spent a day in workshops and came across mothers planning to take Mothers' Day back to its roots in this country, to Julia Ward Howe and her Declaration calling for a Mothers' Day of Peace, and her model of challenging injustice and violence wherever it might be.

There have been, since Rachel's death, others who have urged me to consider the power of mothers. On a radio call-in show out of Washington DC—the only call-in we have done—I was nervous but quickly heartened when two of the first calls came from mothers of Evergreen students who had learned of Rachel through their children.

Then came one from a kind man who told me that I was talking to the wrong people in Washington DC—that instead of trying to communicate with the President, I needed to get in touch with Laura and Barbara Bush—with the mothers of the world. I told the gentleman that I have a great deal of confidence in mothers. And I do. I am bonded to mothers. I feel something deep in our core, something that happens when a child comes into our lives that keeps us grounded in our awareness of the sanctity of that being and by transference keeps us grounded in our awareness of the sanctity of all human beings.

I believe that the policies of this country and the money that follows them in the world should reflect values that most mothers here hold—the sanctity of each life, the equal value of each human being, and a commitment to justice applied equally through adherence to law.

[...]

We in America see the horror of the suicide bombings. We seem to see much less the ongoing violence against the Palestinian people. Our blindness is an enormous contributing factor to this problem. We need to remember that as we have watched the deaths of some of the 773 Israelis who have died since September 2000, there have also been 2,298 Palestinian deaths. In this booklet now dedicated to Rachel—are the names and some of the faces of the children who have died since September 2000—Israeli, Palestinian. We need to remember them all.

The news of the past couple days has left me no choice but to come to you with the hope that some of you will be moved to action this Mothers' Day. I urge you to take your voices to members of Congress, to the White House, to the State Department, to the Israeli Embassy.

Tell them that the International Solidarity Movement and other international human rights activists in Palestine need their support. Tell them that, of course, the Israeli military does not want these activists watching and interfering as it commits one human rights violation after another. Tell them that the United States, which funds the out-of-control military activity in Palestine, should insist that international human rights observers be in the area but that until they do, it is imperative to support the non-violent activists who are there now. Tell them that the timid response from the US and British governments to Rachel's death and that of journalist James Miller, and to the shootings of Brian Avery and Tom Hurndall gives Israel the green light to establish these new, harsh tactics to further intimidate the non-violent activists.

It has been pointed out to me that the response to date by the US and British governments to these incidents is sending a chilling message to human rights activists round the world. Our government must take a much stronger stand.

There have been times when I have been quiet because I felt there were others who knew more. There are some who would like to quiet me now and who would like to quiet the power of Rachel's message, too.

I am no longer intimidated by experts and critics and certainly not by the name-callers. After all, my daughter stood in front of a bulldozer in order to protect the Palestinian home of a family with three young children. I believe that I can speak out and that I have a responsibility as a mother to speak out and to demand that the experts, the policymakers, Congress, and the White House reflect our values—our beliefs in the sanctity of each life, in the equality of each human being, and in justice and the rule of law.

14

CRACKDOWN ON ISM

OPEN LINE WITH THE CHIEF OF STAFF
Transcript from Israeli Military Radio (Galei Tzahal), 16 April 2003

On Passover Eve, 16 April 2003, at 08:00, the programme Open Line was broadcast, during which the Israeli Chief of Staff, Lieutenant-General Moshe Yaalon, spoke with soldiers and commanders about current events. The Chief of Staff also addressed questions by the programme's presenter, Dalik Vilenitz, about ISM, from which the following is excerpted.

Dalik Vilenitz: One of the conclusions from the whole course of the intifada, and we're seeing it now in the war in Iraq, is the question of the IDF's image. The IDF is currently facing problems, one of which is the overseas volunteers. I'm talking about the ISM organization, whose people are in the territories, on the combat line. Some of them have been injured, which has led to strong shock-waves throughout the world. How is the IDF coping with this matter?

Chief of Staff: First of all, you said intifada. Intifada, this is the Palestinian story. I claim that this isn't an intifada, because an intifada is a people's uprising, while here what we have experienced since September 2000 is a proactive attack and a strategic decision

Photograph by an unidentified ISM activist.

by the current Palestinian decision-maker, who took a decision to embark on a terror assault against us. And this is connected to that organization, ISM, an organization with volunteer activists from all over the world, who prepare their peace activists, and they came here after accepting the Palestinian story.

Ostensibly, as they see it, we are the aggressors and they are the victims. In factual terms, the ones who started this aggression are the Palestinians. Those who initiated the incidents in Rafah, in a place where unfortunately two of those activists were wounded, were the Palestinians. An American woman activist was killed there by an IDF bulldozer which did not see her and a British activist was wounded in the head, apparently by our forces, although we are unable to authenticate this conclusively, who entered an area where a terrorist was standing and firing at our forces. One of our snipers fired towards the terrorist who was shooting at him, in an area where we have responsibility under all the Israeli–Egyptian agreements. There are incessant terror operations there, stemming from the Palestinian terror organizations' need to smuggle weaponry from Egypt into the Palestinian-held area, and they now find it hard because of our operations there.

And all of a sudden these activists appear in the area. On the face of it, they are protecting the Palestinians from us. First of all, they create the negative image we have, because it certainly strengthens the Palestinian story, which according to my understanding is fabricated in this context. And as a result of this, they also impede the operations of our forces. As for the bulldozer story, the bulldozer was being used in an operation intended to flatten the ground so the terrorists would not be able to approach the axis of our action on the Israel–Egypt border. It did not see the activist, who was standing in a dead zone in terms of vision, and she was killed.

Their spokesperson says about this that the bulldozer was supposed to destroy a house and that she was protecting the house. "A lie." Their spokesperson reported that the bulldozer drove back and forth over the body. We saw the body, regrettably she was killed, and no such thing happened. We also encountered an incident in Jenin some time ago, during operations to arrest an armed terrorist, and he was in the office of that organization.

I have just given an order to remove the organization's activists from the area, firstly for their own benefit—they are endangering their own lives in a superfluous way—

but are also creating provocations that injure our freedom of action on the ground. And so it's advisable that they get out of the area.

END OF TRANSCRIPT

With thanks to the anonymous translator.

ARMY BACKTRACKS ON DETAILS ABOUT MILITANT ARREST AT INTERNATIONAL SOLIDARITY MOVEMENT
Associated Press, 29 March 2003

JERUSALEM—The Israeli army on Saturday withdrew its claim that a gun was found during a search of a West Bank office of the International Solidarity Movement, a pro-Palestinian group.

Israeli troops raided the office in the West Bank town of Jenin on Thursday and seized a wanted member of the militant Islamic Jihad group.

Originally, the army reported that a pistol was found in the office during the search. On Saturday, the army withdrew the allegation, saying only a weapon was found in the building, which also has apartments and the offices of two other international organizations.

"The information originally released was wrong," an army spokeswoman said. It was unclear where exactly the gun was found.

The army alleged that the Islamic Jihad member, accused of planning several attacks against Israelis, was being sheltered by the International Solidarity Movement.

The group, however, said there were clashes outside their office on Thursday when the man appeared in the stairway. A volunteer invited him into the office because he looked hurt, the group said.

"He looked terrified, was soaking wet and appeared to be in pain. Concerned about his welfare … he was brought into the apartment," a statement from the group said. "He was given a change of clothes, a hot drink and a blanket."

The group said the man spoke Arabic and none of the members in the office could communicate with him. Shortly after he entered, Israeli troops arrested him.

He is still being held and has not yet been charged.

[…]

GAZA VISITORS MUST SIGN WAIVER IN CASE ARMY SHOOTS THEM
by Chris McGreal, 9 May 2003, Guardian

The Israeli military yesterday began obliging foreigners entering the Gaza Strip to sign waivers absolving the army from responsibility if it shoots them. Visitors must also declare that they are not peace activists.

The move came hours before an autopsy on James Miller—the British cameraman killed in a Gaza refugee camp—confirmed that he was almost certainly killed by an Israeli soldier, despite the army's assertions to the contrary.

Yesterday, the British government demanded an Israeli military police criminal investigation into Miller's death and the shooting of another Briton by the army in Gaza, Tom Hurndall, a peace activist.

Mr Hurndall is in a coma with severe brain damage after being shot in the head by an Israeli soldier last month as he attempted to protect a small child from gunfire. The Foreign Office minister, Mike O'Brien, called in the Israeli ambassador to London to press the demand, which diplomatic sources portrayed as a ratcheting up of pressure on the Israeli government.

"On the basis of the evidence we've seen, we feel this case is so serious that we are asking for a military police investigation," said a Foreign Office spokesperson.

The waiver to enter Gaza requires foreigners, including United Nations relief workers, to acknowledge that they are entering a danger zone and will not hold the Israeli army responsible if they are shot or injured. The army document also warns visitors they are forbidden from approaching the security fences next to Jewish settlements or entering "military zones" in Rafah refugee camp close to the Egyptian border where Miller was shot dead on Saturday.

He was the third foreigner killed or severely wounded in the area in recent weeks, besides numerous Palestinian civilians hit by Israeli fire, many of them children. The army invariably claims the victims were caught in crossfire. Palestinians say most of the shooting is indiscriminate and reckless, or worse.

The latest victims include a one-year-old boy, Alian Bashiti, shot dead in his home in neighbouring Khan Younis refugee camp on Wednesday.

Yesterday, Israel's forensic institute issued its autopsy report which backs up the accounts of witnesses who say that Miller was killed by a shot from an Israeli armoured vehicle. A video of the shooting also appears to undermine Israeli army claims that Miller, 34, was caught in crossfire and that soldiers shot in his direction in response to incoming fire from a Palestinian gunman nearby.

The film shows three journalists in flak jackets and helmets, clearly marked with the letters TV. They are shouting "Is there anyone there? Is there anyone there? We are British journalists." A single shot is heard and then another followed by the sound of Miller groaning after he was hit. There is no sound of crossfire.

Yesterday, the army said it had yet to receive the report and therefore could not comment.

The military also now requires visitors to Gaza to declare that they have no affiliation to the International Solidarity Movement (ISM) which is close to becoming a banned organisation since it was revealed that members met with two British suicide bombers days before the attack on a Tel Aviv bar last week in which three people were murdered.

The ISM acknowledges that the bombers—Asif Hanif, who blew himself up, and Omar Sharif, whose bomb failed to explode and who is still being hunted—attended one of its meetings but says the organisation had no idea of their intent.

A Hamas militant was killed in a helicopter missile strike in Gaza City yesterday.

© *The Guardian, 2003. Reprinted with permission.*

TWO BRITONS STILL HELD AT EREZ BORDER CROSSING
Update on detention of two British activists at Erez border crossing
International Solidarity Movement, 9 May 2003

It has been twenty eight hours since, at 8:30 PM on Thursday evening, May 8, 2003, two British Internationals were detained at Erez border crossing at the entrance to the

Gaza strip. The Internationals are Nick and Alice. Both have been held at the crossing with no arrest and no charges. The police have actually refused to arrest them. There is no reason to arrest them. There are no charges pending.

Neither Nick or Alice have had any sleep. There is no place to sleep at the border crossing. Nick was interrogated for many hours by the Shin Bet (Security Services).

They are being told that they are being deported. Alice has said that their plans were to leave the country anyway. However, the pair would like to go back to Rafah to collect the remainder of their belongings, say goodbye to friends and then leave the country as planned by boat from Haifa.

Nick and Alice are being held as part of the overall execution of a plan to remove ISM from the West Bank and Gaza. The plan targets Internationals heading to Gaza in particular. Upon arrival at the border crossing, one is presented with a form to fill out. It absolves Israel of all responsibility in the case an International is injured or killed and in addition forces the International to waive all basic rights.

Nick and Alice signed this document.

They have asked that people call Erez on 08 6741557 to inquire why they are being held illegally and when they will be released. For UK, please call THE FOREIGN OFFICE 020 7008 1500. Also contact your MP and Prime Minister

For Israel contact

Israeli Minister of Interior, tel: +972-2-629- 4701; fax: +972-2-629-4750

Israeli Foreign Minister, Silvan Shalom, fax: +972-2-5303704

Defense Minister, Shaul Mofaz, fax: +972-3-6916940, 6976990

Prime Minister, Ariel Sharon, fax: (+972-2) 566-4838 or 651-3955 or 651-2631

ISRAELI FORCES RAID ISM OFFICE

International Solidarity Movement, 9 May 2003

FOR IMMEDIATE RELEASE

Israeli forces raided the ISM office this morning, confiscating equipment and material and snatching three women. At 12:30pm on Friday, May 9, approximately 20 military vehicles, army jeeps and a large armored personnel carrier (intended for many arrests) surrounded the ISM media office in Beit Sahour. Dozens of soldiers, border police and civilian police officers raided the ISM office, confiscating all computers, not only in the ISM office but in the nearby office of the Palestinian Centre for Rapprochement. Files, CD, and photos were all pillaged, while soldiers broke equipment and damaged office space. Israeli forces kidnapped Palestinian volunteer, Fida, American volunteer, Flo, and a worker with Human Rights Watch visiting the office. At the time of this writing, Fida has been released, and the Internationals seem to have been moved to the office of the Israeli Ministry of Interior, most probably for deportation.

The Israeli government has declared an open war on international peace and human rights workers. Israeli forces are doing everything in their power to specifically prevent the nonviolent resistance to their military rule. The stepped-up harassment of Internationals and journalists in the Occupied Palestinian Territories is nothing short of a further attempt to shield the international community from the brutality of daily Israeli military actions against the Palestinian people.

The ISM, however, has no plans to leave the Palestinian areas or to reduce our actions or our efforts. We need your help. Please protest:

In the US contact your congressperson, the State Department and the White House using this link: http://www. cflweb. org/congress_merge_. htm or http://www. congress. gov. Also call the State Department and demand action: STATE DEPART-MENT 1-202-647-5150.

For UK, please call THE FOREIGN OFFICE 020 7008 1500. Also contact your MP and Prime Minister.

For Israel, contact Israeli Minister of Interior, tel: +972-2-629-4701; fax: +972-2-629-4750.

Israeli Foreign Minister, Silvan Shalom, fax: +972-2-5303704; e-mail: sar@mofa. gov. il.

Israeli Defense Minister, Shaul Mofaz, fax: +972-3-6916940, 6976990; e-mail: sar@mod. gov. il.

Prime Minister, Ariel Sharon, fax: (+972-2) 566-4838 or 651-3955 or 651-2631.

For Canada: Minister of Foreign Affairs Bill Graham, House of Commons, Ottawa ON K1A 0A6; Fax 613-996-3443.

Everyone, contact the Israeli embassy in your country

See our website: www. palsolidarity. org for more ways to help or get involved.

For more information, please call [number withheld]

ENDS

ISRAELI FORCES SNATCH, BEAT AND ARREST ISM VOLUNTEERS
by Radhika Sainath, 11 May 2003

Osama★ and I headed out of our apartment yesterday at approximately 6PM to take personal accounts from refugee families whose houses are frequently occupied by Israeli soldiers. As we walked we heard repeated bursts of live ammunition fire in nearby downtown Tulkarem. Concerned that Israeli Forces or the Border Police were shooting at children—as we have repeatedly witnessed in the past—we called a third ISM volunteer, Charlotte, to the scene to witness and deter any potential human rights violations.

Upon arrival in Tulkarem's main street we viewed a burning hummer (military jeep) stuck in the middle of the road, and three armored personel carriers (APC) and multiple jeeps wildly circling the city. However, what most concerned us was a family's car that contained three small children under the age of twelve parked meters away from the burning vehicle. The army had confiscated the car keys and instructed the family to stay inside, effectively using the father and his small children as human shields. The crying children were clearly terrified of being shot so we agreed to stay with the family and try to speak with the soldiers in an attempt to retreive the car keys.

Two local journalists soon joined us and minutes later an army jeep started to back up in our direction. Given the Israeli Army's recent policy of targeting and shooting Internationals, I began to feel concerned for our saftey. Suddenly, the back doors of the jeep opened and soldiers jumped out, grabbing Osama and the journalists and shoving Charlotte to the side. Once inside the jeep Osama reported being grabbed by the commander, who beat him in the head, after which the other soldiers threw him on the floor and forced him to cover his face with his T-shirt. While putting their rifle butts on his chest, the soldiers demanded to see his videotape, stating,

"We will kill anyone we see on this tape." The journalists were also beaten on their chest and neck.

While the men were in the jeep Charlotte and I spoke to the man being used as a human shield, offering to accompany his children to the hospital. As this was happening an APC approached us and I used our megaphone to ask the soldier to return the family's car keys, as they had nothing to do with the burning hummer and were being collectively punished. Suddenly an army jeep pulled up to us, the commander opening his door, politely asking "What do you want?" and "Come closer, I can't hear you." Sensing a trap Charlotte and I decided to distance ourselves from the jeep as fast as possible. However the army jeep, joined by a large jeep, roared in front of us.

A dozen heavily armed and entirely male army force surrounded us, grabbing for our cameras and violently pushing us to the ground. Several soldiers grabbed Charlotte and me—causing bruises on our arms and legs—and forced us onto a jeep going to the Tulkarem DCO and military base. The jeep carrying Osama and the journalists arrived approximately fifteen minutes later, and Osama dropped to the ground in pain, his leg convulsing in spasms.

While Osama was taken into a military shelter two policemen arrived and demanded that we go with them to Ariel. I insisted that we would go nowhere unless accompanied by a female officer as the manner of our detention by several male soldiers had already been conducted illegally. The soldier who grabbed me had said, "You are a very beautiful peace activist", and earlier that day another soldier said, "Give me a kiss", which made me feel threatened. After much debate the policeman agreed to call a female soldier who accompanied us to Ariel police station.

Osama was released, unconscious, to Thabit Thabit hospital from the DCO after an epileptic fit caused by the Israeli Army's beatings. The journalists were released this morning. Charlotte and I were released under bail at 6:30PM on condition we do not return to "Samaria" for fifteen days. We await our deportation hearing with the Ministry of Interior.

*Osama is a Palestinian volunteer with the International Solidarity Movement and a journalist. He is not involved with any political groups, but has repeatedly been harassed by the Israeli military.

ISM UPDATE
International Solidarity Movement, 14 May 2003

Reports are coming in that Nablus is again under siege. Earlier today, seven Israeli jeeps, a tank, and an APC entered Nablus for an unknown reason. As schools let out some children began throwing stones at the tank. Soldiers fired live rounds directly at the schoolchildren. Thirteen people have been injured. At least one child is in critical condition with a bullet wound to his chest. For more information call Saif at [number withheld].

Alice and Nick have arrived in the UK after having been deported from Israel. They were detained at Erez checkpoint in Gaza last Thursday.

Charlotte and Radhika have been released on bail with the stipulation that they not travel to the occupied territories. They are awaiting a deportation hearing. Osama was released from the hospital the day after his arrest. He has not been re-detained. Charlotte, Radhika, and Osama were arrested in Tulkarem on Friday as they attempted to guard a civilian family who were trapped in their car and being used as human shields by Israeli forces.

Flo remains in custody and is awaiting a deportation hearing.

ISM ACTIVISTS DETAINED BY ISRAELI MILITARY
by Radhika Sainath, 23 May 2003

[Refugee Camp, TULKAREM] Two American ISM volunteers and one Palestinian were taken by Israeli Forces at 9:45AM this morning after accompanying schoolgirls to their homes. Mike Johnson, age 52 from Washington, Matteo Bernal, age 22, from Kentucky and Osama Qashoo, 21, from Qalqilia are currently being held at the Tulkarem DCO.

ISM volunteers arrived to the Tulkarem refugee camp at approximately 7AM this morning, witnessing dozens of schoolgirls on their way to school amidst a heavy military presence including three tanks, multiple armored personnel carriers, a D-9 bulldozer, hummers and jeeps. About fifteen girls between nine and eleven years old were stranded on their on way to school, crying and paralyzed in fear from the Army's sound grenades and random firing of rubber bullets. The ISM volunteers informed the Israeli Military of their decision to escort the girls out of harms way. The army agreed to let the volunteers take the children home and did not instruct them to leave the area.

Upon attempting to leave the camp at 9:45AM, after having led the schoolgirls to safety, Israeli Forces stopped the volunteers, refusing to let them leave the camp under the pretext that the area was a military zone. A large truck and a military jeep arrived, at which point the three volunteers were taken to the Tulkarem DCO. The two Americans were transferred to Ariel Prison where they are currently being held.

Johnson and Bernal are the sixth and seventh foreign ISM peace activists to be taken by Israeli forces in the past two weeks.

ISM DEMANDS ISRAELI RETRACTION AND APOLOGY OVER MIKE'S PLACE BOMBING ALLEGATIONS
The International Solidarity Movement demands a retraction of statements made by the Israeli Ministry of Foreign Affairs and a full apology
International Solidarity Movement, 3 June 2002

FOR IMMEDIATE RELEASE

The Israel Ministry of Foreign Affairs website makes the following accusations against the International Solidarity Movement (ISM).

The Ministry of Foreign Affairs states that "ISM members take an active part in illegal and violent actions against IDF soldiers. At times, their activity in Judea, Samaria and the Gaza Strip is under the auspices of Palestinian terrorist organizations". This is incorrect. The International Solidarity Movement does not and has never worked under the auspices of, or in cooperation with, any armed Palestinian resistance group. The ISM does not undertake any activity in the Occupied Territories this is violent or illegal. On the contrary ISM activists have been harmed by and threatened with harm by Israeli army personnel.

In connection with the two British suicide bombers the Ministry of Foreign Affairs states that "The two terrorists were careful to establish their presence in Judea and Samaria by forging links with foreign left wing activists and members of the International Solidarity Movement (ISM)". This is incorrect. No ISM activist had contact with the two men in the West Bank. Their sole contact was a brief social encounter in Rafah in the Gaza Strip and no "links" were "forged" in short time. See attached press statement for full details.

Immediately after the suicide attack on Mike's Place Israeli intelligence stated that the men had entered the Gaza Strip posing as international peace activists with the ISM. In their report of June 3 Israeli investigations now prove that "On April 24, 2003, the terrorists entered the Gaza Strip via the Erez checkpoint, along with the Italian woman journalist and additional Italian journalists, which greatly assisted them in avoiding suspicion at Erez". The ISM has been shown to be innocent of this false accusation by the Israeli government.

The Ministry of Foreign Affairs states that "It has become clear from the investigation of the Italian journalist that the terrorists exploited foreign left wing activists in the Palestinian Authority (PA) areas for the purpose of covering their movements throughout Judea, Samaria and Gaza. Even though the latter were unwitting, they in effect were accomplices to terrorist activity". This is incorrect. The Italian journalist was interrogated by the Israeli authorities and has subsequently been found to be unaware of their intentions and so is not guilty of being an accomplice. Similarly the ISM activists in Rafah were entirely unaware of the men's intentions to commit an attack in Israel. Moreover ISM has not been approached for questioning by the Israeli authorities in connection with the contact they had with the suicide attackers. Further to this the only contact ISM had with these men was a brief social meeting in Rafah, not in the West Bank and it has been proved that the men used a journalist as a cover for their movements. It is important to state that since it's founding ISM activists have been denied entry to the country and many have been deported. Moving around the Occupied Territories is not made easier as a peace activist.

The Ministry of Foreign Affairs states that "None of the persons involved—neither Palestinian nor foreign—bothered to contact any official body, despite their familiarity with the terrorists, even after they understood that they were involved in the attack, until they came under ISA investigation." This is incorrect. ISM held an open press conference a few days after the attack on Mike's Place and explained the circumstances under which the activists in Rafah briefly met the British men. The ISM has never been approached by the Israeli authorities in connection with an investigation.

ENDS

ISM MEDIA COORDINATOR DEPORTED AND BRITISH SCHOOL TEACHER BARRED FROM THE OCCUPIED TERRITORIES

by International Solidarity Movement, 1 August 2003

Today Judge Barron, presiding over the cases of Michael Shaik and David Watson, both of whom have been denied entry to Israel, issued her decisions. Michael Shaik's appeal has been denied, and the deportation order stands. David Watson has been granted provisional entry to Israel as a tourist, on the conditions that he not enter the Occupied Palestinian Territories, engage in political activities, or communicate with the International Solidarity Movement.

Both cases have also had a freeze action placed on them until Monday, which means that the two will continue to be held in detention until then, in order to give both prosecution and defense a chance to appeal Barron's decision to the High Court.

ISRAEL TO DEPORT EIGHT INTERNATIONAL PEACE ACTIVISTS

International Solidarity Movement, 17 July 2003

FOR IMMEDIATE RELEASE

Today Tel Aviv District Court Judge Nissim Yeshaya upheld the deportation orders of eight International Peace activists who were working with the International Solidarity Movement (ISM). Of the eight activists, Tubias Karlsson (Sweden), Tarek Loubani (Canada), Fredrick Lind (Denmark), Bill Capowski (USA), Daniel Knutsson (Sweden),

Alex Perry (UK), Saul Reid (UK) and Thomas Pellas (France), four were arrested on July 9 while at a camp on Palestinian land in the village of Arrabony near Jenin slated to be confiscated by Israel for the building of the separation wall, and four on July 10 while helping to remove roadblocks near the city of Nablus calling attention to the restrictions on Palestinian freedom of movement under the Occupation. They were subsequently issued deportation orders by the Ministry of the Interior.

The Israeli military has claimed that the ISM and all peace activists are a security threat and the lawyer for the state used this as the argument for why the activists should be deported. No evidence as to the illegality of the defendants' actions was presented. Signed affidavits that the presence and work of ISM is important were submitted by prominent Israeli organizations and individuals such as Bat Shalom, MK Yossi Sarid and several Israeli professors. The judge sided with the state lawyers saying that under Israeli law the Ministry of the Interior has unlimited power to deport and revoke visas of Internationals.

The policy of punishing international peace activists without any evidence other than labeling them a security threat is an expansion of Israel's policy of using administrative detention to punish Palestinians the military labels a security threat. Currently there are over 1,000 Palestinians being held in administrative detention after having secret evidence used against them. Administrative detention is an indefinitely renewable six months of captivity. Many Palestinians have now been held in detention for years without any charge or knowledge of when they might be released.

After the ruling, a lawyer for the eight defendants requested a one week stay on the deportations to allow time to file an appeal. The request was denied. Two Israeli citizens were also arrested with one of the groups of activists. Both were released without charge. Some of the activists reported being kicked and otherwise abused while interrogated after the arrests and at least one was severely beaten after they stopped eating in protest two days ago.

For more information please contact:
Huwaida [number withheld]
ISM Media Office [number withheld]

ENDS

PRISON BEATING
by Tarek Loubani, 17 July 2003

The following was scribbled on a piece of paper by Tarek and passed to Huwaida via a lawyer during court proceedings for the deportation of eight international peace activists on 17 July. The hunger protest referred to was begun on the evening of 15 July.

I had forgotten what love was. My world was one of anger, rage and hate. As the 5 or 6 police officers each took a turn hitting me, all I could think of was hate. There could be nothing else. All of this started when Captain Ya'kov (Yoki) Golan came into our room and asked if we were on hunger strike. "We're not eating" we replied. A few police thugs swarmed the room and started to take anything. Capt. Ya'kov started to talk about how we were nothing, to which I replied, "Shut the hell up and don't you dare talk to us like that. You can't break me. You can't break any of us." "I'm not just going to break you; I'm going to destroy you." We all laughed.

We were strip searched 3 times in the next hour and then they came for me.

"Where are you taking him?" The other seven protested on my behalf. They cared more about me than I did. I came to terms with the fact that I was going into solitary, and finally approached the police. "I'm ready," I declared melodramatically. That's when the first hand came. They grabbed my shirt and pulled me to the ground in front of the cell. I did nothing. Even if I wanted to, I had lost track of all my appendages. All I knew was that they were all limp. The hitting started, and I filled the halls with screams of pain.

As I was up against the wall, with one man stomping on my leg, another bending my arm and another two or three pulling and hitting elsewhere, I caught a glimpse of the faces and entered that other world.

I can't do anything now. The guards who were involved all smile when they pass our cell. And all of this over the only act of resistance we can do: going hungry. One thing hasn't changed though: none of us will be broken.

Tarek

"WE ARE ALL PALESTINIANS"
by Avi Zer-Aviv, 19 July 2003

Dear Friends,

I have been hiding out here in Tel Aviv the last few days, recovering from a really turbulent few weeks and of the bitter news that my friends are being deported from Israel now.

Already five of the eight detained Internationals have been deported, following the Tel Aviv District Court decision upholding the Interior Ministry's decision that these human rights activists pose a "security threat". The judge seemed unsympathetic, ordering the immediate deportation of the activists, dismissing a request to allow for one more week to file an appeal.

My friends looked sickly as they arrived in court this last Thursday. They had already been sitting in Ariel settlement jail for one week, enduring poor treatment, the denial of their medical rights, some physical violence by prison guards, and a raid of their jail cell, confiscating their valuables.

Sadly, they were treated much better than most of the Palestinians sitting in the cells with them. In my one night in Ariel settlement jail, I shared a cell with two Palestinians, both being held for weeks awaiting a court decision for minor infractions that would at best receive a slap on the wrist had they been Israeli Jews.

The issue is not a bunch of Western kids serving time for trying to remove road-blocks in isolated Palestinian villages, but rather 36 years of occupation that has left a rotting scar on the lives of millions of ordinary people trying to make a decent liveli-hood. The issue is the family who graciously hosted me in their home for two nights in the town of Iraq Bureen outside Nablus, displaying Israeli bullet holes left by recent incursions covering their front door, bedroom closet and kitchen. Their village has been without open roads for months, and the delivery of basic milk, water and food hampered without good reason.

All of this in a lookout surrounded by Israeli settlements, military outposts and watchtowers, and daily make-shift checkpoints set up right in the village itself. The only justification Israel uses to stay here is the tired and lame mantra of security or terror, all the while ignoring the fact that their presence is the real fuel for growing despair and agony.

Let us not forget the real issue in the commotion of our experience as seasoned or unseasoned peace workers. Let us not forget that even as I was arrested and put in an army jeep, a call came in on the radio dispatch requesting permission for an ill Palestinian woman to pass a checkpoint so she can seek medical treatment. Let us not forget the dozens of Palestinian men I saw each day standing out in the blazing heat, being denied freedom of movement as punishment for attempting to enter their villages through the fields and around the checkpoints that would turn many away in any case.

As an Israeli–Canadian Jew in Palestine, I have come to witness and document count-less human rights violations in the occupied territories, and come to the conclusion that Israel is moving closer to becoming a totalitarian state with a warped moral compass. 'Never Again', a famous slogan symbolizing Jewish self-determination after the holocaust, need not be replaced with 'At Any Price!' Yet many Jews still see Israel as The Golden Child that can do no harm. They send money, support Israeli policy unconditionally, swallow the propaganda whole, not realizing that their Golden Child has become a bully!

Israel's greatest threat is not the Palestinians, nor Iraq, nor the United States, but rather biting its own tail in the name of reactionary military policies that serve only the army generals who make up the previous and current governments here. We, as Jews, must remember how much we have suffered so as to transform that pain to compassion, generosity and understanding. Otherwise, we are destined to fall prey to the victim–victimizer dichotomy, asserting that we are either prey or predator.

Today, I say, 'We Are All Palestinians.'

OCCUPIED PEOPLES HAVE A RIGHT TO RESIST

by Tom Wallace and Radhika Sainath, 28 July 2003, Jerusalem Post

'We have all committed ourselves to the practice of nonviolence and do not assist anyone in committing acts of violence.'

As volunteers with the International Solidarity Movement and as individuals devoted to human rights and justice, we must address recent statements maligning us, our movement and those who have given their lives standing up for the principles we espouse.

We are unwavering in our commitment to nonviolence.

Due to these beliefs, we oppose the illegal Israeli occupation of the West Bank and Gaza. As a result we have come under heavy fire in the Occupied Territories and in the media. Israeli officials and several right-wing Israeli and American pundits have embarked on a campaign to discredit ISM, by attempting to equate ISM's principled and active support for Palestinian rights with terrorism.

In one such attack, 'ISM: Support Unit for Terror', journalist David Bedein falsely asserted that ISM works 'in alliance with those who choose to kill people in order to advance their goals.'

Our goal is to end the military occupation and bring peace and justice to Israelis and Palestinians. ISM is not linked with political parties or armed groups. Our partners are Palestinian, Israeli and international peace and human rights groups and Palestinian communities.

ISM believes in the dignity of every human being. Consequently, we strongly oppose violence against all civilians. This includes all acts of terrorism, whether perpetrated by a state, group or individual. We have all thoroughly committed ourselves to the practice of nonviolence and do not assist anyone in committing acts of violence.

Although our movement is completely nonviolent, we must recognize that independent nations and occupied peoples have security concerns and rights to self-defense and resistance as specified under international law.

Rights are rights and are not up for negotiation. But rights to self-defense and resistance should not be turned into justification for illegitimate violence against civilians.

While others condemn and criticize we provide a viable alternative by demonstrating that nonviolent resistance can succeed.

We are Christian, Muslim, Jewish and Hindu. We are grandparents, students, professionals, nuns and ministers. We are also Israelis. Two weeks ago 10 ISM volunteers were arrested during acts of nonviolent civil disobedience. Two of the arrestees, Avi Zer-Aviv and Aviv Kruglanski, are Israeli and as such were released; the rest remain in jail, or were deported. They were removing roadblocks and setting up peace camps. They were not assisting terrorists.

We do assist medical personnel, pregnant mothers, farmers and children targeted by Israeli Forces on a daily basis. They are human beings being humiliated, tortured, beaten, arrested, shot, and killed for attempting to go to school, see a doctor or tend to their land.

Opponents of ISM claim that the movement's goal is to impede the army's job in stopping terrorism and even act as an accomplice to terrorist activities.

Does anyone honestly believe that thousands of volunteers from Tel Aviv to New York City, many Jewish, would spend their vacations to come and spread terrorism?

Many of us have paid a price for our commitment. James Deleplain, 74, sustained a broken rib and punctured lung after settlers beat him during the olive harvest. Tom Hurndall, 21, was shot in the head while moving children out of harm's way from an Israeli sniper. Brian Avery, 24, had his face blown off by an Israeli armored personnel carrier. And, of course, Rachel Corrie, 23, was run over by a bulldozer driven by an Israeli soldier while attempting to protect the home of a Palestinian physician from illegal demolition.

No one was held accountable for these violent attacks on civilians.

Instead, we get lies and distortions. Rather than investigating and correcting Israeli army actions to better protect civilians, the Israeli government is trying to expel foreign civilians who are monitoring human rights abuses, implicitly giving a green light for further attacks on human rights workers.

In its attempt to smother voices of dissent Israel is rapidly moving away from the democratic values it espouses toward policies reminiscent of dictatorships in Argentina and the USSR where, in the name of security, thousands were arrested, exiled and killed for their politics.

The growing international nonviolent movement offers one of the best hopes for achieving an end to the Israeli military occupation and a just peace for Palestinians and Israelis. If the Israeli government is successful in its attempt to eliminate the nonviolent resistance to its illegal policies, what alternative does that leave for those justifiably opposed to its military occupation?

15

HERE TO STAY

THE FOREIGNERS WHO BRAVE ISRAELI BULLETS
by Ken Lee, 1 September 2003, Aljazeera.Net

One warm August day, Juliana, a US citizen from New York, prepared herself to be gassed and shot at by Israeli soldiers.

Along with about 60 other international activists and 200 local Palestinians, she joined a brazen daylight attempt to tear down part of Israel's apartheid wall in a West Bank village near Tulkarem, where hundreds of farmers have been denied access to their land.

That day, 28-year-old Juliana became one of the first casualties of steel-core rubber bullets, baptised with a bloody purple welt on her right forearm.

Seven other foreign nationals participating with the International Solidarity Movement (ISM)—the activist group with the largest number of foreigners demonstrating in the Palestinian territories against Israel's occupation—went down with similar injuries along with two Tulkarem locals.

"I actually saw [the bullets] coming right at me," she says, gesturing in a spiral motion. "But when you spend some time here and you see what Palestinians go through all the time, you can't let yourself get freaked out about [getting hurt]."

Photograph by Abdel Karim Dalbah.

Death and danger

Such self-assuredness in the face of danger comes just five months after US activist Rachel Corrie, an ISM volunteer, was crushed to death under the shovel of an Israeli bulldozer on 16 March.

Israel claimed the driver did not see her. Corrie was wearing a fluorescent orange jacket in broad daylight while attempting to block the demolition of a Palestinian home in Rafah, Gaza Strip.

Although her killing devastated the movement and the activist community worldwide—shattering the notion for some that foreign passports offer physical immunity here—the tragedy appears to have strengthened ISM's resolve a half-year on.

Since then, the ranks of the Palestinian-led movement have swelled and the media are taking them more seriously.

Its coordinators insist non-violent, direct-action protests—such as barrier demonstrations, roadblock removals and marches on checkpoints—are the most effective strategy to exposing the often brutal measures of the 36-year Occupation.

ISM's first fatality heralded a particularly bloody string of injuries to its activists less than 30 days after Corrie's death.

More than two weeks later, Brian Avery, another American, had his left cheek nearly torn off after heavy-calibre fire was sprayed in his direction from an Israeli armoured personnel carrier in Jenin.

Six days later on 11 April, a round fired from an Israeli military watchtower in Rafah pierced the skull of British volunteer Tom Hurndall. He remains in a coma with severe brain damage.

"What happened to the activists made me feel more compelled to come," says Juliana, who works as a video editor in New York.

Diverse backgrounds

Other activists here this summer, whose diverse backgrounds stretch from college-aged anarchists to senior members of clergy, expressed similar motivations.

"It didn't deter me," says Philip, 66, a grandfather and retired probation officer from Manchester, England. "I realised the Palestinian people were in larger danger and they needed our support."

Hits to the ISM website during that fateful month peaked at more than five million, while incoming phone calls and inquiry emails jumped from around two to ten a day, according to ISM co-founder Huwaida Arraf.

More than 1,500 volunteers from around the world have participated with the movement since it started more than two years ago, and Arraf expects that number to reach 2000 in the next few months.

About 15% to 20% of ISM activists are Jewish.

"The volunteers take what they've seen out here and report back to their communities and in turn recruit others; it's a snowball effect," Arraf explains. "The tragedies reaffirmed our commitment to struggling against the Occupation in the face of such lethal force. We were never under any false [impressions] that just because we're nonviolent the Israeli military won't use violence against us."

Unfounded accusations

Israel insists Avery and Hurndall were caught in exchanges of gunfire with Palestinian militants. Eyewitnesses say no clashes occurred at either scene, arguing they wouldn't have been there in the first place had there been any fighting.

Like Corrie, both victims were wearing brightly coloured jackets while trying to assist the local population.

ISM has been repeatedly denounced by Israel as abetting what it calls terrorist activity.

A *Jerusalem Post* article on 1 August quoted a senior security government source as saying the ISM receives funds from both the Palestinian Authority and Hamas.

But Arraf vehemently denies any connection. And one unfounded allegation—that a pistol was found in an ISM office in Jenin—was officially retracted by the Israeli Army in March.

Others in the international community have praised the work of its volunteers. A Canadian member of parliament, recognising the efforts of Corrie, Avery and Hurndall, has nominated the movement for a 2004 Nobel Peace Prize.

Changing tactics

This summer marks a departure from the group's activities last year.

Because of Israel's massive Defensive Shield Operation in April 2002, volunteers were bogged down with humanitarian and relief work, ferrying food and medicine to Palestinian civilians trapped under curfew and escorting ambulances through checkpoints.

This year, ISM has staged mass demonstrations on their terms—at least 30 already against the apartheid wall alone, part of their Freedom Summer campaign.

The rash of injuries has no doubt weeded out some of the movement's faint-hearted.

Still, many ISM volunteers report having doubts about just how far they would go, having deeply questioned the risk involved and the movement's tactics. The spectre of Corrie's death, it seems, still haunts.

"I'm not willing to go as far [in direct actions] as others have gone and I prefer not to get arrested," says Mark, a 42-year-old library researcher from Canada who did not give his last name for fear of deportation. "I wouldn't put myself in [any life-threatening] situations."

But what some may perceive as recklessness is key to ISM's strategy. Coordinators know that without media presence, a significant portion of their work largely goes unnoticed.

Audacious acts

That calls for pulling off some audacious acts, like spray painting New York City-style graffiti saying Made in Berlin on sections of Israel's roughly $2 million-per-kilometre wall in Qalqilia as Israeli soldiers stand by bemused, cradling M-16s.

Yet, paradoxically, the more cameras are there, the less likely the Israeli occupying forces are to respond with lethal force, Arraf points out.

But no amount of coordination can handle situations that go awry.

At the Tulkarem wall demonstration, the Palestinian youth became caught up in revolutionary fervour and broke an apparent understanding not to unleash a hailstorm of stones.

They shattered the windows of an Israeli army jeep that pulled up on the demonstrators, while just missing some of the activists—who were forming a line to shield the Palestinians supposedly cutting the wire mesh behind them.

"I was trembling, I thought someone was going to get seriously hurt that day," says Eva, a 25-year-old German musician who was filming the demonstration, arrested four days later at a West Bank sit-in.

"Before I came, I asked myself, 'Aren't I more useful [to the Palestinian cause] alive than dead?' Fear is still a factor."

Asked whether she believed it was just a matter of time before another foreign volunteer is killed, Arraf, the ISM co-founder, replied with slight indignation:

"[That] question is seeking to place more value on an International's life than a Palestinian's. That's a reality of disturbing racism that we're up against. The fact is, there are civilians being killed out here every day."

EYE ON ISM—ACTIVITIES AND OBSTACLES
by the International Press Center–Palestine, 1 September 2003

The International Solidarity Movement (ISM) has become a very well-known name and has been directly associated with the Occupied Palestinian Territories and the Israeli Occupation. Many media outlets, mainly Israeli and US, have made efforts to smear this movement and distort their true goals.

They spread lies about its members, exploiting the weak support ISM has and the media blackout Israel is imposing in the Occupied Palestinian Territories.

What is the ISM?
The ISM, in its own words published on its website (www. palsolidarity.org), is "… a movement of Palestinian and International activists working to raise awareness of the struggle for Palestinian freedom and an end to Israeli occupation, utilizing nonviolent, direct-action methods of resistance to confront and challenge illegal Israeli occupation forces and policies".

The nonviolent methods include protests against Israeli troops, standing in the face of bulldozers that try to demolish Palestinian homes. ISM members sometimes spend nights in a house marked for destruction, as well as escorting Palestinian municipal workers who fix infrastructures wrecked by the Israeli war machine. All these actions can be summarized as being "human shields".

Most ISM members prefer not to use the phrase "human shield" at all. They prefer other terms, calling what they do "direct action", "non-violent protest" or "solidarity and communication". "Human shield" sounds distastefully passive and limited to them, as if all they do is put their bodies in front of a bullet. Activists are quick to tell you that human shield work encompasses a wide variety of activities, from escorting ambulances to participating in protests. Still, the basic premise of human shield work justifies the expression: the underlying rationale is that no one cares if a Palestinian dies, but if an International is shot it will cause an uproar. The very presence of human shields can ward off bullets and draw the world's attention. And if one of these activists dies, the world's attention will be drawn to the situation.

What do others say about ISM?

The "human shields" activists in Palestine have chosen sides in the most bitterly divisive foreign policy issue in America today. They say that Israel's presence and tactics in the occupied territories are morally unacceptable. American and Israeli critics regard them as bleeding hearts or worse, who are defending "terrorists" and (literally) standing in the way of Israel's legitimate defense needs. In April 2002, Jay Nordlinger, managing editor of the conservative *National Review*, denounced the human shields activists, writing that they "aren't 'peace activists': They're supporters of the Palestinian war on Israel, who want the war to succeed."

Not surprisingly, the Israeli government is also strongly opposed to the movement, regarding it as "biased and playing into the hands of Israel's enemies". Spokesman of the Israeli Embassy in the United States Mark Regev calls the human shields "misguided", adding that "the ISM are so one-sided they are almost mouthpieces for Arafat's propaganda." Israel has recognized several obvious activists, refusing to allow them to enter the country.

Regev added that the activists don't look morally to the conflict, claiming that human shields must also be provided for the "Israeli innocent civilians who are being slaughtered".

The activists retort that such answers ignore the basic political reality: Israel is an illegal occupying power, which undercuts its claims to be acting in legitimate self-defense when it operates outside its pre-'67 borders. (Israel captured the occupied territories, comprising the West Bank, the Gaza Strip and the Golan Heights, from Jordan, Egypt and Syria in the 1967 war.) They reject Israel's claims that it exercises special care not to harm civilians as absurd: they say the very nature of the Israeli military presence in the occupied territories relegates Palestinians to a wretched life. Israeli troops, they charge, routinely engage in acts that have nothing to do with self-defense and everything to do with brutalizing and humiliating Palestinians.

International human rights groups such as Amnesty International and Human Rights Watch, as well as the Israeli human rights organization B'tselem and Israeli journalists such as Amira Hass, support the activists' sayings, finding that the Israeli military has engaged in persistent human rights violations in the West Bank and the Gaza Strip, including collective punishment, assassinations, destruction of homes, indiscriminate fire directed at civilian targets, beatings, detainment of medical personnel, unjustified restrictions on movement, and other such practices.

Who are they?

Most of the ISM members in Rafah have been previously involved in peace activities before coming to Palestine. "The idea to come here has been in the back of my head for a long time, but (Rachel) Corrie's murder by the Israeli military brought this idea to the present, so I decided to come," Laura said, explaining why she came to Rafah.

Laura, a member of the ISM in the city of Rafah, explains that the basis of ISM work is to build bridges of communication between the Internationals and the residents of Rafah, but the media overshadowed this aim to the direct resistance action against the Israeli military occupation.

The recent calm situation in the Gaza Strip has presented an opportunity to the ISM members to achieve this goal, so they started participating in social activities and community work in Rafah.

In "Yaboos Charity Organization", ISM members, Mike, Emma, Laura and Noah, attend the summer camp held there for the children of Rafah. Mike and Noah teach the children juggling, while Emma and Laura hold arts and crafts workshops.

Lovely pieces of colored cardboard, with stickers of roses and ribbons placed on them, formed a beautifully colored notebook. "Each one of the children made one of these notebooks, and wrote something in it. We intend to translate these writings and bring them with us back to the USA to show them to the American children," said Emma.

Emma, from Olympia, Washington, the same town from which Rachel Corrie came, hopes to continue the work of Corrie, in creating a children-exchange program between Palestinian and American children. "I hope that some American children would have the opportunity to visit Palestine," Emma added.

In the West Bank, the situation of the Palestinian people continues to worsen. The large area of the West Bank and proximity to Israeli cities, as well the large number of sporadic Jewish settlements built to be the Occupation's partitioning tool of the Palestinian territories. As if that wasn't enough, the Israeli occupying forces (IOF) started the construction of the "Separation Barrier": a huge barrier composed of thick cement walls, eight meters high in some places, deep ditches, trenches and high-voltage electric fences. The barrier is constantly patrolled by IOF jeeps, tanks, armored vehicles and fortified guard towers. The barrier is supposed to extend for 590 kilometers along the West Bank. However, the IOF have rerouted the barrier to snake into the Palestinian-owned lands, diving as deep as six kilometers in some sections. This twist in the barrier led to the complete isolation of nearly 220,000 Palestinians from their lands and from other Palestinian cities.

The ISM activities in the West Bank, at the time of this report, revolved mainly around this barrier, or "Apartheid Wall", as the activists call it. Many activists have been wounded, arrested, deported and detained by the IOF troops and policemen when they protested such a wall.

Eva, from Germany, told IPC on the phone that the Palestinian people lack a lot of basic human rights and they're suppressed by the illegal Occupation, and that's the reason that drove her to come to Palestine and join the ISM.

"My family has been very supportive of it [my travel]. My friends in Israel are part of peace groups and they completely support what I'm doing and they're also against the illegal Occupation of their country and what their government is doing in their name," Eva said.

What Eva tries to convey to the world by working in Palestine as a "human shield" is to show the world the Palestinians' spirit "that always stands up and never gives up, always is brave and keeps on going". A personal aim of hers is to bring back a detailed picture of the Palestinian people to her country, "so Palestinians could actually be re-humanized, not just numbers in the second report of the eight o'clock news, lying in the bottom and mentioned only in one sentence".

As for the IOF's attacks on her, Eva mentioned that she was arrested while documenting ISM peace activists trying to prevent the Occupation's wall construction in the village of Mas'ha.

"I was arrested in Mas'ha, trying to film and document Internationals trying to stop the construction of the second stage of the wall, which the Israeli government has claimed it will not start for a period of six months, since they claimed that the first stage of the wall is done. This piece of the second stage of the wall, as I understand, is to be or still to be last part. In any case, it's an embarrassment for the Israeli government, that's why it was very important for them not to have this documented. The house of the family that supposed to be passing it was destroyed because the wall was supposed to go through their front yard, and behind the house there was a fence for the next settlement, so this family would be literally locked in between fence and wall, separating this family from their village, and before that, the family got a notice that they'll be able to leave their houses three times a day."

Eva intend to continue being a peace activist after she returns home, as she is filming a documentary about the life of the Palestinian people and their daily suffering under the Occupation, and will be spreading it around the world.

As for Greta, from Los Angeles, United States, her contact with the Palestinian people and Palestinian cause is more personal. Greta is married to a Palestinian, a refugee from 1948. Her children are Palestinian Americans.

As for her reasons for coming to Palestine, she said, "One is because my children are Palestinian Americans and their father is a refugee of 1948, and they can't come back to see where their father was born and where their father was raised, so I came in their place. The second reason is I'm so ashamed of being an American and what Americans have done. I came so as to bear witness to what's happening to the Palestinian people."

An interesting reason for Greta to come also is because "... when three billion dollars of my tax-paying money as an American comes to Israel, it's time I took a stand against what the Israeli government is doing."

Greta added that she's trying to compensate for the United Nations' shield that should be protecting the Palestinian people from the IOF: "… there should have been a United Nations shield. We shouldn't have to be doing this, but we are because we care and are more passionate about the Palestinians and what's happening to them."

Greta was wounded in the village of Aneen, when she, along with other ISM peace activists, tried to open the gate separating Palestinians from their farms and lands, which were separated from them by the Occupation's separation barrier.

Despite being wounded, Greta says that she protected the Palestinian people, because Israeli soldiers fired rubber-coated steel bullets at them instead of the live bullets which are usually shot at Palestinians when there're no cameras, no Internationals and no media present at the place.

Answering a question about the ISM being smeared by some US and Israeli media outlets, and associating them with supporting terrorism, Greta replies, "The only terrorists I've seen here the past months are the Israeli army and the Israeli policemen, and I fail to see any other terrorism that is happening on the West Bank except for the terrorism against Palestinians. In July, the very first month of the ceasefire, 11 Palestinians were killed and only one Israeli was killed. So, how long can you do that without speaking out and saying you want your freedom? I think the ISM if anything is the opposite of terrorists. They've tried to do everything they can. I think the Israeli army has killed us, arrested us, deported us, detained us, and not allowed us in. So exactly who is being terrorized?"

In the end, Greta commented that she has been advocating the Palestinian cause and suffering for the past 30 years, and that when she returns home, she intends to write articles, show pictures and talk to groups about the suffering of the Palestinian people, and make sure that the people understand that there's another side to the conflict, and that this side, which the Palestinian people belong to, is the side of justice.

Conclusion

The International Solidarity Movement (ISM), though recently established, has exerted tremendous efforts to expose the cruelty of the Israeli occupation of the Palestinian territories, and the inhumane conditions they impose on the people. The movement had been the subject of criticism and slander by many Western media outlets, who tried to drive it out of the equation by associating it and its members with terrorism. The Israeli Occupation has killed, wounded, arrested and detained members of this movement, who continue to do their voluntary work because they believe that the Palestinian people, after 55 years of silence, must have a voice, a very loud one, in order for the whole world to hear. The ISM is the Palestinian people's voice to the world.

WALKING TOWARDS GUNFIRE: THE PEACE PROTESTERS WHO STAND UP AGAINST VIOLENCE

by Johann Hari, 1 August 2003, Independent

In the hills of Palestine, next to a village called Aneen, three groups of people stood this Monday afternoon amid clouds of tear-gas and the boom of bullets to yell at each other. I was standing on one side of Israel's new "security fence" with the largest group, a band of 100 Palestinian villagers and 80 members of the International Solidarity Movement (ISM), the organisation that brings committed Internationalists from across the world to support non-violent Palestinian resistance. On the other side were Israeli protesters, disgusted by their own government's inhumanity; and in between us stood a group of teenage soldiers fighting an old man's war they barely seemed to understand.

Their job was to guard the wall that is being built deep into the West Bank, splitting Palestinian land in two, dividing farmers from their fields, chopping families in half. Even the ultra-pro-Israeli George Bush, as he shared canapés with Ariel Sharon in Washington DC over the last few days, has condemned the building programme as a terrible mistake.

The ISM and Palestinians came on Monday to symbolically destroy a patch of this immoral barrier. Two ISM negotiators began the protest by telling the troops what they were here to do—and with that, the destruction of one patch of this steel construct, which is three times the height of the Berlin Wall, began. Within seconds, five people had been shot with rubber bullets, including two of my friends; and then there was a descent into an angry, chaotic mess.

One person glided through the spluttering and bleeding that followed with an infectious sense of total calm. Her name is Huwaida Arraf, a 27-year-old Palestinian-American who, with her Jewish husband Adam Shapiro, founded the ISM two and a half years ago. As I saw her talk calmly and firmly to an Israeli soldier, asking for an explanation, I thought of the Vietnam film *Apocalypse Now*. There is a character in the movie called "Wild Bill" who is described as "one of those guys that had that weird light around him. You just knew he wasn't gonna get so much as a scratch out here."

Huwaida has that weird light. Most Palestinians resist the Occupation in their minds but not with their flesh: they still flinch when an Israeli gun is turned on them, they still retreat when a soldier howls that they should. Huwaida walks towards gunfire with an air of tranquil certainty that she belongs here and the soldiers, with their fences and guns and tanks, do not.

Over coffee the day before the protest, she explained to me how she does it. "I am stronger than some soldier turning his tank barrel at me. When I stand in front of him, unarmed and in peace as I walk around my own city, I know that he is the weak one. Non-violence is much more threatening to the Occupation because it shows we are morally strong." She continues, "You know, at a demonstration against the closure of the Bir Zeit University on the West Bank, we marched in protest, and they opened machine gun fire on us. We stayed standing. When the dust cleared, we carried on marching forward with the students who just wanted to go to school. We chose not be frightened of an occupier who chooses massive and disproportionate violence."

The ISM is to our day what the International Brigade was to the Spanish Civil War. Left-wingers from countless countries have gathered here with nothing to unite them but their hatred of oppression; the ghost of George Orwell is no doubt smiling on them. The ISM's actions are mostly solid and practical: for example, they march Palestinian children to school during Israeli-imposed curfews because, as one ISMer explained, "Nobody can justify sealing children in their homes for months on end and denying them an education. Nobody." Sometimes, they reach for the symbolic: last week, they painted the words "Return To Sender" on an Israeli tank.

Already, the movement has generated myths and folk-heroes. I visited Rafah last week, the Gaza Strip town where an Israeli bulldozer killed 26-year-old American Rachel Corrie as she tried to protect the house of an innocent Palestinian doctor. The town looks like it has been hit by a vast bomb. Rubble and the possessions of newly homeless families are strewn like rubbish across the streets. The patch of dirt and earth where Rachel died is now a site of near-pilgrimage, and hers was only the first of three ISM deaths so far this year. Yet despite all this danger, there are now nearly 200 ISMers in Palestine who could just as easily be lolling on a beach in Ibiza, and more are expected throughout August.

Predictably, the Israel defence establishment has tried to bulldoze the ISM's reputation. They have claimed that the group are not "in favour of human rights, as they claim" but "pro-Palestinian"—a fatuous distinction. They have even tried to link the ISM to Palestinian terrorism with a series of silly charges that crumble on the slightest analysis. A claim circulated by the Associated Press (and reported gleefully in US right-wing circles) that Kalashnikovs had been found in an ISM office was completely retracted by AP and even the Israeli army itself when it emerged that it was totally false. Two British suicide bombers did, it is true, meet some ISM representatives in Gaza earlier this year, as anybody can; but nobody has suggested that the ISM knew their purposes, or that they offered them more than a cup of tea. That is the sum of the Israeli government's rather pathetic charges against the ISM.

Before I joined the group in Aneen, I braced myself for the possibility that many of the ISM's members, understandably disgusted by the Occupation, would question Israel's right to exist alongside a Palestinian state at all—a political stance I am very uncomfortable with. My fears were totally unfounded. A few ISMers I met believed in a binational solution—one big state of both Israel and Palestine—but most of the people I spoke to argued strongly for a two-state solution.

There are people who want to destroy Israel and push the Jews into the sea, and we must never underestimate the danger they pose; but the ISM is definitely not on their side. When one lone protester in Aneen tried to chant, "Bush, Sharon, you should know/We are all the PLO", he was universally shot contemptuous looks and told to shut up. If this conflict were the other way round and the Palestinians were oppressing the Israelis and denying their right to national self-determination, I have no doubt that most of the current ISMers would come to protect the Jews. If only the Jewish people had had such friends for the last two millennia, there would be an awful lot more of them alive today.

As the shouting died down and the sting of tear-gas died away, a Palestinian man named Mohammed Aktar turned to me and shook my hand so hard I feared it would snap. "Thank you for coming," he cried. "We used to think that nobody cared and we were alone in this fight. We thought the world had forgotten us. Now we know that there are people everywhere who think we matter, who know we are human beings and not animals. Now we know that this Occupation must one day end."

FIGHTING THE CONSPIRACY OF SILENCE
by Huwaida Arraf, May 2003, Al-Ahram (abridged)

The newest threat to Israel's massive "security" establishment is an unarmed, multi-ethnic, multi-national entity called the International Solidarity Movement (ISM). This Palestinian-led movement of Palestinian and international activists has now come under direct attack by Israeli forces and the Israeli government.

First there were the attacks against activists—threats, intimidation, shooting and killing. Then Moshe Yaalon, the Israeli Chief of Staff, stated that the Israeli army would arrest and deport all ISM activists. The ISM office in Beit Sahour was raided and equipment and files were damaged and looted by Israeli soldiers. Any foreigner wishing to enter Gaza must now sign a form releasing the Israeli army from its obligations under international law, and even Israeli law, to protect civilian life.

How can the "Middle East's only democracy" sanction murder by agents of the state in this way, and get away with it? Only with the conspiracy of silence of the international community.

ISM is a danger to the Israeli project of occupation, discrimination and apartheid-like rule, but not because Internationals stop bulldozers or tanks with their bodies. ISM is a threat because we've created the space for Internationals to see it, live it, and speak out about it. But Occupation is not going to be defeated by words alone; occupation, oppression and domination are going to be dismantled the same way they were erected, through the action of people—through civilian-based resistance.

Together with Internationals this struggle must be taken up. Yes, there are many "buts", and no, there is no guarantee for success. So, why should we Palestinians take up the struggle in this way?

There are many reasons.

Because this form of struggle relies on our greatest strength and resource—ourselves and our national community. And this form of struggle places control in our hands and upon our shoulders—even if they tear-gas us, even if they shoot at us, even if they erect walls and fences—it is only up to us if and when to stop and on what terms.

Because our goal of a free Palestine should reflect the values and morals of ourselves as a people and as a community, and our struggle should reflect these values. Committing suicide is not one of these values, nor is killing any civilian. This tactic only aids and supports the expansionist efforts of Israel. Our struggle must be based on our legitimate rights and values and we should not cloud or distort that claim by resorting to the tactics of our oppressors.

Because the Israeli military can meet violence with violence. Non-violence is altogether harder to deal with in this way. This was apparent during the first Intifada when the violence of the Israeli response led to international outcry and internal Israeli debates over the government's use of force. Now, we have massive international solidarity for the Palestinian people, realized on the ground by the ISM. Such a massive movement significantly affects foreign governments because their own citizens are mobilized to act in support of the Palestinian people.

Because Israeli occupation is based on control—the proliferation of checkpoints, roadblocks, identity cards, imprisonment, intimidation and violence. Only by rejecting these methods of domination can we overcome these tactics—the violence of this Intifada has only created more of these elements of control. We must utilize a strategy that challenges and dismantles these means of control.

The International Solidarity Movement was created to provide the Palestinian people with a resource—international protection—and a voice—with which to use nonviolent action to resist an overwhelming military force. The ISM is now under direct attack from the Israeli military and government—slander, threats, arrests, raids, and violence—and we don't expect the attacks to let up. This should not dissuade, but rather motivate people into action. The ISM will continue bringing international civilians to the Occupied Palestinian Territories and will continue to organize with the belief that the hearts, minds and collective action of a united civilian force—Palestinians and internationals together—can defeat an oppressive military force.

We call on people everywhere to join us.

EPILOGUE

A LETTER FROM AN ISRAELI RESERVIST TO ISM

Hi,

My name is Danny Dworsky. I volunteered to the IDF August 1976 and served my full tour until my honourable discharge in July of 1979. Since 1992 I have served as an army reservist agent for the Military Justice Department (METZACH) since 1992. I am a first Sergeant and my military ID is DN BDRK 2297771.

If the ISM is guilty of anything, they are guilty of making things not as bad as they could be. They support nonviolent means for Palestinians to further their cause and they more often than not slow the progress of the gigantic hole we in the Israeli establishment are digging for ourselves. In bringing Israelis and Palestinians together in a common goal of achieving peace and justice, ISM often provides that little bit of sanity and hope that so often deter us from acts of desperation, rage, and revenge.

Although I am not a pacifist or worse a left winger, I have spent enough time with these ISM people to determine that they are not only harmless to the state of Israel, they may very well be all that we have between who we claim to be and finding ourselves becoming something far beyond our own worst nightmares of persecution and extinction as a people. That being quite simply put "the bad guys".

Last October I investigated armed paramilitary settler gangs that had been "allegedly" assaulting, looting and terrorising Palestinian farmers during the olive harvest in the village of Yousouf. These attacks were carried out often in broad daylight in full view of Israeli Police and IDF armoured and infantry patrols.

Palestinian families picking olives were cursed and shot at. Their tools and donkeys were confiscated by settlers pointing and poking unlocked and loaded automatic weapons. "White people" and "war tourists" were beaten. Those with cameras had them ripped out of their hands or struck away from their faces with rifle butts or metre long steel construction bars.

I reported all of these offences to my superiors in Haifa—I had captured many of these scenes on film. Because of the weird confidence of the settlers and the absolutely bizarre behaviour of law enforcement people on the scene, I also kept copies of these materials for myself. These in turn were copied and handed off to an ABC News correspondent at the town of Yanoun a few days later. I managed to capture the faces of local police and soldiers as well as the numbers on the vehicles that brought them to the scene. All police deny having seen, heard or even having found the place. This is a lie.

At the first sign of trouble I had called the Ariel police department and they were on the scene in less that 20 minutes. The soldiers were less than three feet away from the police. The two policemen, who claimed over the phone that they couldn't find the place, were leaning against their patrol car between me and the settlers when I was told that if I pursued the matter further and didn't mind my own business, I could expect to have a bullet fired "accidentally" into the back of my head.

ISMers keep Sharon and Mofaz's IDF and lunatic settlers from carrying out ethnic cleansing. These ISM people are my heroes. They save lives. They are practicing the purest form of what the great Rabbis called "Tikkun Olam"—"It is upon all Jews to repair the world". As a Jew I owe a terrible debt to the humanity of these volunteer peacemakers who are paying my tab with their blood.

My family is available and our home is open to every one of these people. They know that they have a hot meal and a bed waiting for them anytime they need it.

I've been to funerals and hospitals for relatives and dear friends, students and young children lost to suicide bombers. If I thought for a second that the ISM had anything to do with enabling terrorism by dilution of security measures, I would not be so accommodating.

Daniel M. Dworsky
Atlit, Israel
October 2002